It Happened Like This

VICKY FOSTER

It Happened Like This

MY TESTIMONY

BLOOMSBURY CIRCUS
LONDON · OXFORD · NEW YORK · NEW DELHI · SYDNEY

BLOOMSBURY CIRCUS
Bloomsbury Publishing Plc
50 Bedford Square, London, WC1B 3DP, UK
29 Earlsfort Terrace, Dublin 2, Ireland

BLOOMSBURY, BLOOMSBURY CIRCUS and the Circus logo are trademarks
of Bloomsbury Publishing Plc

First published in Great Britain 2024

A catalogue record for this book is available from the British Library

ISBN: HB: 978-1-5266-5658-2; EBOOK: 978-1-5266-5657-5; EPDF: 978-1-5266-5656-8

2 4 6 8 10 9 7 5 3 1

Typeset by Newgen KnowledgeWorks Pvt. Ltd., Chennai, India
Printed and bound in Great Britain by CPI Group (UK) Ltd, Croydon CR0 4YY

To find out more about our authors and books visit www.bloomsbury.com
and sign up for our newsletters

AUTHOR'S NOTE

The events described in this book are not told chronologically. As this may cause some ambiguity, and as this book includes events of a sensitive nature, I would like to acknowledge that my ex-husband does not appear in the book in any way.

For Edna and Doreen

'Here leaves unnoticed thicken,
Hidden weeds flower, neglected waters quicken'
                                        - Philip Larkin

Part One

Blood

There is a man. He is running. He is running towards something, but from here we can't see what. We do know there is danger, and he is running. Every muscle in his body tensed as he moves. Every sinew strained. He is not running away. He is running towards, and one hand, shifting at his side, curves around something cylindrical, carrying it with him as he moves.

Somewhere else there is a woman, doing something. But we don't know yet what it is. Only that she exists, though sometimes she doubts it herself.

WOMAN

I want to not love you. I do a lot of this. Wanting not to love. Love pouring out of me anyway. It has been my downfall, or so I thought for a long time. Now I see it was not love, but the things I thought had to come with it. I don't want you taking up space in me, and yet here I am, insides dropping open in that way they've learnt to do. Space opening up between my heart and lungs and spleen. Space that doesn't exist and yet is there anyway. I wonder if this can be what causes all the tummy aches. I wonder if this is why, some mornings, I'm so heavy. The weight of more people than myself is being dragged across my pillows to find the floor. I wonder why I can't shut it off. I wonder if I would, if I could.

VICTIM SUPPORT NATIONAL HOMICIDE SERVICE, *LIVING WITH LOSS* REPORT, PUBLISHED MAY 2019

As well as highlighting emotions that remain over time, the research highlighted a number of ways that bereaved family members viewed themselves as permanently changed and with no hope of life returning to how it was. They felt that the incident had changed their personality and that they are now a different person. Although they may have better or worse days, many bereaved family members stated that their lives and their family lives were forever changed and that they will live with the effect of the crime for the rest of their lives.

Female, AC: 'Life will never be the same... They get easier but there are some days where you're stronger than others. There's days of anger. You don't put the past to rest. It's always there. So definitely I don't think anyone is ever the same after a murder. No one is ever the same.'

Male, R: 'I think it's [incident] always going to affect us... We've got to carry on and do what you need to do. You can't just stop because something bad happened. If you stop and think about it, we'd both be emotional wrecks and wouldn't be able to do anything and there'd be two children suffering in it as well.'

WOMAN

Five Things I Know About Blood:

1. In the right conditions, large quantities of blood can be leaking from your body for twelve continuous hours, and you will not die.
2. The sole of a shoe that has been scrubbed by a determined person can still have traces of blood detectable on it, but these traces will not be adequate to determine a one hundred per cent match for DNA. This may mean blood is thicker not only than water, but also than cleaning products.
3. The phrase 'blood is thicker than water' suggests that ties to family members are stronger than ties to non-family members. I think this holds true, whether you like it or not, except in a case where someone has murdered one of your family members, and then your tie to them can become just as strong as it was to the family member they have murdered. You almost definitely will not like this.
4. When I was a kid, it wasn't unusual for some of the boys I knew to pair up, then cut themselves on purpose, so they could press the small, freshly made wounds together, and having done so, declare themselves 'blood-brothers'. According to Wikipedia, they were replicating a ritual that's been going on for centuries.
5. In primary school, blocking a toilet with tissue paper and being sought out as the person who did it, might be a bit embarrassing, but if the toilet is blocked with blood-stained sanitary products, being sought out as the person who did it becomes shameful.

LORD JUSTICE LATHAM SPEAKING DURING SG'S APPEAL
AGAINST HIS MURDER CONVICTION: R V GALLANT,
ENGLAND AND WALES COURT OF APPEAL (CRIMINAL
DIVISION), 21 MAY 2008
On the 9th November 2005 in the Crown Court at Hull the appellant was convicted of murder and sentenced to life imprisonment with

a minimum term of 17 years. His co-accused, James Gilligan, was also convicted of murder and received the same sentence. A third defendant, Shaun Wilson, pleaded guilty to an offence of assisting an offender and was sentenced to 21 months' imprisonment. The appellant appeals against conviction with leave of the full court.

WOMAN

I'm trying to negotiate a way to still be in this world. Therapy sometimes feels like a very clever conjuring trick — one you play on yourself, or at least collude in. We know the world can be a bad place. We discuss it at length. We know very bad things happen here. We know they have happened repeatedly to me. We have examined, forensically, whether this has been my fault, and concluded, logically, that it has not. But it's strange how you can know something logically, in your brain, and still not really feel that it's true. It's been taking some time for this particular idea to sink in for me.

I couldn't let go of the suspicion that maybe therapists were just telling me what they thought I wanted to hear about fault and blame, and were trying to give me the gift of not accepting any. I'd begun to think that must just be what therapists do, to get you through. But then my son started his recovery from addiction, and I began to hear how people in his support groups speak. I realised they talk, all the time, about the need to take responsibility for their actions and the effect they've had. I also saw them as they shared things that had been done to them, helped hold the space as they recognised they weren't to blame for those. In turn, something in me shifted. I realised that maybe therapists don't just tell you what they think you want to hear, and maybe it really is true that I am not to blame for the things that have happened to me. As my current therapist points out, only people we have already established as malevolent have been telling me it's my fault.

But this presents a new problem. When I believed that all these bad things that happened to me, happened because of something in my behaviour, something about me, I also believed that therapy could be a way of making sure they didn't happen again. I had been

6

thinking, I now realise, that I could take the bad thing about me and change it. But if the bad thing is not inside of me, then I have no control over it. And this, it turns out, is worse. This is terrifying.

THE SUN WEBSITE, 7 JANUARY 2020
'HAD TO HELP'
Convicted murderer says he 'didn't hesitate' to tackle London Bridge terrorist during murderous rampage
A CONVICTED murderer has told how he tackled the London Bridge terrorist.

Steve Gallant, 42, was on day release at a prisoner rehabilitation event when Usman Khan launched his deadly attack at Fishmongers' Hall.

He brandished a narwhal tusk handed to him by fellow hero Darryn Frost and chased Khan on to the bridge, where the terrorist was shot dead by cops.

LETTER I WILL NEVER SEND TO SG
It's been sixteen months now since this started, but I'm picking up the phone again to call my son. I'd like to be asking how his day's going, what he's found in the shops, what he's having for his tea. I'd like to be calling just to tell him that I love him, or a joke I heard today, or something someone told me that I thought he might want to know. I'd like to just be calling him, but I'm not. I'm calling about you. Again. And it's been sixteen months now.

DAILY MAIL ONLINE, 8 JANUARY 2020
[. . .]
Speaking publicly for the first time about Khan's rampage, Gallant said he heard noises downstairs and went to investigate despite 'orders to stay in the conference hall'.

In a statement issued through his lawyers, he said: 'I could tell something was wrong and had to help.

'I saw injured people.

'Khan was stood in the foyer with two large knives in his hands.

'He was a clear danger to all, so I didn't hesitate.'

Using a chair and narwhal tusk handed to him by civil servant Darryn Frost, who revealed last month how he had also risked his life to take on the attacker, Gallant tried to hold Khan back.

He said: 'Khan also showed us the bomb around his waist in an attempt to frighten us.

'We then chased him on to London Bridge and restrained him until the police arrived.'

LETTER I CAN'T SEND TO BARRIE

One of the things I've thought about a lot is cigarette butts; the ones in the ashtray of the car that day when we got in to go somewhere. I don't remember if I was pregnant, or if the baby seat was strapped into the back seat. The back seat has blurred. The rest of the car has blurred. I remember sunlight through the windscreen, the heavy scent of hours-old tobacco smoke in the car, and cigarette butts in the ashtray.

Neither of us smoked, and as far as I knew, the car had been sitting out on the street all night, locked and empty. It hadn't smelt like that when we'd left it yesterday, and the ashtray was definitely empty then too. You looked as surprised as I did. Then you said somebody must have broken into the car and smoked some fags in it.

'Nothing's gone,' I said. 'Nothing's damaged.'

'Maybe I left it unlocked,' you said, 'and someone just needed somewhere warm to sit for a while.'

It wasn't until years later that something triggered the memory and I started to repeat your story. Recognition met my lips as I spoke and shushed me for a while. I remembered how, after we split up, neighbours told me they had sometimes seen you leaving the house late at night, alone, while I was asleep. I realised the story I was repeating was a lie, and I didn't tell it again. But I think about it now, from time to time. The lie. The people who just wanted to sit somewhere warm for a while.

HULL LIVE WEBSITE, 7 JANUARY 2020
The truth behind London Bridge terror 'hero' – The Hull murderer, his firefighter victim and the prostitute dumped in a skip
[. . .]

For the past 15 years, the name Steve Gallant has been synonymous with the gratuitous violence Barrie Jackson suffered that night.

But in an extraordinary twist, he was catapulted into the headlines once again after saving the lives of countless innocent citizens during the London Bridge terror attack.

He was quickly branded a 'hero' by those who were unaware of his horrific past – until now.

Barrie had been sprayed with CS gas and beaten to the ground with a hammer by a gang of men – including Gallant – who wanted revenge after he was cleared of the attempted murder of a 64-year-old Hull prostitute.

The prostitute was attacked in Staples car park in November 2002 and left for dead in a nearby skip, until a scrap metal collector found her with a broken jaw, fractured nose and wounds to her forehead that were caused by being stamped on.

In October 2003 Jackson, a father-of-two, was acquitted of attempted murder.

But he was found guilty of attacking Rosaleena Capell, who was left with severe facial injuries after she came across Jackson punching his elderly father in Albert Avenue and tried to intervene.

Just a month after his death, Jackson had been due to appear in court for intimidating a witness during the trial.

After a city-wide police hunt, Jackson's murderers were finally found.

The attack was deemed to have been pre-meditated and co-ordinated, as the gang had laid in wait for Jackson, and continued to attack him despite him trying to run away.

A post-mortem revealed every bone in his face had been broken.

LETTER I WILL NEVER SEND TO SG

A man appears in my living room. He is holding a hammer in one hand and a narwhal tusk in the other. He wasn't here a second ago, and he's only alone briefly. He is quickly joined by two other men. One wears an explosive vest. He is dead. The other wears no face. He is dead. I am not dead. I am suddenly very alive, in the way that a frightened animal is suddenly very alive. You know the way I mean? You know how everything is suddenly very physical? Very visceral? You can smell the iron of your own blood in your veins. The air thickens around you. But, what am I saying? Of course you know. You're the man with a hammer in one hand and a narwhal tusk in the other.

I'd seen your face before, but it was only a passing blur. I'd made myself not pay attention, which is unusual. Trying not to pay attention is one of those things that doesn't usually work. It's like an oxymoron. Don't think of the pink elephant. You know. But somehow, I'd managed to make it work on you. Maybe it was a self-defence thing.

I've got this theory. I used to tell it to my kids when they were small and I'd got angry: your brain can only hold so many things at one time, and Mummy's brain is really full up of things, and that one little thing you did was too much for it, and I'm sorry, I didn't mean it.

You were sort of one of the things that was filling up my brain at that time, when I was trying to explain this to my kids. Not you directly. The things you did, with that hammer. I think my brain didn't have room for your face then. It hasn't had room for it for the last fifteen years. But now, here you are. Forcing your way in. You appear in my living room.

SARAH COMPTON, FACEBOOK
OMG paramedics couldn't find the victim's mouth horrific

MR WHITE, *HULL LIVE* COMMENTER
Gallant did the world a favour, sadly lost 18 years of his life in prison. Typical HDM reporting

MEDIATOR, *HULL LIVE* COMMENTER
I would rather have Gallant and Gilligan walking the streets of Hull than Barry Jackson.

MAILY JOANNE, FACEBOOK
he was a sick beast, he deserved death, look up on what he did to that poor woman

WOMAN
I remember the first time it happened. Or I have a memory, and it is the first time I remember it happening. Other people have told me it happened before, but I don't like to rely on other people's versions of events if I can help it. So, I have a first memory of it happening. His name was David, and when I was ten years old, I thought I loved him. If I'd have named it, I would have named it love. But I probably didn't name it then. I just felt it. Hot and strong, gushing through me sometimes.

One day at school he was talking to me in the playground, and I liked it. It was nice. He was smiling and being kind, and then he just punched me. Full in the belly. I remember his face when he did it, and I remember that's when the hot, gushing feeling came. If I were to name it now, I'd probably call it sympathy, or empathy, or compassion. I'd seen the way his dad humiliated him in the street. I'd heard what his dad did to him inside the house. I got it. I understood.

Another day at school, I was running. I used to be a good runner. Fast. I won races on Sports Day. I was running on the field, playing with my friends, and then suddenly I was falling through air, legs flailing, skirt ripping, eyes watering as I bumped along the ground. The harshness of it at my face. I said it wasn't his fault. It was an accident.

I remember I saw him once, in the middle of the worst time. I was standing outside my tiny house, in my scruffy clothes, one of the kids in a buggy, and he was walking home from work. I knew this because he was wearing scruffy clothes too. The kind you wear for manual labour. It was the time of day to be walking home from a job like that.

I said, 'Hiya, David,' and he looked at me. His lips started to rise in a smile, and at first I thought he was pleased to see me. Just because it was me. Because of school and everything. But then I realised it was a sly kind of smile.

He said, 'Do you live here?'

And I said, 'Yes,' and his sly smile grew wider as he carried on walking past me, not even breaking his stride.

VICTIM SUPPORT NATIONAL HOMICIDE SERVICE, *LIVING WITH LOSS* REPORT, PUBLISHED MAY 2019
Emotional and psychological impact
The unexpected death of a loved one by homicide can have a wide range of short- and long-term emotional and psychological consequences on co-victims. For example, a study conducted by Norris and colleagues found that 26% of family members bereaved by homicide could be considered clinically distressed. Evidence also shows co-victims of homicide are at higher risk of developing long-term depression, long-term and lifetime PTSD symptoms, as well as long-lasting anxiety, panic syndromes, compulsive behaviour and obsessive revenge seeking.

Moreover, Mastrocinque and colleagues reported that co-victims who lost their loved one to a homicide between three and sixteen years ago still suffer from sleepless nights, anxiety, and fear for their own and others' safety.

ANOTHER WOMAN
The first time, she comes only as a reminder of fresh fag smoke, the faint aroma of the air freshener she used to keep at the bottom of the stairs, and another smell I can't quite place but that is unequivocally

hers. She is only passing through. It is months before she appears, and I see her like this, rolling the trim white body of a cigarette between the thick rings on her still-strong fingers. The knuckles protruding and awkward, the skin soft.

She hasn't physically touched me since she started visiting like this. I don't know if she can, even though she appears as solid as life, sitting here now in what is somehow half her living room, and somehow still my office. She doesn't lift her eyes before she speaks. There's no indication at all that she intends to say anything. Her words just move towards me across the room:

'There are thousands of women, right now, with these words printed somewhere in their house: "Fridge pickers wear bigger knickers" and "A moment on the lips, a lifetime on the hips". They'll be printed on pretty, kitsch little fridge magnets, bought from pretty, kitsch little shops in seaside towns. They'll sometimes still raise a smile from me – I'm a sucker for a silly rhyme. But really, we shouldn't let the silly, pretty, rhyming kitschness of it all suck us in. They're the fucking patriarchy at work, even when these magnets have been crafted by women, wrapped in soft lavender tissue paper by women, and gifted, lovingly, from one woman to another woman she really, deeply cares about. They are self-surveillance, self-regulation, self-flagellation: I must not be hungry, I must not enjoy the pleasure of fat and sugar on my lips and tongue, the warm, comforting feeling of it in my stomach, the rush and swell of it in my bloodstream. I must not eat what tempts me, because I must conform. And that goes right back to Eve. To all of men's evil deeds being placed, as a burden, on the shoulders, tongue, between the teeth – oh, how it is time for those aching jaws to clamp down – of women.

'Do not buy these wares. Or else, buy them and burn them – although by the rules of supply-and-demand capitalism, the buying-and-burning model may become self-perpetuating. Do not buy these wares. If you already own them, burn them. If anyone you know owns them, burn theirs. All signs, symbols and kitsch fridge magnets of the patriarchy must be burned. Forthwith.'

She never spoke like this when she was alive, and I wonder at the change in her. Did she even know what the patriarchy was before she died? Supply-and-demand capitalism? She used to buy all her shopping daily on Holderness Road, a five-minute walk from her house, and then wheel it back in her shopping trolley. She didn't learn how to use a cash machine until after my grandad died. She never swore in front of me, unless it was singing along to those rude songs they used to play at the end of parties in the eighties. The smoke dances in the sunlight from the window and I follow it back to its source, follow the cigarette back to her face. A raised eyebrow.

I often felt like she was reading my mind when she was still alive. Now that she's not, it's even harder to know. I don't want to speak because sometimes she disappears without warning, and I wouldn't want it to be with a question like that hanging in the air. Not the one about the patriarchy; the one that lies behind it; why didn't we ever talk like this when you were here? And the one that lies behind that; why didn't you know this when you were here? And the one behind that; wouldn't life have been easier then?

LORD JUSTICE LATHAM SPEAKING DURING SG'S APPEAL AGAINST HIS MURDER CONVICTION: R V GALLANT, ENGLAND AND WALES COURT OF APPEAL (CRIMINAL DIVISION), 21 MAY 2008
The deceased, Barrie Jackson, died on the night of the 24th April 2005. The appellant believed that the deceased had been partly responsible for an assault on his girlfriend some eight days previously. The prosecution case was that on the night of the 24th April, he arranged with the co-accused Gilligan to meet and attack the deceased who was known to be drinking that night in a public house known as The Dolphin. There would appear to be no doubt that the appellant was waiting outside The Dolphin when the deceased emerged after a violent incident inside the public house. There is equally no doubt that Gilligan's white van had been seen parked in the area shortly

before the deceased emerged, and was driven to the scene very shortly after the incident which culminated in the deceased's death began.

LETTER I WON'T POST TO KARL TURNER, MP

When I hear what you've been saying on the radio, I'm furious. By now, there's been a week of this coverage. I call the show producer, ask them why they're doing this. I cry on the phone. I don't mean to. It's humiliating. It's like I'm melting. People talk a lot about holding it together. I've never thought too much about it before. Holding it together. But now, it means something. I am not holding together. It's like my edges are melting. Everything's leaking out. I got through the first night OK. The stories of what he had done on the bridge. The stories about that other night. The grisly, gory details. All of them following in a chain one after the other, like someone has found something shiny at the edge of a lake, and pulled. This is what has come out. These are all the things that follow.

DAILY MAIL ONLINE, 8 JANUARY 2020

Convicted murderer who helped fight off London Bridge terrorist Usman Khan with a narwhal tusk could be in line for a medal as Boris Johnson praises his 'gallantry'

[. . .]

The Prime Minister told the Commons he was 'lost in admiration for the bravery' of Steven Gallant and others who helped members of the public during the attack last November.

His remarks came after Labour's Karl Turner asked Mr Johnson to pay tribute to his Hull East constituent for taking on Usman Khan, who embarked on a killing spree armed with two knives.

THE SUN WEBSITE, 9 JAN 2020

A convicted murderer who helped fight off the London Bridge [terrorist] with a narwhal tusk could be in line for a medal for his 'gallantry'.

Steven Gallant, 42, could be in line for a gong after Boris Johnson praised his bravery while fighting off Usman Khan in the attack last November.

[. . .]

Speaking in the Commons at PMQs Mr Turner said: 'In 2005, my constituent Steven Gallant did a bad thing for which he is serving a life sentence in prison. But on November 29 he was the third man on London Bridge.

'He wrestled the knife-wielding murderous terrorist to the ground so that police marksmen could shoot him dead. Steven is rightly serving life in prison.

'But will the Prime Minister congratulate and pay tribute to Steven for his bravery that day, which no doubt saved lives?'

The Prime Minister replied: 'I'm lost in admiration for the bravery of Steven Gallant and indeed others who went to the assistance of members of the public on that day and fought a very determined terrorist.

'It's not for the Government to decide these things but it is my hope that that gallantry will in due course be recognised in the proper way.'

HULL LIVE WEBSITE, 8 JANUARY 2020

[. . .]

[Hull East MP] Mr Turner told *Hull Live* after PMQs: 'In my experience as a criminal lawyer, sometimes good people do bad things.

'In 2005, Steven Gallant committed a terrible offence – but on November 29 he acted in a way tat [sic] most of us would not have had the courage to do.

'Convicted criminals must always pay for their crimes and he is currently doing so – but we must also encourage rehabilitation.'

He added: 'Given the fact that Steven is taking part in the Learning Together programme and has been appropriately cateogrosed [sic] as not a risk to the public, it is clear that his rehabilitation is well underway.'

JACQUES VERLADD, *MAIL ONLINE* COMMENTS SECTION
Each year on this date they will remember the occasion with a
ceremonial parade displaying the narwhal rampant and the fake
suicide vest

TTORLER, *MAIL ONLINE* COMMENTS SECTION
Even a murderer can be the right man in the right place at the
right time.

KIRSTY WOODSMITH, FACEBOOK
Well I say he has done the world two favours and should be let out.
Barrie Jackson was jailed for viscously attacking a woman when
drunk and although he was acquitted we all know he was the one
that beat that elderly prostitute to death and dumped her in a bin

WOMAN
I did a bad thing once. I slipped a chunky, triangular Toblerone
bar up the slack sleeve of my fake Naf Naf jacket in Kwik Save on
Holderness Road. Then I left without paying. I did another bad thing
once. I goaded two girls in a classroom argument until they erupted
into, not violence, but physical contact. It probably wouldn't have
happened without my help.

Another bad thing: I once watched as some of my friends smirked
at each other, scissors in hands, while another friend, her long
blonde hair swinging almost to the floor, sat on a kitchen chair one
lunchtime. I sensed what they were going to do. I didn't speak.

Bad things make me think of teenagers. Old enough to sort of
know what they're doing and doing it anyway. Bad things are things
that bad girls or bad boys do. I once went into a takeaway with the
group of bad boys I used to hang about with, back when I was a
bad girl. It was the summer holidays. We'd been knocking about
unsupervised for weeks, doing bad things. But this was the worst.

One of them lifted the charity box from the counter in the pizza shop, tucked it up under his T-shirt, and when they started to run, I ran with them. We got halfway down Holderness Road before I made them all stop. Give me the charity box. Took it back. I stayed in most of the rest of that summer. Paid a sort of penance, I suppose. It had gone too far, but at least I'd taken it back. There are some bad things you can't take back.

VICTIM SUPPORT NATIONAL HOMICIDE SERVICE, *LIVING WITH LOSS* REPORT, PUBLISHED MAY 2019

Many family members bereaved by homicide report a major deterioration in their physical health following the crime. For example, previous research found that 83% of participants stated that their physical health was affected and 75% reported that the physical health of their family members was affected as well, including suffering from stress and anxiety.

Casey also found that many bereaved family members reported developing health conditions such as cancer, stroke, heart disease, high blood pressure as well as other family members dying shortly after the homicide took place. Research suggests that common physical effects of homicide on co-victims include high blood pressure, weight loss, weight gain, appetite loss, sleep disturbance, gastrointestinal problems, decreased resistance to infectious diseases, cardiovascular diseases and cancer. Besides, it has been found that co-victims suffered disturbance in sleep including nightmares and irregular patterns that continued for over a year following a homicide, whereas impairment in memory and loss of concentration lasted for much longer than in normal grief. Moreover, after the crime occurred all family members bereaved by homicide reported physical complaints such as headaches, cardiac problems, stomach and bowel problems, tiredness and sleeping problems, as well as loss of appetite. Also, many participants reported being stressed all the time because of the crime, which may cause above mentioned physical symptoms.

In addition, the homicide of a loved one has been found to aggravate existing physical conditions.

It has also been found that over the years following homicide, physical symptoms gradually lessened or even disappeared for some bereaved family members. However, for many, physical symptoms remained or reappeared during, for example, the criminal justice process. Another study looking at the needs of co-victims between around three and sixteen years after the homicide found that participants reported feeling physically sick, especially around significant dates.

Homicide has also been linked to co-victims' premature mortality. Some research reported significant numbers of homicide co-victims dying within the first few years following the incident.

LETTER I WILL NEVER SEND TO SG

In the hours before you appeared in my living room, I had been out somewhere. I don't remember where, but that's not important. Where I had been is not part of the story. But I remember I arrived home feeling good. Light and happy. The freshness of the outside world on my skin and hair as I entered back into the safety and warmth of home. Do you know what I mean? Do you remember that feeling? It seems very important to me, looking back, that I remember it. Because now, it seems the unlikeliest of feelings to have been feeling, under the circumstances.

Did you ever buy those little bottles of bubbles they used to sell in corner shops? They came in all the primary colours – red, green, yellow, blue. The little white plastic ring in the lid was too flimsy to make bubbles, or else the liquid was too diluted, not enough detergent to water. You could wave the little ring around as fiercely as you liked, purse your lips to coax the gentlest blow. Bubbles did not come. Or only the ones no bigger than suds in a washing-up bowl came. Tiny, inconsequential things you could have conjured on your own tongue with spit. And yet, somehow, once in a while, one of you kids would have got the bottle where the mix was strong, would shake the white ring when the wind was in just the right direction, and out of nothing, a beautiful, brilliant bubble would be born. You'd all stop to watch it. The way the wild slick colours shimmied on its surface. You'd watch as it floated only briefly, then landed on the path – somehow surviving the grit, intact, then lifting in another breeze, carried precariously across the road to land on the neighbour's red brick wall. Somehow still whole. We watched. All us kids watched. You are next door's cat. Leaping from an unseen place to pop that bubble.

Simon would rather not have conjured you. He's the nicest man I've ever met, and he loves me. A lot. The last thing he would have wanted to do was bring you into our living room. But the task had fallen to him. The kind of scenario that plays out across the country countless times each day: people like you making messes. People like Simon and me, cleaning them up. Call it what you like. Some people might call us mugs, but it's the same as doing the housework. I'd just rather live somewhere nice. Sometimes that means cleaning up other people's messes.

After you arrived in my living room, I got angry. But I've never been good at anger. Not like you. I reckon you could teach me a thing or two about anger. You and the man you killed. You were both good at it. You were probably a good match. Some people pick up weapons when they're angry, but me, I try to reason it out, and I found myself thinking a lot about weight.

Atlas was a hero, hoisting up the sky onto his great shoulders, and holding it there, infinitely. Can you really compare one short, sharp snapshot of disregard for consequence, with a long, sweeping stretch of moments that bend out before you, without end? A long, sweeping stretch of moments of struggle and pain. Have you heard that analogy, the one that does the rounds on social media, about the lecturer and the glass of water? He asks one of his students to come to the front of the class, he fills a glass of water, and he asks the student to hold it.

'Is it heavy?' he asks.

The student laughs. 'Of course it's not heavy.'

'Good,' says the lecturer. 'Now I want you to stand there for the rest of this session, with your arm outstretched, holding the glass of water.'

By the end of the session, the student's arm is aching. It's a demonstration of why we shouldn't hold stress, why we should put it down, offload to friends or therapists. And he's right, things get heavy.

I wonder how many glasses of water a murder weighs. Maybe it's the equivalent weight of the person who died. Barrie probably weighed about the same as ninety-eight glasses of water. The student wouldn't be laughing in the first place if he had to hold that.

How much does possibility weigh? Or potential? Google gets confused if I ask it – turns up results like 'what is a potential prize-winning fish weight?' or 'rapid changes of weight after a headstand' or 'how much weight you could potentially lose in a week'.

My children weighed seven pounds, fourteen ounces (four glasses of water) and eight pounds, ten ounces (four and a half glasses of water) when they were born. Now they probably weigh about eleven stone (seventy-seven glasses of water) and thirteen stone (ninety-one glasses of water). Does the proportion of your children's weight that you carry get smaller as they grow? Am I always holding the eight and a half glasses of water that they weighed, combined, when they were born? Or does it get heavier? Am I now holding one hundred and sixty-eight glasses of water?

Let's go with the first option; one hundred and sixty-eight glasses of water seems unmanageable. If they had two parents, we'd be holding half each – four glasses of water, two in each hand, for the rest of our lives. And of course, we'd get to put them down sometimes, when they were both asleep, or when they were both in school or nursery, or at work. As long as they were OK there. As long as we knew they were content and fulfilled and happy and safe, with people around who could look out for them. But when none of those things apply, then you're carrying these four glasses of water each, or if you're a sole parent, then you're carrying eight glasses of water, for the rest of the time.

I got confused after that. Lost track of my own thoughts. I get confused a lot since you appeared in my living room. My brain is too full again. Too full of you. The man I spent fifteen years avoiding. My greatest accomplishment to date. Shattered. You just won't go away, will you? Boris, he loves you. Karl Turner MP, he loves you. Turns out, even the Queen loves you. But not me. I don't love you. I've been working very hard not to hate you, and I really, really wish you would fuck off.

LORD JUSTICE LATHAM SPEAKING DURING SG'S APPEAL AGAINST HIS MURDER CONVICTION: R V GALLANT, ENGLAND AND WALES COURT OF APPEAL (CRIMINAL DIVISION), 21 MAY 2008

As is so often the case, the evidence relating to the incident itself was somewhat confused. A witness, Gary Green, saw a person, whom he did not identify as the appellant, spray CS gas into the deceased's eyes: the deceased started to run away, but was chased by the man with the spray who was swinging a hammer at him. He then described a van approaching and coming into contact with the deceased who fell to the ground. The man with the hammer continued to attack the deceased. Gilligan got out of the van and joined in the attack, there was then confusion during which he saw someone stamping and jumping on the deceased.

LETTER I WOULD LIKE TO SEND TO PRIME MINISTER BORIS JOHNSON

I'm fairly certain you don't know my name, despite various emails sent to you, on my behalf, by my MP, Dame Diana Johnson. I, of course, do know yours. Boris. Good old Bojo with the flapping hair and the flapping arms, contrived to make sure that anybody looking looks anywhere but your face. But I'm not so easily tricked, Boris.

I'd already been paying close attention to the way your eyes slide away while you're speaking. The slight smirk that plays along your lips even when words on the most serious subjects are leaving them. I'd developed a serious aversion to those traits long before they began to taint words on matters related directly to me.

Now, I'm not one of those people who don't think political matters have personal impacts. I've spent a lot of hours in the waiting rooms of Children and Adolescent Mental Health Services buildings, or on the phone, trying to make doctors' and dentists' appointments. I know what it's like to need those services and find them unavailable, over-subscribed. I've also spent a lot of time at home on my sofa, incapacitated by one event or another. So I've had a lot of time to think. But much as I had come to dislike you, and much as my life had been impacted by decisions made by you and your political associates, I could not argue that I had been singled out.

Until this day, when you took something of mine into your mouth. You took the thing I had been chewing on many a long night. Many a long, sleepless night. You know the way your jaw can work, when you're in the halfway place between the daytime world and your unconscious self. The place in your bed where the dark stuff creeps in, the dust in your sheets, the itch in your sheets, the uncomfortable things you don't want to let in, the things that daylight holds at bay, that busyness holds at bay. But when the daylight and the busyness are gone, there are things that itch out into the sheets and crawl there, over your skin. These things, I had gathered them up and worked them in my jaw like a chunk of well-chewed meat — you know that meat that won't be chewed away? You know the kind of meat that will not be got rid of in any civilised kind of way, will not be disposed of without you opening your mouth, without you hiding the action of your jaw with your hand, but everyone at the table can see it anyway? You know the kind of meat you might spit into a napkin and wait for someone to take away at the end of the night?

But there is nobody to take it away, and the napkin is my sheet. And every night when I climb in and lie down, and try to leave the day in sleep, try to leave the day unconsciously, when I am halfway there, this meat has found its way into my mouth again, and I am chewing it. I am chewing, and it is well chewed by now, and this is how intimate this thing was. And you opened your lips, those smirking lips, and you took it in. And as you held it there, just a few seconds, your eyes did the sliding thing, and God, I hated you then.

THE GUARDIAN WEBSITE, 18 OCTOBER 2020
Murderer who tackled London Bridge attacker with narwhal tusk to have sentence reduced
[. . .]

Steven Gallant, who was praised for risking his life to stop the attack, has been granted the royal prerogative of mercy, an extremely rare case of absolution for a convicted murderer.

Gallant, 42, will see the 17-year sentence he received in 2005 reduced by 10 months, and could go before a parole board next June to rubber stamp his freedom, the *Mirror* reported.

The Ministry of Justice said the Queen was advised to grant this pardon as a result of Gallant's 'exceptionally brave actions [. . .] which helped save people's lives despite the tremendous risk to his own'.

DAILY MAIL ONLINE, 18 OCTOBER 2020
[. . .]
The monarch used the power on the advice of Lord Chancellor Robert Buckland.

A spokesman for the Ministry of Justice said: 'The Lord Chancellor has granted Steven Gallant a Royal Prerogative of Mercy reducing his minimum tariff...'

The final decision ultimately rests with the parole board, but it is highly unlikely Gallant will be denied his freedom.

It is understood he has been a model prisoner who has expressed remorse for his crimes and has not faced any punishment or loss of privileges for the past 10 years.

Jack Merritt's father David, 55, welcomed the news.

He told the Daily Mirror: 'Steve fully deserves this pardon, or reduction in sentence.

'It is fantastic. He was very close to Jack and he turned his life around and reformed. I am really pleased for him.'

HULL LIVE WEBSITE, 17 OCTOBER 2020

[...]

A statement issued by [Gallant's] solicitor, Hull lawyer Neil Hudgell to the Sunday Mirror, said: 'Steve feels a debt of gratitude to all those who helped him to achieve a Royal Prerogative of Mercy.

'He is passionate about using his knowledge and experiences to help others steer away from crime.'

[...]

Now he has been given a rare second chance. The last known murderer to be given a royal pardon was nearly 25 years ago when former IRA leader Sean O'Callaghan, who died in 2017 aged 63, was freed.

He had been jailed in 1988 for killing a female soldier and male colleague in a 1974 mortar bomb attack. But he had also been a police informer and claimed to have thwarted a plot to murder Charles and Diana in the 1980s. He was released as part of a Royal Prerogative of Mercy by the Queen in 1996.

The most high-profile royal pardon was awarded posthumously to Alan Turing in 2013, overturning the wartime codebreaker's 1952 gross indecency conviction for a then illegal homosexual relationship.

The Mirror reported Royal insiders saying the Queen 'acts on the advice of Her Majesty's Government' when signing off such pardons.

WOMAN

I always say that I'd like to be buried in one of those compostable coffins with a tree attached. In one of those woods where they do that kind of thing. Let's not get into the practicalities of it. I mean,

I've got no idea how much that costs compared to the standard coffin, the standard crematorium, the standard closing of the standard red velvet curtain. The click and whoosh of a standard cremation chamber.

I saw a dead body once. Was shocked by the way she seemed to be waiting. I thought that I'd see her and think, *Oh yes, an empty shell, as I expected*. But I didn't see that. I saw that she looked strained, like she wanted to get out. Like she might still be in there. For a while after that, I understood cremation. The click, the whoosh, the sudden and certain letting go. Two thousand degrees. A raging inferno of release. But those images passed and now I think that feeding the earth is probably still the best way to go. Slow and steady. The way I measure out kibble for my dog each morning. Not so bad to be lying somewhere dark and peaceful while you slowly ebb out of your body and find your way to the next place. Not so bad. There are worse ways to go.

KAL SCOTT-G, *DAILY MIRROR* COMMENTS SECTION
it's the queen's County.

she owns a police, courts, prisons, army's she can do what ever the hell she wants.

ANONYMOUS, *MAIL ONLINE* COMMENTS SECTION
Set him free and give him a weekly stipend for life.

TOSHI1218, *HULL LIVE* COMMENTS SECTION
[. . .]and all I kept hearing was he fully deserved it . I'm not saying this is right but one nasty person gone . As for Steve Gallant he has nearly served his time and will be out slightly earlier than Gilly with this act of bravery and I can honestly say that the two men will leave the Prison service and will never ever be in trouble with the system again

the victim's family support the move, it says it in the article – the Queen wouldn't have done it otherwise.

LETTER I WON'T POST TO KARL TURNER, MP

I got through it OK the first night, the news stories, the retweets, the Facebook comments. I got through it OK, surprisingly, but my son didn't. We spent the next night in A&E. But we got through that. Then we all got through you asking Boris Johnson in the House of Commons about honour and recognition. We got through the stories about that in the papers, on Radio 4 and on the national TV news. We got through it. But you don't stop, do you? You're on Radio Humberside today. They're holding a phone-in about whether Steven Gallant should be pardoned, and you're their star turn. I call the producer. I want to know why you are doing this.

They can't speak for you, obviously. But they do tell me you were phoning in direct from your surgery in your constituency office. I know where that is. It's at the top of my old street. I passed it every day of my life as a kid. You're in my old stomping ground. I know where you are, and MPs' surgeries are for asking questions. In five minutes, I'm in the car. Coming to see you. The door is locked when we arrive, but when we knock, someone answers. I tell her I'd like to speak to you, but I don't tell her why. You come to the door. You let us in. I tell you who I am, and your face is a picture.

Back when Barrie was first accused of attacking Carol Ives, a strange thing happened in my brain. I wasn't particularly well-read back then, but I'd done Shakespeare at school and loved him. When I began to find out about the things Barrie had been doing while I wasn't looking, Shakespeare came back to me. I'd lie in bed, not sleeping, and hear Lady Macbeth: 'Look like th'innocent flower, but be the serpent under't.' Or Macbeth himself: 'I am in blood stepped in so far, that go back were as tedious as go o'er.' I don't know when it stopped, but it was a long time ago. Then when I tell you who

I am, and see your face, he comes back: 'Never shake thy gory locks at me.' Just like that, I'm Banquo at the feast, and you, well, I don't know who you are yet. But you tell me to sit down, and I realise I'm about to find out.

VICTIM SUPPORT NATIONAL HOMICIDE SERVICE, *LIVING WITH LOSS* REPORT, PUBLISHED MAY 2019
Due to the intensity and unrelenting nature of grief from the loss of a loved one through homicide, family relationships may suffer.

As well as difficulties within relationships between partners, other relationships within families are affected long-term. Homicide tends to have an effect on the relationship of younger members of the family with the others.

In some circumstances children were placed in the care system, which resulted in losing all contact with family and friends.

Moreover, homicide can affect relationships with extended family and friends. Often extended family learns about the death from the media. This leads to directing their anger onto the immediate family members and has a negative impact on relationships between family members.

Furthermore, as close friends can find it challenging or do not know how to support bereaved family members, they can struggle to maintain close contact and distance themselves from the family. This in turn reduces social support, which is much needed for coping with the impact of the crime.

Van Wijk and colleagues found that shortly after the homicide almost all bereaved family members who participated in the research avoided other people and places where they could run into familiar people, with some staying indoors so they did not have to talk about the victim and what happened. However, as the years went by, even though bereaved family members became more selective of their friends, they increased their social interactions. They were also able to talk about the victim, although some found it still difficult more than five years after the crime took place.

Co-victims have also reported feeling isolated, lonely and lack of understanding from friends and family who reduced communication with them because they did not know how to approach the bereaved or what to say. The ability to trust other people is also affected. For example, co-victims reported being less able to trust other people and to teaching their children not to trust other people.

MEMORY

There's a detective on the phone. I've crammed myself into the tiny stairwell, behind the kitchen door, which I've closed, so the kids hopefully can't hear me talking. Last night I pressed the red button, and this detective is not happy.

'That button is only for Barrie Jackson. You can't just go pressing it whenever you like—'

'I'm sorry, but—'

'I had armed police officers turn up there last night. Blue lights. They could have knocked somebody down and killed them. I had a man with a samurai sword at the top of your street last week. We thought it was serious.'

'I didn't know what else to do. He'd locked me in. Smashed my phone.'

'Who had?'

'The man you removed from my house?'

'Your new boyfriend?'

'Yeah.'

'You can't go pressing the button every time you have a domestic.'

'I was trapped in the house. He'd smashed my phone. I tried to climb out of the window, and he dragged me off the windowsill. He wouldn't let me move. The kids were in bed. They could hear everything.'

He's quiet for a few beats, and when he speaks, he's not as angry.

'OK. Well, you shouldn't let him back in the house then.'

'I know that. I won't.'

'Where is he now?'

'At my dad's house.'

'No, I mean, where's your boyfriend?'

'He's at my dad's house. My dad picked him up from the police station last night. He's staying at my dad's.'

This time he's quiet for longer. I hold my breath. Have I given too much away? Maybe this piece of information is enough for him to guess at what my dad said to me on the phone this morning – that I must have done something to make my boyfriend behave that way. That I must have started it. That it can't always be everybody else's fault.

Maybe this piece of information will be enough for the police to say I shouldn't have the red button any more. I'm a scammer. A liar. I make men do the things they do to me, and everybody should just ignore me from now on. But when the detective speaks again, he's changed completely. He is fatherly and concerned. He is full of warmth for me now.

'Look, listen, if there's anything I can ever do for you, you let me know, OK? You've got my number.'

There is some relief in this for me, for a while. He might not know it, but with those few seconds of warmth, he has done something for me, and at the time I was grateful. But now, looking back, I'm fucking furious.

LORD JUSTICE LATHAM SPEAKING DURING SG'S APPEAL AGAINST HIS MURDER CONVICTION: R V GALLANT, ENGLAND AND WALES COURT OF APPEAL (CRIMINAL DIVISION), 21 MAY 2008

Other witnesses also described a man having something which looked like a gas canister, and an attack including stamping on the deceased whilst he was lying on the ground.

[. . .]

The appellant's account was that he accepted that he was the person with the CS canister. He was not intending to do more than confront the deceased when he came out of the public house. The deceased however made as if to attack him, so he sprayed his face with gas. He accepted that he then punched and ultimately kicked the deceased whilst he was on the ground. He denied that any of the phone calls, which he had accepted he had made to Gilligan, were anything to do with organising an attack on the deceased. When the deceased was on the ground, and Gilligan's van had arrived, but before anyone else was involved, he left the scene, taking a hammer from the rear of the van in case any friends of the deceased tried to attack him.

LETTER I WOULD LIKE TO SEND TO PRIME MINISTER BORIS JOHNSON

What I hated most was that you will never have the palate to taste what you were holding there, poised carefully between your back teeth, so that it was barely touching your tongue. It was distasteful to you, I'm sure, and so you must've held it there, like that. But even if you had held its rough body against the long, wet expanse of your tongue, exposing it to the full force of all those tastebuds, spread out like pores, like the nodes of lungs, so that you could breathe it in, you would not have had the palate to taste what it was. It takes years. It takes a lifetime to develop a sense of taste that can comprehend all that earthy, astringent complexity.

You won't know what it feels like to scratch around in the dust at the pit of your belly, looking for something, looking for something you can grab hold of. But your fingers are just scrabbling in dust. In fact, scrabbling is too strong. Your fingers are just moving listlessly in empty air, and the dust is moving in tiny motes between them, too small to grasp, too small for scrabbling. But you realise that your fingers should not stop at the pit of your own stomach, that the world does not stop with the boundaries of your body now. That there are two beings, two more bodies, who can't be allowed to fall through the dusty membrane of your belly. You've got to hold onto them, you've got to hold onto them tight and close. You've got to pull from this nothing-dust something to nourish them. Something to keep them close. Because we all know what can happen when children are 'ill-raised, ignorant, aggressive and illegitimate'.

ITV WEBSITE, 7 DECEMBER 2020
Hull mum opens up about London Bridge terror attack 'hero' who killed her ex-partner
Vicky Foster, who has two children to Mr Jackson, was one of the millions of people to share videos of three men fighting Khan on London Bridge with items including a narwhal tusk, before it was revealed Gallant was among them.

ITVX WEBSITE, 22 DECEMBER 2020 [NOW DATED 7 DECEMBER 2021]
Vicky Foster, who has two children to Mr Jackson, was one of the millions of people to share videos of three men fighting Khan on London Bridge with items including a narwhal tusk, before it was revealed Gallant was among them.

'It just stops you in your tracks. It's kind of a retriggering of trauma, I now understand, but at the time it was really scary. I was having flashbacks, nightmares, couldn't get out of bed, couldn't concentrate. It very quickly became a nightmare for us.'

[. . .]

Ms Foster has now recorded a radio documentary about the incident called 'Can I Talk About Heroes?' which premieres tonight.

[. . .]

Ms Foster says she is now accessing counselling that was not available to the families of victims of homicide 15 years ago.

HULL LIVE WEBSITE, 22 DECEMBER 2020
In the documentary, 'Can I talk about heroes?', Vicky addresses the way society creates heroes and her experience with both Jackson – who was a firefighter and often seen as a hero but who also had run-ins with the law – and Gallant, who killed Barrie but was now seen in a heroic light for his actions on London Bridge.

She said in the Radio 4 documentary: 'Because Gallant had now been labelled a hero, I felt like I wasn't allowed to be angry either at him or at the situation or the processes that had led us to that point.

'I felt like you can't speak out against a hero, which in itself is difficult, but for me it linked back to my experiences with Barrie because he was a fireman and seen in that way and that made it difficult for me to tell people about what was going on.

'We miss the fact that someone can be a hero in one minute and something totally different the next minute. Heroes are people at the end of the day and people are capable of all kinds of things.'

WOMAN

Is it always like this for women? I'm wondering. We are, after all, used to this inadvertent opening up. Blood. Leaking out from us monthly, beyond our control. It will come when it's coming, and we can't stop it. And you men, with your fists and your weapons, you think you know about blood. If it wasn't so bad, it would be funny. I almost pity you. Almost. Not quite. I almost pity myself; all the women opening up without consent. All the women who are softening against their will. Cervix lining shedding. All kinds of shells shedding. Almost, but not quite. The strength there is in softness is what stops me. An old oxymoron.

The head of a sperm will repeatedly bludgeon the outer shell of an egg in order to fertilise it. The pre-cum will have softened it first. Chemical foreplay. I'm sure that might seem like hard work to some people. *The hard work is done now. Fertilisation achieved.* The fast, brutal shock of it. It's not what I'd call hard work. The softening, the shedding, the smooth embedding. The blossoming, the blooming, the feeding and the keeping warm. The long, long, unending stretch of it. Don't talk to me about blood and grind.

ACCOUNTSWIZARD, *HULL LIVE* COMMENTS SECTION
Wow. Never read so many lies.
   She's remarried but she's also divorced.
   Forgets to mention she had a restraining order on Jackson.
   Clearly forgot about him throwing her down the stairs when she was pregnant.
   Why make Jackson out to be an angel when we all know he was a thug?

MUM TO TWO, *DAILY MAIL* COMMENTS SECTION
After reading the whole article I don't think I would have spoken to the press if I was this lady.

JOHN BEACHELL, FACEBOOK
funny how she's so upset she's already remarried! The man has done his time and proven to be a hero so yes been released 10 months early is what he deserves!

CYMRAES1990, *DAILY MAIL* COMMENTS SECTION
If my husband was like that I'd have probably kept quiet and not gone to the press about this. . .

SOMWHEREINGB, *DAILY MAIL* COMMENTS SECTION
It's not like his sentence was halved. Why begrudge one year?

MANDY, LONDON, *DAILY MAIL* COMMENTS SECTION
The last think I would have done is go to the papers with this. As now everyone knows how vile her husband sounded.

LETTER I WILL NEVER SEND TO SG

It takes hours. I'm not exaggerating. We're on the phone and I'm on Google Maps and she's on Google Maps and we're both trying to figure out which bit of blue or brown the other person is talking about. Geography has never been my strong point, but it's not just that; not just the actual time on the phone. It's the thinking it all through. Where do I not want to bump into you? Anywhere, that's the truth. But that's not an option. Neither is the whole of Hull. Which bits then? I already know I want to include my house, the street with all the pubs where all the people I know drink. The thought of seeing you there, celebrating with your friends – maybe celebrating your release. That street is definitely on the list. Where else?

The university, where I've been a student for the last four years, where my granny was a cleaner, where I dream, one day, of having my own office. Where the wedding dos of my dad and brother were held; me in a shiny cream-coloured dress, scuffing my tights on the parquet flooring with a Coke in my hand. Me in a red satin dress, swilling whisky and Coke as I raise my arm to gesture at my sons. That's on the list. Where else? As much space around us as I can manage, that's where. We'll wait and see whether or not it's signed off. Apparently, they usually go through no problem, if it's reasonable, which this is, and if probation have agreed, which they have. But not every offender is the nation's newest hero, are they, so we'll wait and see.

I feel guilty about it at first. Like, who am I to say where you're allowed to go and where you're not allowed to go? Live and let live. If I've got a problem with you, then that's my problem, isn't it? Isn't that the modern way of thinking? What if there are places within those lines we've drawn out that you love? I have to talk myself back out of this. And when I have, I feel better, because I really, really do not want to bump into you, and I don't know the effect it will have on me now, after the last year. More than that, much, much more than that, I really, really do not want my kids bumping into you. Those beautiful boys who, right now, have just about managed to heft this huge weight, along with all the other weight they were already carrying, up onto their shoulders. Not only hold it but begin to walk around with it. I do not want you near them. Not if I can help it. Not on our patch.

It's not until much later, when it's all done, and the relief has settled on me – it's like that feeling when you step off an aeroplane from somewhere cold into somewhere much warmer – that I begin to realise you imposed an exclusion zone on me once. Not a lifelong one, but a long one all the same. It had places I loved in it.

It had the doctor's surgery where I attended all my antenatal appointments. Where I'd arrive with my burgeoning bump, and my burgeoning two-year-old son and my big, strong, firefighter partner, and we'd walk in, like a picture of health, and sit in the waiting area until it was time to go into the little room with the desk and the bed and the contraption thingy that they put on your stomach. Where we all held our breath as the white noise rose up into the room, and then, like something familiar we'd been waiting on for a long time, like something that had been brewing in the distance, waiting to show itself to us, the underwater hiss and thump of our new child's heartbeat. We held it there, the three of us. In the quiet.

You took that place from me. And the greengrocers and the butchers where I'd arrive, pot-bellied, on my bike. Jack would be in the seat on the back, his little fingers playing over my jumper as I moved. His cheeks would be flushed from the ride and the park and the thought of what we'd have when we got home. I'd buy thick, green, sturdy cabbage, and tiny little pasta shapes for chicken soup. It was our stopping-off point on the way between the other places we loved. The planning place. The what-shall-we-have-for-tea-tonight place.

You took that from me, and I was glad to give it. Because I've always thought – it was one of my first thoughts when I heard where you did it – that maybe that brought him comfort as he lay dying in the street. I've thought, often, of that. Would it be possible that he still had some awareness of where he was, when everything else was slipping away? Remember that place with the heartbeat and the bumps and the tousled soft hair of a small boy who's just woken. I was glad to give it. Now you can give this place to me.

VICTIM SUPPORT NATIONAL HOMICIDE SERVICE, *LIVING WITH LOSS* REPORT, PUBLISHED MAY 2019

Persistent anxiety, fear of violence and for the safety of their family members

The majority of emotional and psychological effects of the homicide have endured and are shown to be long-term. Several years after the incident many bereaved family members feel anxious and fearful, not only of violence but for the safety of other members of their family. Participants also reported particular fear for their own safety when the offender is released from prison. The research found that anxiety and feelings of fear persist.

Female, AN: 'I guess I'm a lot more apprehensive and a lot more sort of scared about things than I used to be, fearful of things happening... Since it [incident] has happened to me and my family I think you know it just makes everything else so possible. I realise quite how fragile life can be now whereas before I didn't.'

LETTER I CAN'T SEND TO BARRIE

When I spoke to the police, I thought I was doing you a favour. Honestly, deep down in my heart, I thought I was helping you. Not just you. All of us; you, me, the kids, and anybody else you might come across while you were in one of those dark phases. I knew you wouldn't see it that way, but I don't think that pretending things haven't happened is helping. I thought it was very possible you'd done whatever it was they thought you'd done. And I don't believe in lying for people. I don't think it helps anyone. If you've done something, better to face it, change what needs to be changed, make right what needs to be made right. And I didn't want to be made a liar of. I didn't want to collude with you, in whatever it was you'd been doing. I was of course very, very scared of you by then, too. But it turns out those two things can live side by side in me — fear and concern — there is space for both. Later I'd have to explain this in court, but I didn't know that at the time. I only knew what I needed to do right then.

I answered every question. Told them everything they wanted to know. I thought it would help everyone, but most of all, I wanted it to help the kids. I had always seen the good in you, and I wanted to get back to that. I wanted them to have some of that, even if they had to wait a long time for it. Even if they had to wait fifteen years for it. The police took my statement, and it took hours and hours and hours, and it's a good job my mum lived next door and could look after the kids.

It was twenty-five pages long when it was finished, but everything I'd said was true. Later, the female detective who came to my house a lot would tell me that until they spoke to me, they didn't think it was you. I carried a lot of painful guilt about that for a long time, and now I see it just plain wasn't true. All that jabbing in my gut. All that uncomfortable manoeuvring around it. Unnecessary. I took her at her word when she said it but, looking back, it doesn't really sit right with the fact that you were already in a police cell when they came and knocked on my door. I didn't call the police; they came to me.

Once I started looking back, I got angry at myself a lot; all that taking people at their word, all that trust and openness. But as I got older, I began to see just how young I was. It was seven weeks after my twenty-third birthday when they knocked on my door that night.

Anyway, the statement was twenty-five pages long when we'd finished. After I'd signed it, they brought it straight to you in an interview room, in a police station somewhere. The next day, two things happened:

1. They came to my house and fitted a panic alarm and cameras.
2. They let you go.

THE SUN WEBSITE, 3 JULY 2021
A convicted killer who tackled the London Bridge terrorist could be free within weeks after being pardoned by the Queen.
[...]

A source told the *Sunday Mirror*: 'A decision will be made on Monday. He could be out in three weeks if things go OK.

'But Steve is desperate to keep a low profile whilst settling outside. He's turned his life around and wants to keep on probation's good side.'

John Samuels QC, of the Prisoners' Education Trust, previously said: 'He deserves the opportunity to start a new chapter in his life.'
[...]

Last year, Gallant said he wants to start a charity when he gets out of jail to help rehabilitate fellow cons.

He has struck up a bond with civil servant Darryn Frost, 38, who helped him battle the knife-wielding extremist and the two kept in touch after that.

Speaking after the attack, Gallant said: 'Special thanks to Darryn. Had he not passed me the tusk the situation could have been worse.'

METRO WEBSITE, 7 JULY 2021
Murderer who tackled London Bridge terrorist to be freed from prison
Although Mr Gallant is seeing freedom earlier than expected, he will have to live under a licence which includes a curfew, a requirement to stay at a designated address and an exclusion zone ensuring his victim's family avoids contact with him.

Mr Gallant's solicitor Neil Hudgell said: 'When I first met Steve he struck me as a hugely articulate and reflective person with a wealth of insight into the prison system.

'He is a shining example of reformation not only for himself, but others he has helped.'

HULL LIVE WEBSITE, 6 JULY 2021
Hull murderer and terror attack 'hero' granted early prison release
Steven Gallant now wants to make a 'positive contribution' to society.

[. . .]

At the parole hearing, it was heard how the panel considered the contents of Mr Gallant's dossier, prepared by the Secretary of State.

Mr Gallant's community-based Probation Officer and Gallant himself also gave evidence to the panel, and the board heard a victim impact statement for his original crime, which was 'considered carefully'.

The parole statement said: 'The panel had the benefit of a victim personal statement which conveyed clearly the impact of Mr Gallant's crime and the long-term consequences of his offending.

'The contents were considered carefully by the panel which also took into account the views expressed about licence conditions which might apply if Mr Gallant was returned to the community.'

In what was his second parole hearing, it was heard how Gallant was 28 at the time of the murder, and at that time had a 'willingness to use violence and weapons, misuse of drugs and alcohol, his lifestyle and choice of anti-social friends, having some unhelpful attitudes and ways of thinking, and difficulties with regard to relationships.'

However, he is now 44, has managed to improve his education, and has undertaken a number of accredited programmes to address key aspects of his offending behaviour.

The parole decision said: 'The courses addressed issues connected to his thinking and problem-solving skills, the link between his use of alcohol and his violent behaviour and his attitude towards the use of violence and aggression. He had also completed an accredited programme to enhance his understanding of the impact of his offending on victims, their families and the wider community.'

LETTER I CAN'T SEND TO BARRIE
What I've learnt now about death is that people soothe it. Death brings people, and they soothe the rough edges. But when a man

who has been stalking you for two years has just been beaten to death in the street, when you were terrified of that man, when he has almost beaten a woman to death, when he has been shamed, and you have been shamed, and somewhere inside of you (though you speak of this to no one) you know there is still love for him, then people do not come. People do not speak, because they don't know what to say.

I'm glad I was hard by then. I'm glad I was numb by then. I'm glad that the man in my house who continued to control and belittle me could not get through that hard shell by then. Because it was the only way to stay alive.

Maybe that's why, when the front-page headline, the day after you died, was 'Violent End for Violent Man', I said things like, 'Not violent enough, if you want to add it up,' and when people didn't know what to say, I spoke instead, and what I said was, 'It's a relief.'

And in some ways, it was a relief.

The unwinding of the wires that had twined their way along my windowsill to the camera there, set for recording your weekly visits, the ones you weren't supposed to make; that was a relief. The lifting down of the heavy box on top of the fridge and its accompanying strung red button, designed to be worn around my neck; that felt like a relief. Being able to walk down the street without watching out for each car that passed, without listening out for sudden movements, without scanning and scanning and trying to slow my breathing; they were all a relief. To pretend there was an ending; that was a relief.

But all that relief was a lie. It was a prelude. A pause, in which I managed to remove the man still inside my house, managed to find a job, managed to stand up straight for a few months, begin to feel like a normal person again. Those few months were a relief.

I don't remember what I dreamt of in that time. I don't remember what I did. Those months are still a blank to me. But if I've learnt anything, it's that those blank spaces can suddenly fill and bleed back into your days at the most inconvenient times. So, there's that to look forward to. I remember I had to tell the kids what had happened.

Three and five, they were, and before I asked the family liaison officer to leave and not come back, she did tell me one thing. Under no circumstances should what I told them be anything but the truth. I'd hoped I could give them something softer. Something much softer, after everything else. But apparently that was wrong. My story of an accident would not suffice. So, I remember that I told them the truth. But I don't remember what it felt like. I don't remember if I felt.

I remember crying only twice. One time in my house, when the man in my house was there, and I was supposed to be cooking tea, and he was vicious, and I didn't cry again at home. One time with my nanna in the street. I didn't mean to. She'd come out to say goodbye as I got in my car, and the tears began to come, and I ducked my head beneath the metal crook of the doorframe, and I sat down, and I did not look back and I drove away. I was fool enough to think that was my crying done.

I do have memories of disembodied dreams. I don't know when I dreamt them. Only that I did, and in them you were bound by rubber hose. You were thrashing against it, and it was holding you. Otherwise, you were crammed, arms pinned to your sides, in a tiny makeshift bed that was jammed against the weighty metal stretch of a nuclear missile. These things were holding you, in my dreams. But they did not hold you in real life. Nothing held you there.

LILLIAN BELL, FACEBOOK
After 16 years in prison this man deserves a break,,how he turned his life around,,,,I hope Mr,gallant gets to have a chat with Jack the son off the firefighter,,will do them both good and a relief for Mr,gallent

FLOWERGIRL, *HULL LIVE* COMMENTS SECTION
Jackson was a bully boy to women and only women. . . . Steve hope u do well in the future u have served your time now time to make a new life

RIPPER 1, *HULL LIVE* COMMENTS SECTION

[…] Killed two bad eggs

    Swish, reply to Ripper 1: not true the police shot one

    Ripper 1, reply to Swish: Joint effort. Gallant restrained him. A copper shot him. Still a good result

    Swish, reply to Ripper 1: I know Stevens my son

ANOTHER WOMAN

I'm getting hot under the collar, and she is staying calm. Implacable. That's making me more hot under the collar.

    I say, 'My point though, is that they can't have it both ways.'

    She smiles and turns away towards the window where the chaffinch is back, puffing out his bright red chest and laying his head first on one shoulder and then the other.

    I try again. 'Do you see what I'm saying? It can't be "but that's just what men do" when they do something bad, and then "not all men" when you mention that they keep doing it. Can it?'

    She doesn't turn her head, or any other part of herself towards me. But she does speak.

    'It's another one of those paradoxes you keep thinking about, isn't it?'

    I don't ask how she can possibly know what I've been thinking about. Must be the same way she knows all the things she knows now. Or maybe I told her. Time passes in strange ways when she's here, and I can't always remember what either of us said after she's gone. The bashing against the window starts again, and I look across. Now she has her head tilted down to meet one shoulder, watching him. She looks perplexed.

    'I think he's attacking his own reflection,' I tell her.

    'Don't you feel a bit sorry for him?'

    'I suppose so. He's going to hurt himself.'

    'He sees his own reflection and thinks it's an intruder in his territory.'

'Yes, I think so. Someone said I should put up a picture of a cat. That might stop him. But I don't like cats.'

LORD JUSTICE LATHAM SPEAKING DURING SG'S APPEAL AGAINST HIS MURDER CONVICTION: R V GALLANT, ENGLAND AND WALES COURT OF APPEAL (CRIMINAL DIVISION), 21 MAY 2008

Gilligan accepted that he was there, and was the driver of the van. He agreed that the van came into contact with the deceased and the deceased then fell. The appellant fell on top of the deceased, punching his face. He, Gilligan, was trying to pull the appellant away, he saw the appellant kicking the deceased in the face and head up to four times. He played no part in the attack.

The pathologist, Professor Vanezis described severe injuries to the facial bones of the deceased and a fracture of the skull which were all consistent with stamping and kicking injuries. It was possible that a hammer could have been used to cause one of the injuries. It was the injuries to the head which caused the deceased's death; but the pathologist was unable to say which particular injury or injuries either caused or contributed to his death.

[...]

'So where does that leave the issues in the case? Let's take Steven Gallant. He denies there was ever any plan in advance. He accepts that he did use violence on Barrie Jackson by punching him and kicking him, but he denies involvement with anybody else in doing that. He denies that any physical violence by him was a cause of the death of Barrie Jackson and he denies any intention to cause serious harm, although he admits he did intend to cause some harm.

LETTER I WILL NEVER SEND TO SG

I thought I was going to write another angry letter. I can feel anger like a burn in the pit of my stomach. All that money wasted on Gaviscon, that I could have saved up for something special.

The thing is though, anger isn't going to make it into this letter. I knew as soon as I started typing. Probably I'm too tired again. It's after 1 a.m. again. I'm writing a letter to you again. Maybe I'm running out of anger now. It wasn't all yours in the first place. Some of it was. You do deserve it, but not all of it. I made the mistake of writing to Barrie first, that's the problem. When I think of you, I think of him. I think my anger for him is mostly burnt out too now. I can't keep it up.

The thing is, I think I know why you might want to be a hero. Someone told me the other day that you're a dad, and if that's true, it would make sense to me. I watched *3:10 to Yuma* earlier. Saw Christian Bale give up his life so his son could have a hero for a dad. Do you see I would have liked that for my boys too? Can you see that? When Barrie was on remand, I wanted him to get fifteen years. I wanted him to straighten himself out in prison. Come out changed, given the chance. But that wasn't to be, was it? Found not guilty, and then you did what you did, and now we don't even have that, such as it is. Such as your child will have to live with. I've been angry about that, but I'm just sad about it now, more than anything else.

There are lots of things that have been taken from my boys, but you took their dad, and any chance they ever had of having a dad who found his way back. He could have done what you did on that bridge that day. It's exactly the kind of thing he'd do. But you were the one still walking about, still breathing in and out. I wonder if you've done therapy around that in prison. Maybe. I don't know.

I've done a lot of therapy about guilt. I've been carrying all this guilt for other people's actions. Including yours. I've been thinking for a very long time that I was bad. And I was ashamed. That's what the therapy is about.

Sometimes I remember things that have been done to me so vividly that I think I would rather die than keep seeing them. I've struggled with that – the climb back up from it. It happened today. It was Sunday and we'd been for a walk on the beach, and as we were driving back, it happened. I tried to keep it in, but I couldn't.

I had to turn the radio off and say it. At least I've learnt something. Telling someone when it happens is the thing that could save my life – and I've learnt to throw myself that ring when I'm sinking. Luckily, I've got someone who will listen, help me remember these things are not my fault. That I didn't do them. That these moments will pass.

I wonder if you have these moments. I wonder what it is you cling to when they come. If they come. Maybe you don't have them at all. Maybe somebody who feels it's their right to take away someone's life, someone's brother, someone's father, uncle – maybe someone who feels so certain of what their feelings entitle them to, will never have a moment like that. And still, I'm glad I'm me and not you. Sometimes.

Other times I wonder what it would be like to let go with a hammer in my hand. But I'm the kind of person who worries, years and years later, about a thoughtless thing I once said in a conversation. About that time I misjudged the effect of sticking a freshly sharpened pencil into the back of someone's hand at school. Everything in me tenses when I remember that. The way I didn't think about it until after it was done. Didn't recognise what the consequences might be. I'm starting to feel sympathy for you. But not much.

I was fifteen, and the result was a tiny red mark in the back of a quiet boy's hand. You were a grown man who kept going and going and going and going and going, until you'd killed a man. Taken a person's whole life and all their possibilities away from them. And all my sons' possibilities to have any kind of dad ever again. It's not the same thing. I need to remember that. I wish I didn't have to remember any of it.

Part Two
Mud

Part Two

There is a man. In his hands he holds a thick lump of clay. His thumbs work over it, around it, crafting and shaping. He is creating something. Moulding it. Whispering into the mud as his fingers move. The shape of a figure, half-human, begins to emerge. Stumpy arms, the nubs of legs. It leans into his lips and listens.

WOMAN

The problem is the softening. To have been soft. To have given. To have given in. Lain down. Allowed someone to come in. The problem once you've given, and given, is then to be able to give again. I have sometimes had to claim back pieces of myself, and found, when they returned, that they bore fingermarks. A kind of scar that always links me back to the people who made them.

I do the work. Every day, I do it. It's what keeps me going. Physio for the brain. You get used to old scars and injuries like you get used to anything else. But they will never go away. The body doesn't forget. A sudden movement, a shift in mood, words or gestures, something that echoes another place, another person. Even when you've tricked your mind into an almost forgetting, almost all of the time.

The problem now is with welcoming. With welcoming anyone in. There is softness still to be defended, that will not withstand pummelling.

FIVE THINGS I KNOW ABOUT MUD

1. Mud is technically a liquid or semi-solid; soil and water mixed. Over long periods it can harden and compress to form rock. At this point, it might seem permanent, fixed, but it's probably best for everyone if we all dispense with the idea that anything is going to stay the same forever.

2. When wet, clay is a kind of mud. It's malleable when wet and hardens when dried, all the imprints of everything that touched it baked in, evident.

3. The cliffs at Withernsea and Tunstall, and a lot of the East Yorkshire coast, are formed from clay. It's unstable. Easily eroded. Carried away by the action of the waves repeating and repeating against it, because it never gets a chance to dry out fully. The creeping fingers of the sea don't give it a chance.

4. The bed of the river Humber is a wide expanse of wet mud, constantly shifting, rearranging itself, banks forming, and reforming. There are places along its edges where it's safe to

walk, and other places where the mud is so deep and unstable that you can't stand, for fear of being sucked in.

5. The form a riverbed takes is dictated by what is carried in the water that flows over it. Deposits will be made as it passes, and the bed will form its own geography. This geography, along with flow dynamics, will influence the course of the river, where it ends up, whether it survives, and it's not easy to control what comes floating down a river, what's caught up in the water as it moves. It's like stopping the rain or the weather or the passing of time.

LETTER I CAN'T SEND TO BARRIE

I didn't think I was going to go out with you. I'd been all poised to say no, despite the pressure you and your friends and my landlord were piling on. You seemed nice enough, but I just didn't want to go on a date with you. Maybe what changed my mind was the way you swanned into the pub where I was working and bought pizzas for everyone. Or maybe it was because of my squeaky shoes. Maybe I was just embarrassed to keep walking across the bar with my cheap fake-cork platforms squeaking away like they did, every time you made an excuse for me to come over to your table. Maybe it was your persistence. Maybe that was something I liked. Did I just want someone who would hold on and not let go? The human equivalent of a pit-bull. No, I don't believe it was that. It was the way you held yourself, I think, that did it.

Anyway, whatever it was, let's call this our '*Sliding Doors*' moment. Because I said yes, and after that nothing was ever the same. Will never be the same again. Which is, in itself, a stupid thing to say, because it was twenty-two years ago now, so how could everything possibly be the same? For one thing, I would never get away with those shiny, brown flared trousers now. Ah, the nineties. And being nineteen. And being able to subsist on a diet of frozen meat pies and pints of smooth and never gain a pound. You see? This is the patriarchy at work. I'm talking about being able to maintain the ideal weight without thinking about it, when I'm meant to be talking about what happened. I'll tell you what else I blame the patriarchy for: the fact that I nearly described that moment, me saying yes, as the seed of the way we began to unravel each other. But that's just conditioning. That's the hangover of things you used to say to me.

You: 'Why are women like monsoons? Because when they come, they're warm and wet, and when they leave, they take half your house.'

HOME OFFICE, DOMESTIC ABUSE STATUTORY GUIDANCE, JULY 2022

HM Government: Transforming the Response to Domestic Abuse Consultation Response and Draft Bill, January 2019

FOREWORD BY HOME SECRETARY AND JUSTICE SECRETARY
THE IMPORTANCE OF TACKLING DOMESTIC ABUSE

Domestic abuse destroys lives. It is a cruel and complex crime that can affect anyone, leaving physical and emotional scars that can last a lifetime.

No one should have to suffer the pain of this abhorrent crime, particularly at the hands of those closest to them. Children should not have to witness violence and abuse in their own homes. We have a duty to support victims and prevent people from being hurt.

That is why the government has committed to introduce a Domestic Abuse Bill, which will provide a once-in-a-generation opportunity to transform the response to this terrible crime. In March 2018, we set out our legislative proposals for this landmark bill, alongside a package of practical action. We consulted on these, seeking views from victims and survivors, support organisations and frontline professionals, to harness their knowledge and expertise.

WOMAN

Sometimes a huge chunk of the cliff at Tunstall or Withernsea will be lost overnight. A crash that probably nobody will hear, and someone wakes with the windows of their wooden chalet a foot or so nearer to the sea than when they went to bed. More often though, it's gradual. Slow and steady. The waves repeating and repeating themselves against the permeable clay of the cliff. A minuscule amount lifting away into the sea. Solid to liquid suspension, maybe later to gas. What happens to the particles of cliff then?

LETTER I CAN'T SEND TO BARRIE

It's like I've fallen into a dream, it happens so fast; the transition from dreamy, drunk, footloose, fancy-free nineteen-year-old girl to house-girlfriend. Each morning I clean, even though most of the rooms don't have carpets or furniture. I scrub, I shine windows, I peg out clean washing in the rubble of the back garden. I even iron your underpants. And in the front garden, I dig and water, I plant and sow. You build a sturdy wooden fence, post by plank – a picket fence. We paint it green. Along its edge my flowers begin to bloom – poppies, lupins, lobelia – and by then, I'm blooming too. I know because people actually stop me in the street and tell me. And if there are nights I leave in the dark, shivering and afraid, we don't talk about them. I'm usually back by lunchtime – my dad tells me I'm over-reacting, I need to think about my child – and I walk back in without mentioning whatever it was that sent me running.

You can't hold those kinds of things in forever, though. I manage two and a half years before it all comes spilling out over the thick black lines of police statement pages. My name printed neatly at the top of each, beside the date. My looping signature at the bottom. The length of that statement seemed to be one of the things you were so angry about when you made that phone call. Obviously, you wanted to scare me. You wanted me to know that you knew about the panic alarm and the cameras. You wanted me to know that all you had to do was cut the phone lines and I was fucked. But you also wanted me to know that you'd seen my statement, all twenty-five pages of it, before they let you go.

In the months that followed, I used to think the police were tapping my phone lines. I had the little tape-recorder thing that I was supposed to use every time you rang me. But there was something else. A click on the line when I was talking sometimes, a change in the tone. Maybe it had always been there. I don't know. But it was enough to make me change the way I spoke. Just in case. Corrections in inflection. Omissions. Additions. Curating an image in a different way to the way I might normally have performed for my friends. It was like a policeman was always listening, to all my conversations, and I needed them to know where I stood, and that it was not with you.

It's the little things, isn't it? You said in court that if you did have Carol Ives' blood on your shoe, it could be because you always parked your car in that car park when you went into town to pay your phone bill. Always done it, you'd said, and that was a lie. We used to do things like that together, when we were together. I didn't work, and when you were teaching me to drive, I drove us everywhere, for the practice. If there was a bill to be paid, I drove us there to pay it. And I never drove to that car park.

It's the little things. The way they slide in between bigger things, like grit in gears. Doubt, for example, can be so slight. A change in the tone of your thoughts. Beyond reasonable doubt, a judge will say. You were good at creating doubt, and also at sweeping it away. All the time I knew you. A story might be outlandish, but it was told with such conviction that people went along with it. I went along with it for a long time. For a long time, a lot of the time, I didn't have doubt. But when it came, it came crashing in.

HULL DAILY MAIL, FRONT PAGE, MONDAY 11 NOVEMBER 2002
63-year-old woman left for dead in rubbish skip
CITY CENTRE: A 63-year-old woman was fighting for her life today after being battered and left for dead in a rubbish skip.

The woman was found behind the Staples Office Superstore, in Myton Street, with severe facial injuries and missing teeth.

Police are urgently appealing for witnesses to come forward.

The victim was found just after noon yesterday after a man scavenging for materials heard a murmuring sound coming from the skip in the store's loading bay.

He immediately called an ambulance and the woman was taken to Hull Royal Infirmary.

Doctors today said her condition was life threatening.

The woman, who is white with dark hair and lives in the city centre, was also suffering from hypothermia.

Police believe she may have been in the car park all night.

She was wearing a sheepskin coat.

Although she has been able to talk, officers say she is incoherent and has been unable to give any information about the attack.

Detective Chief Inspector Malcolm Redmore said it was unclear how many attackers they were looking for.

The area at the back of Staples was cordoned off yesterday as forensic teams searched for clues.

Police are searching the surrounding area, which is in the city's red light district.

WOMAN

By the time I was eighteen, I'd been told so often there was something wrong with me that I didn't even question it. It had laid down in me like bedrock. A fact. Indisputable. And I had to try and compensate for it if I ever wanted anyone to love me. Cook better meals. Keep the house cleaner. Be prettier. Be nicer. Smile more. But most important of all: I must make allowances. I couldn't expect to be loved by a person unflawed when I was so corrupted. I had to accept what was coming. I knew this, but just in case I didn't, I was constantly reminded.

I don't think I could say any man ever beat me. I never felt the crack of splintering bone, or the sticky ooze of blood. Never the sickening wrench of a ball joint uncoupling from a socket. The odd well-placed punch. Hands around my throat. The odd well-placed word or story. Often walls or household objects were bruised, but I was almost never marked externally. Most of what happened to me happened on the inside.

MEMORY

The nurse tells me, in a voice which I have always believed was kind, that my bikini days are over. I set the tone, I suppose, when the consultant removed the dressings. I looked down at my exposed midriff, nurses and doctors crowded around the bed, and I laughed. Probably it was the size of the moment. It had grown bigger every time someone reminded me it was going to happen, then again with every face that appeared around the bed. I don't like big moments. Especially not ones that involve my midriff being exposed. Especially when that midriff has so recently been sliced right open – pubic bone to breastbone – and I am about to see what that is going to look like for the rest of my life.

It turned out that I didn't have a belly button any more. They'd gone right through the middle of it – someone had – I don't know who. And not only that; the long line wasn't straight. It was wonky. And so I laughed and said, 'You could have gone round it!' And that was how I set the tone for the nurse to say my bikini days were over. But the thing is, my bikini days never really got started. There is one shivery picture of me, on a beach in Cornwall, arms crossed over my stomach, and I don't quite know if you'd call it a bikini, but I'm definitely wearing a two-piece. I think I'm about fifteen in that picture. Seven years and two children later, I've never felt the urge to recreate that moment. So, to be more accurate about it, my almost-bikini day was over. Singular. But it had been over for a long time when the nurse said these words.

GROWN-UP TO 10-YEAR-OLD ME

Girls are horrible. You can't trust them. Sneaky. Liars. Boys might be boisterous, but at least you know where you are with them. Have a fight, get it all out of their systems, and then it's done. Girls are nasty though. Spiteful.

GROWN-UP TO 14-YEAR-OLD ME
I don't want to hear about it. It's about time you learnt to be grateful. And it's about time you learnt to keep your mouth shut as well. Nobody wants to hear your whingeing. If you don't like it, you know what you can do.

GROWN-UP TO 12-YEAR-OLD-ME
Don't come crying when you've wound him up. What do you expect?

GROWN-UP TO 9-YEAR-OLD ME
You lying little bitch.

WOMAN
It's 5 a.m. and I've just woken from a dream. Simon woke me, a soft hand at my back, like he has so many times. I catch myself still whimpering as I wake, the pictures in my head beginning to fade. Me cowering in my dad's bedroom, holding a baby. I have been trying to get the baby to sleep, but she will not rest. Things keep going wrong. There is a man. He has been screaming at me in the night, every time I have tried to steady my hand to place a scoop of milk powder into the plastic bottle, to steady the baby against my chest so that she can sleep, to rest the soft plastic teat in her mouth in a way where she can find suction. I have moved her to another room, to try again, because I think he is sleeping.

At the moment Simon wakes me, the door of my dad's bedroom is opening cartoon-slowly, the sound of a man's footsteps, the creaking of the floorboard I remember from the inside of the door.

My arm frozen, the warm milk running down my wrist. I wake with these images burning against my eyelids in the dark, the burning low-down ache of period pains in my belly – so similar to those tightenings of the womb in the days when my babies were small, when I was still bleeding, when my body tried to reset itself. It's all jumbled up. It makes no sense, and yet, it also makes perfect sense.

EARLY INTERVENTION FOUNDATION REPORT (PUBLISHED FEBRUARY 2020): *ADVERSE CHILDHOOD EXPERIENCES: WHAT WE KNOW, WHAT WE DON'T KNOW AND WHAT SHOULD HAPPEN NEXT.*

Introduction to ACEs

Adverse childhood experiences (ACEs) are traditionally understood as a set of 10 traumatic events or circumstances occurring before the age of 18 that have been shown through research to increase the risk of adult mental health problems and debilitating diseases. Five ACE categories are forms of child abuse and neglect, which are known to harm children and are punishable by law, and five represent forms of family dysfunction that increase children's exposure to trauma.

What are the 10 ACEs?

The 10 original ACEs are:

- physical abuse
- sexual abuse
- psychological abuse
- physical neglect
- psychological neglect
- witnessing domestic abuse
- having a close family member who misused drugs or alcohol
- having a close family member with mental health problems
- having a close family member who served time in prison
- parental separation or divorce on account of relationship breakdown

WOMAN

I shocked some people at a party a few weeks ago when I told them I used to get bathed in front of the fire when I was little. Not shocked, probably more like surprised. When I said it was only for a little while until we got a shower installed in the kitchen, they laughed. So I threw in the part about the toilet being in the back garden for good measure. I didn't say that the back garden was really a back yard, or that the yard used to run onto the tip. I didn't mention the smell – ammonia and dirt and dead things – or the mouse that used to live in the cupboard under the stairs. You've got to know when to stop, I find. You've got to learn to judge the levels of likely acceptance, and when you'll be going too far.

I didn't tell them that house was my dad's punishment for my mum. She'd had an affair with her driving instructor and left him when I was four. She told me it was because he wouldn't let her go swimming on her own (didn't want other men to see her in her swimming costume) and because he used to turn the light out when she was reading (he wanted to be able to concentrate better on what he was watching on TV). I know there was more to it than that, but these reasons are good enough for me.

LETTER I WILL NEVER SEND TO SG

There are things you believe will never happen to you. Things that exist in some other dimension; not fiction, but all the same, nothing to do with you. You learn about them when you're small, but as you grow, you stop considering them in your day-to-day life, in the same way you no longer see faces in the wallpaper, no longer check inside the wardrobe for the monster who makes himself out of your hanging clothes, no longer wonder what moves in the shadows between your bedside lamp and the side of your bed. These things exist only in the flare of pixels on TV screens, in the ink of newspaper print. They are confined. You are protected.

But then the world cracks, and all the things you thought were nothing to do with you come flooding in. Once one is there, they can all be there. You question everything for a long time. The world has to re-prove its stability to you after that. It takes a significant period of relative calm for you to begin to settle. For me, it took fifteen years, and just as the earth had firmed beneath my feet, along came you again.

Last night I rose from my bed to write down memories of things Barrie did before he died. A way of emptying my head. Gaining some peace. When I returned, slipped beneath my duvet, I slept soundly, restfully. Deeply. And woke to realise I'd been dreaming of you.

The dream starts with me spitting rage at you; you taking it, accepting it, knowing it's yours; me eventually running out, softening. Then a crisis happens. I don't remember what. Something where we're thrown together, needing to react against a common enemy. I remember the warmth and the strength of you beside me. The brush of my arm against your shoulder as we move to act. It plays and plays in my head as I lie in bed the next morning, waking.

It shakes me, the way my mind has betrayed me in my sleep. I feel as though my sleeping self has let down waking me, who is insisting on not accepting you as some kind of saviour. I want to be clear. Analytical. Precise. I want to be given the right to choose how I feel about you. But against the weight of the Queen, the prime minister, the press, it seems my mind, at rest, has succumbed. I tell myself I've been watching too many episodes of *Buffy*; the way an enemy slips into being an ally and back again. Try to convince myself that it is only this, and tiredness. But of course, I know what it's really about.

HULL DAILY MAIL, PAGE 6, MONDAY 11 NOVEMBER 2002
Inquiry's deal for firefighters
AN INDEPENDENT inquiry into the fire service, set up to head off a national strike over pay, was expected to recommend firefighters should receive a 'substantial' wage rise.

But any increase would be in return for major reforms of the service, including increased flexibility and improved partnerships with other agencies.

The interim findings of the inquiry, chaired by Sir George Bain, were being delivered today to the Fire Brigades' Union, local authority employers and the Government.

And union leaders were being told no reforms would mean no pay increase.

The union, which is seeking a 40 per cent pay rise, said it would not be prepared to consider reforms which would 'negatively affect terms and conditions.'

'The review has always been a distraction and nothing more,' a Fire Brigade Union spokesman said today.

LETTER I CAN'T SEND TO BARRIE

You are holding my hand. Harry lies in his plastic crib a foot behind where you're standing. I'm not quite with it. Feeling strange. It's the anaesthetic, I tell myself, knowing it's not true. I have, after all, done this before, but I don't say anything about it. Earlier on, hours ago now, before the epidural and the emergency section, I told the midwife I didn't feel well. Something strange was happening. I'd suddenly begun to shake all over. I was shivery, lightheaded. She told me it was nothing to worry about. I said it hadn't happened last time, and she said every birth was different. I can tell she is getting a bit exasperated with me, so, I don't say anything now. It is, after all, a big operation, and I have, after all, not slept for the last twenty-nine hours. I have, after all, just brought a whole new life into the world. I look over to where the plastic crib lies, behind your shoulder.

As I look back, I interrupt something. Your eyes dart back to me, away from the midwife. There's something in them.

'What's wrong?' I say.

And you say, 'Nothing. Everything's fine.'

My gaze must slip away again, because when I look back, I see you nod towards the floor, below the bed. The midwife comes around to look, and this time I watch her eyes. She does her best to hide it, but I still see panic.

The rest of that day is a blur to me. I think my son was born at around 11 a.m. I know now that you were nodding towards the spreading pool of blood below the bed. Blood that had leaked from me and through two hospital mattresses. I know that I went into theatre three times that day. That though I was conscious for the first two operations, I passed out before the third, and I didn't come round until the next day, in a different hospital, in an intensive care ward. I know that I hadn't been stitched up right after the C-section, and that, though they stitched me up right on the second try, I was still bleeding internally. To find out where I was bleeding from, they eventually cut me from pubic bone to the top of my rib cage. Pinned me open like that while they determined that my spleen was ruptured. Then kept me alive, like a running tap, blood and plasma flowing in from a drip, blood and plasma flowing out from, well, I've never thought about it before, but I suppose from my whole torso.

I didn't get to hold our son until two days later. The Sunday evening, when I finally got transferred back to the maternity hospital. They'd prepared me for the fact that I wouldn't be able to breastfeed. A body can't go through that kind of thing and still produce milk, they said. Only, they were wrong, because mine did. I fed him every drop of food he had after those first two days, propping him with pillows to protect my scar. It felt like a miracle. I felt like a miracle. I felt like I was living a life I shouldn't have got. I was somehow blessed. I don't know why my milk came in. I don't know why I didn't die.

I hadn't been home from hospital long when you woke, while I was mid-feed, in the middle of the night. You'd been drinking. I asked what you'd said, but your eyes were blank. I asked again, and you said it would have been better if I'd have died. And then you punched me, just missing my baby's head. Just missing my healing scar.

RAB MARTIN, *HULL LIVE* COMMENTER
I have a friend whos in jail for murder an although he did kill some one he handed himself in pled guilty an doing the full sentence an he's very remorsefull . . . one night of stupid madness an it's ruined a lot of lives . . . an he's not a bad guy just fuxxed up in a major way ..

WILLIAM GALLAGHER, *HULL LIVE* COMMENTER
Yip I no a few guys who I was in with that tht exact same thing happened too 1 stupid night and there doing a 20year! Crazy like! There was a few I was in with who deserved to be where they were but a couple of m8s who I did feel sorry for.

ANNRSMITH50, *HULL LIVE* COMMENTER
She clearly has a very selective memory about her late violent partner & what a 'perfect' example her late partner was to their children.

HOME OFFICE, DOMESTIC ABUSE STATUTORY GUIDANCE, JULY 2022
Impact on Victims – Livelihood
Many victims can be made homeless by domestic abuse. Annual statutory homelessness statistics for 2020 to 2021 show that 12% of households in England recorded 'domestic abuse' as their main reason for being homeless or threatened with homelessness.

Victims who are homeless are vulnerable to being further targeted by perpetrators of both physical and sexual abuse. Survey research conducted across England reported that some homeless women had formed an unwanted sexual partnership to get a roof over their heads or by engaging in sex work to raise money for accommodation.

The risk of homelessness can prevent a victim from leaving a home shared with a perpetrator, a victim may remain living with the perpetrator to avoid homelessness for them and their children.

Victims may suffer from the effects of economic abuse resulting in unemployment, diminished employment prospects, debt or coerced debt, or poverty. The impact can lead to devastating and long-term consequences and can severely limit access to finance and financial independence.

WOMAN

Gratitude meditations every morning have begun to feel like a lie. I say the words in my head, try them out loud. They're empty. Shallow. Like Alexa is saying them. Like I'm a robotic voice, spouting the words that have been pre-programmed. Who programmed Alexa? Didn't I read something about how it had to be a woman's voice because people wouldn't feel right telling a man what to do? Anyway, that's me now. Sitting in my office, on my own, in complete control of my own time, telling myself how grateful I am, while rage, steady and strong, burns me from the belly up.

I take a breath. I am grateful for my children. I am grateful for the food I eat and the roof over my head. I am grateful for my MacBook and the incense I'm burning. I am grateful for my body. I am . . . fucking raging. I am fucking raging and I don't know what to do about it. It can't come out because people think I'm absolutely bonkers if it does. You see their faces change. Their eyes slide away. They don't want to hear about my rage. And yet, here it is. Spilling out in all the wrong places. I'm having an emotion malfunction. Like my nipple's popped out on stage. Or I've shown my knickers. It's inappropriate. But yes, Boris and Karl Turner are talking about Steven Gallant in the House of Commons and saying they're lost in admiration. Yes, both of these things are true. Ha. Hahahahaha. It's so funny, isn't it? It's a funny old life, isn't it? What a turn-up, eh? What a turn-up for the books?

MEMORY

There's a rugby player close at my heels. Turn, assess. Not at my heels any more; he's on the other side of the road, and more careful than me. That's what's holding him up. Four lanes of traffic separate us now, and that should be enough. It's just as well, because I've seen him on the rugby pitch, caked in wet mud, running, and I'd have no chance of outpacing him if he was on the move again. I've just learnt that he's got arms like a vice, so I'm calling him Vice-Arms in my head. I don't want to find myself clamped by them again, so even though I'm panting hard, my legs are still moving. I'm not slowing. He's still stopped, waiting for a gap in the cars. I'm into the bushes before he's onto the road. I know exactly where the fence is; I'm up and over and into the park in no time. It would be too dark to run this fast if you didn't know where you were going. But I do. Home turf. It's only a few-minutes' sprint across a flat field to the next set of gates; they can spill me out onto the street of houses that are nearly home.

These gates are higher though. More of a challenge, but I'm well-practised. I get my foot in at the handle, stretch up to the spikes on top, avoiding the vandal paint, and pull myself up and over. Thank God I'm not in a skirt. It's a long jump down from the top, but no other way of doing it. It jars my ankles and legs and takes me a second to recover, but I'm fine. And there's no chance of Vice-Arms catching me now. He's probably forgotten all about me, and how, five minutes ago, he had me in his grip and didn't want to let go. He's probably safely back inside the pub with his mates. I can breathe. Straighten my hair. Walk the rest of the way.

I only get a few steps before I realise I've got another problem. There's a car parked on the footpath, off the road, right in my way; and it's a car I know. It belongs to Mechanic-Man. He lives down my street and is always in his garden working on this car when I pass. Everything about Mechanic-Man has always put me on edge. Not enough to stop me sitting and smoking the rollies he makes for me when I'm on my way home from school, but I always make sure that while I'm smoking them, my bum's planted safely on the footpath with him on the other side of a fence. He's constantly offering me lifts or to take me for drives, but the thought of getting into his car . . . nope. I try to stroll by, but the window's down.

'All right, Vicky?'

'Not bad, thanks.'

'In a rush?'

'Just late home.'

'Want a lift?'

'Nah, thanks, I'm all right.'

I've had a lot of lifts in a lot of cars, but this one I will never get into, especially not on my own. Especially not right now, when I've just run my way out of another sticky situation. Never mind that I'm pissed and tired and still a bit scared. I speed up again.

Home, five minutes later, I shout to my mum and head straight to the bathroom, downstairs at the back of the house. Turn on the shower in the cubicle so that the room will fill with steam before I get undressed. I open the bathroom window – a small slit at the top – climb up on the side of the bath, light a fag, lean my arm out as far as I can, press my face into the tiny space to blow the smoke out into the warm, dark air of the backyard.

I shiver, and go back over what happened with Vice-Arms, just before I started running. I can't get the feeling of his arms out of my head. He was so strong, and there was nothing I could have done to get him off. It was just luck that there were so many people about. It had seemed like fun, snogging one of the rugby players. It wasn't every week that I even went back to the pub with them all after I finished work at the stadium. But this week I'd been invited, which was something in itself. To be getting the attention of one of the star players was something else.

I've only been working there a few months and I love it. Some of my friends have worked there for ages, while I'd been selling pizzas in town – my first proper Saturday job. But that had ended after an incident during an afternoon lull, while we restocked the margherita and Hawaiians. My boss had asked me to pass him something from the bottom shelf of an open metal table and when I bobbed down to reach it, he was crouched, looking at me, his penis exposed and erect, pointing towards me through a hole in his jogger bottoms. I'd spent the rest of the afternoon jittery, trying not to catch his eye in the confined space. Trying especially hard not to have to be on the same side of the table as him, cos he'd often push himself up against me if he got the chance. When I got home, there was a message waiting on the answerphone, from his wife, telling me not to go back again.

So when I was offered this job as a waitress, I jumped at the chance. Before the match you'd either be serving chips, sausages, gravy, tea and coffee to spectators, or three-course meals in the restaurant. Then chips and stuff at half-time, and after the match you'd either be on coffee in the exec suite, or – the best bit – serving the players their tea. We knew who all the home lads were, of course, and the arrival of the away bus was always an event. Me and the other waitresses would gather round the window to see who got off, and we'd know which ones we were looking out for, by the time they'd played and come up, shower-fresh, for their sausage and chips.

I'd spoken to Vice-Arms a couple of times in the pub, but that was all. And only briefly. Then tonight, I'd become the focus of his attention, and I had no problem with that, at first. But when he got too forceful outside of the pub and I wanted him to let go, he wouldn't. I wriggled and squirmed. I laughed, thinking he was joking around at first. Then I got angry, and he still wouldn't let go. It was only when I raised my voice, drawing the attention of all the outside drinkers, that he eventually unlocked the arms that had fastened around my waist and would not give. But after he let go and I took off, he'd given chase.

The burning red end of the cigarette reaches my fingers. I've been distracted. It's burnt down, which is a waste. I scrub the tab-end into the brick, wrap it in toilet paper and flush it. Then I undress, get into the shower and scrub away the feeling of those fingers against my skin.

EARLY INTERVENTION FOUNDATION: ADVERSE CHILDHOOD EXPERIENCES: WHAT WE KNOW, WHAT WE DON'T KNOW AND WHAT SHOULD HAPPEN NEXT.
Introduction to ACEs
The fact that ACEs are harmful should be sufficient reason for implementing strategies to stop and prevent them. However,

consistent evidence showing that ACEs also predict poor adult outcomes has made the need for these strategies even more compelling.

EARLY INTERVENTION FOUNDATION: ADVERSE
CHILDHOOD EXPERIENCES: WHAT WE KNOW, WHAT WE
DON'T KNOW AND WHAT SHOULD HAPPEN NEXT.

Summary

It is essential that children's policy and services respond to the fact that understanding, measuring and assessing need is complex, as is responding effectively to complex social problems. We urge caution on the ACE agenda given that:

- Current estimates of the prevalence of ACEs are imprecise. Although we know that childhood adversities and vulnerabilities are prevalent, we do not know *how* prevalent. For example, people are not always able to accurately recall whether they have experienced adversities, such as abuse, in childhood.
- Good data on the prevalence of childhood adversity and wider risk factors is lacking. More accurate estimates are essential for understanding the scale of childhood adversity, in order to plan services and to ensure that effective interventions are available for the children and families who most need them.
- A focus on the original 10 ACEs to the exclusion of other factors risks missing people who also need help. Many other negative circumstances in childhood are also associated with poor adult outcomes. These circumstances include economic disadvantage, discrimination, peer victimisation, low birth weight and child disability. For example, studies show that low family income may be a stronger predictor of poor physical health outcomes than many of the original ACE categories.
- ACEs do not occur in isolation. While ACEs occur across society, they are far more prevalent among those who are poor, isolated or living in deprived circumstances. These social inequalities not only increase the likelihood of ACEs, but also amplify their

negative impact. This means that structural inequalities must be addressed for ACE-related policies, services and interventions to have any meaningful effect.

ANOTHER WOMAN

'You could always sing. It's what you should have done from the start,' she says.

This time, she has the backdrop of that club we used to visit in Withernsea. The long ribbons of gold at the back of the stage, where Ric Owen is singing his heart out. The table brimming with pint glasses and half-pint glasses. It's packed, people moving in a blur beyond her arm, which rests on the deep red velour of the bench seat. She's smiling, eyes sliding over to me as she speaks, and back to the stage, unable to stay off the young singer, who I know she'll always make the effort to go and watch for the rest of her life. He sang at their golden wedding anniversary party.

It was a good day. I remember it. Me and my brother, my mum and her boyfriend, Uncle Phil, Auntie Liz, Nanna and Grandad and all their friends. They had so many friends. Was one of them Ric Owen's mum? His auntie? Everyone was connected to everyone back then. The world was smaller. Safer.

Suddenly the background shifts. It's cold. Wet metal rail tracks fall away to my right, and the towering, solid limestone walls of a station pub rise on my left. Dewsbury. My first job after leaving school, commuting by train every day to work as an admin assistant. The feeling of anxiety is immediate. The wobbly legs, the short breath, the blurred vision. I feel myself sway, reach automatically for my bag – for a fag, or the little brown bottle of Rescue Remedy I used to carry with me everywhere.

'Ah, yes,' she says. 'Fair enough, I'd forgotten about that.'

There was no way I'd ever have made my way onto a stage at that age. We both know it, and she understands. She could sing too, like her mum. But it's not just a voice you need to be a singer, is it?

I glance back at her, and she's changed. She is dressed in faded jeans, ripped at the knees, crouching in her little back garden. Her hands are sunk deep in the soil; the trowel, as usual, tossed away to one side. She lifts her hands to point and I see the dark earth in her nails, almost touching the spiky heads of the thistles towards which she is gesturing.

'Your grandad loved these,' she says.

'I know,' I say, and as I speak, I realise she never said she loved them – and yet they crowded her tiny garden, towering above other plants, throwing them into the shade, stunting their growth.

'Some people call them weeds,' she says. 'A nuisance. But I always watered them anyway. Hung the stuff I wanted – my fuchsias, and that – in baskets on the wall instead. Sometimes you've got to think outside the box – or outside of the tiny patch of earth you've got for planting in.'

WOMAN

There's something very reassuring about labels. Recently I took myself off to Sainsbury's with a list of canisters I needed: size, shape, purpose. When I got home, I raided my kitchen cupboards, pouring out soft white flour, clanking, jangling pasta, a fluid rush of rice grains, into the freshly washed, gleaming glass jars that awaited them. Then I took my favourite pen and thick white paper, wrote out FLOUR, PASTA, RICE, cut out the words and taped them to the jars. The relief I felt was huge.

Now, the satisfaction every time I open the cupboard door is immense. 'Ah, rice, there you are – come sit on the worktop while I chop these onions, stir spices and tomatoes into the pan. Then let me tip you into boiling water, where you will soften, plump and sit steaming under a snug lid until you take your place below curry on the plates I serve up.' You know where you are with labels.

I once watched a man, live on TV, become a murderer. Not here – he wasn't here, in this country – but in America, where news crews can broadcast court proceedings live to the world. I watched as the verdict was read out, saw how his face changed, imagined the impact that would now be felt on his life, the life of his victim's family. I walked away from my TV set feeling satisfied. Justice had been done. Good or bad, people knew where they stood now. I went to my cupboards, opened the door, remembered the feeling of tearing open paper and plastic, of repackaging things, of sticky tape and clear, swooping lettering. I smiled at the rice: 'If I take you now and use this amount of water, apply this measurement of heat for this length of time, you will turn from this one thing to that other thing. Predictable. Reassuring.'

HULL DAILY MAIL, 14 NOVEMBER 2002
SOLEMN SHIFT
FIRE DISPUTE
When the clock strikes 6pm the green watch at West Hull Fire Station comes on duty.

They then wait to be called to action, perhaps to save a life or someone's home.

But last night the night watch arrived at the Calvert Lane station and promptly walked out.

It was the start of the first strike by the Fire Brigades' Union (FBU) for 25 years.

Most of the 50 firefighters picketing at Calvert Lane were not in the brigade then.

Some were not even born.

Talking to them, it was clear that while they are striking for what they believe to be the right reasons, it is not something that sits comfortably on their consciences.

These people signed on to help people, to save lives.

And no matter how strong their belief that they deserve a 40 per cent pay rise for putting their lives on the line every day, they care about what the public thinks.

They worry if someone should die in a fire during the strike, regardless of whether or not their presence would have made a difference, the tide of public opinion could turn. Heroes could become villains.

How would they cope if someone died on their watch?

If the houses over the road caught fire they would rush to the aid of anyone in danger. It is not in a firefighter's makeup to stand by.

Huddled against the cold on their picket line, the firefighters' camaraderie helps them through.

When talks between FBU leader Adam Gilchrist and the local government employers broke down on Tuesday, it was these men who felt it most keenly, because they knew they would be the first on strike when the time came.

The flags and banners on display outside the Calvert Lane station helped tell their story.

One asks: 'What would we be worth if we saved your life?'

The firefighters were supported by their families and children who supported them on the picket lines.

Chris Ogden, 53, is married to firefighter Christopher.

She said: 'I am here to support my husband and I've brought my boy Andrew along.

'If something happens firefighters here will be the most affected. They will have to live with it every day for the rest of their lives.

'But I still think what they are doing is right.'

MEMORY

The ice cube they've given to ease the dry throat isn't working. It aches all the way down to my chest like someone has shoved cotton wool down there – hard. I'm trying to shake the image of an animal pinned to the board of a taxidermist, but the cold metal of the trolley against my back isn't helping. Hands and steel instruments move inside my abdomen. Tugging. A lot of tugging, but no pain. Above me curves white ceiling; at its centre, a raft of electric suns. There's movement all around, beyond my vision. The scuffing of soft plastic shoes against tiled floors. It wasn't like this last time. Something doesn't feel right. Everyone is so busy, and my voice has almost disappeared so that I can't make them hear – wouldn't know what to tell them if I could.

Beyond the white walls lies a corridor leading back to the comfortable labour rooms we just left behind. Women panting and pushing their way into motherhood. Pass those by, and you'll work your way back towards the smiling faces at the reception desk. The reassuring façade that all is under control here.

A few steps more and the slick sliding electric doors will part, opening onto trees. Cars parked in neat rows. Administration buildings. You could be in an office complex somewhere, amongst the careful columns of numbers in spreadsheets and accounting books.

If you could climb in and start the engine of one of these waiting cars, you'd leave through stone gates, onto a busy road that would take you back, back to where this all started only hours ago. Weaving between white lines for ten minutes or so, the houses would move further and further apart. Sunlight would find its way between leaves, and the soft tang of manure would fill the air. You'd turn smoothly onto a neat driveway and walk backwards up the stairs in comfortable soft red pyjamas to snooze again on warm sheets.

Someone speaks, and I'm back on the trolley with the lights in my eyes. The action beyond the foot of the bed intensifies. More green surgical caps appear, and below them I see foreheads creased with tension. Lips in thin taut lines that are trying to give nothing away. I hear a door open, so far away now, at the other end of the room, and a disembodied voice shouting for something. Someone takes my hand, squeezes. Tells me everything is OK. I can't see his lips, only his eyes, and they're saying something else. Something else entirely.

LETTER I CAN'T SEND TO BARRIE
There was a joke you used to tell, about Hedon Road maternity hospital and Hull prison being so close together on the same road. Something about convenience. Something about not having too far to go. You told it when I was pregnant and you were a fireman, and you

73

thought those kinds of things were OK to make jokes about. Neither of us suspected then that there would come a time when our one-year-old son would be bounced on your knee in the visiting room.

In fact, I don't think I remembered that joke at all as we sat there on the hard plastic chairs. I couldn't think of you as a whole person then. You were no longer three-dimensional to me. You had become flat. I had to focus on just one part – the one that I needed to protect myself and the kids from. It's only now I'm starting to put you back together again. A reconstructed man from all these pieces.

I have a very vivid memory of sitting on the rug in the house where we lived when Harry was born. The wide, leaded windows, the polished wooden floor, the leaves of the winter plants in my hanging baskets moving in and out of sight as the wind tossed them. I am sore, still healing. My breasts are heavy with milk. The baby is sleeping. Jack is playing upstairs. The community psychiatric nurse is sitting in the big black leather armchair by the window. You are on the couch. You have just told him you don't need his help any more. That you've realised the only problem in your life is me. That now we're splitting up, you'll be fine.

I am looking at this man, the one I have hoped is going to solve the problem of this darkness in you. The one I'm hoping knows the cure for the fitful blank-eyed nights when you lash out, half asleep; who knows how to make sense of the tales of your violence that have begun to reach me: the erratic, impulsive ways you react (you jumping up and down on the roof of the car of a man who cut us up at traffic lights; you throwing a brick through a workmate's window). But now this man is saying he can't force you to accept treatment. It's your choice. He is talking about discharging you. About typing the paperwork. Winding things up.

Maybe I wouldn't have said what I did, if it wasn't for the rising panic in my chest and throat, the fear that bleached the room of colour. As soon as the words left my lips, I felt the weight of two pairs of eyes judging me, and I felt the judgement they made was that I was hysterical, unsympathetic. The man in the black leather chair said I shouldn't say things like that, and you said, 'See what I mean?'

74

I didn't want to be right. Maybe it was something to do with the fact that my abdomen had recently spent so much time sliced open, with what should be inside exposed to the air, but I'd found this new power of loosening the things I felt in my gut, letting them travel out into the world. At that moment, in that room, what I felt in my gut was that if no one helped us, you were going to end up dead or in prison, and those are the words I said.

THIRTEEN-YEAR-OLD SCHOOL FRIEND TO THIRTEEN-YEAR-OLD ME

Try not to stress about it. Flashers aren't worth stressing about. Just make sure you're not on your own any more if you're walking through the park on the way to school. And if he jumps out of the bushes while I'm with you, I'll tell him it's so tiny that we'd need a magnifying glass to see it anyway.

MAN IN THE POST OFFICE TO FIFTEEN-YEAR-OLD ME

You're gonna get yourself in trouble going about dressed like that.

WOMAN IN THE POST OFFICE TO MAN IN THE POST OFFICE

Young girls don't have any decorum nowadays, and then when it all goes wrong, it'll be some young lad's fault, won't it?

BOYFRIEND TO FIFTEEN-YEAR-OLD ME

If you weren't talking to him all night, giving him the come-on, he wouldn't have done it, would he?

HULL DAILY MAIL, PAGE 2, TUESDAY 12 NOVEMBER 2002
'Attacker may kill next time'

Police today warned the man who savagely attacked 63-year-old prostitute Carol Ives could kill his next victim.

They also urged any women still plying their trade on the streets to work in pairs until the attacker is arrested.

Today Ms Ives, from the city's Walker Street estate, was recovering at the Hull Royal Infirmary after undergoing major surgery to rebuild her shattered face.

Yesterday police issued a gruesome photo of the 63-year-old's battered and bloody face after she was discovered whimpering for help on Sunday lunchtime in a rubbish skip in Myton Street – part of the city's red-light district.

Officers believe she had been left for dead the previous night.

It was an attack which Detective Superintendent Paul Davison described as 'brutal and nasty' while warning the attacker 'could strike again.'

'We have no idea as to the motive which is chilling because there are still girls out there on the street,' said Det Supt Davison.

'As the attacker left Ms Ives for dead, it means he is capable of coldly and brutally assaulting someone.

'She was found by pure chance and we believe he did intend to kill her.'

Meanwhile, Insp Steve Page, of Humberside Police, issued a warning to other prostitutes.

'If girls insist on plying the trade, they should take as many safeguards as possible,' he said.

'We will have a high visibility in the area but there is still potential for danger.'

He suggested women should work in pairs or telephone each other regularly.

But girls say the area needs to have better security cameras if they are to be safe.

'If girls are on the streets then the streets should have more cameras,' said a spokeswoman from Studio 621 parlour in West Hull.

Another Hull parlour owner suggested Ms Ives, who has no history of drug abuse, would not have been the typical prostitute.

'Most of the girls on the street are between 14 and 40 and there to feed a habit,' she said. 'I can't understand why a 63-year-old needs to be on the game.'

'You really need to have your wits about you on the street and this woman was obviously very vulnerable.'

Last night the streets were unusually quiet and it is believed prostitutes may have stayed away in fear of another attack.

Det Supt Davison said: 'We cannot protect these girls 24 hours a day, 365 days a year. But we will work as hard as we need to catch this man.'

LETTER I WILL NEVER SEND TO SG

My uncle lives on a council estate in Hull. Not yours. One of the others. Different part of the city, same type of houses. Same mix of people. My family have lived there since before I was born. It's their home. Their place, and often my place too. But there was a period of time when my uncle had a problem where he lived. There was a group of lads who used to harass him at night. Throw things at his windows while his kids were in bed. Shout, swear, bang on the door. Then one night they set his front path on fire. My brother was about twenty at the time, and after that, he decided enough was enough. Took a couple of his mates and went to confront this group of lads. There was a fight. My brother and his friends walked away feeling like they'd made their point, and thinking that maybe my uncle would get some peace now.

I didn't know anything about it until I got a phone call from a friend early the next day asking if my brother was OK. She panicked when she realised I didn't know what had happened. I had to ring my dad to find out that my brother had walked nearly all the way back to my uncle's house and was just turning onto his street when a car pulled up. Men piled out, and he'd been hit round the head with a metal baseball bat and stabbed three times. My dad had beaten the ambulance to my uncle's house, where my brother was bleeding out on the living-room carpet. It had been a close call, but he'd made it through the night, and was going to be OK.

In the days that followed, a name came to us. Someone said they knew who'd done it, and my dad told me, that for one long night, he fought with himself. Got as far as the front door a few times before turning back. Wanting revenge. Almost setting out to take it. But catching himself. And the following morning the police arrested someone else entirely, who was eventually charged and convicted.

Clearly my dad thought a lot like you, but he didn't do what you did. I don't know why. He used to make us watch a lot of cowboy films when we were kids. Taught us to shoot air-pistols at tin cans and targets, fire a bow and arrow, throw knives at trees. I can still remember the hard smell of the earth as I had to tug out a blade from freezing mud after I missed. His voice, mocking me for not getting it right. He's full of stories about fights he's had over the years, physical triumphs on the rugby pitch.

There are an estimated 1.7 billion TVs in the world. Every one of them will probably have shown an image, not so different to the one of you running down that bridge, at one time or another. A man in action. A man in the midst of movement, in the midst of something 'heroic'. John Wayne. Clint Eastwood. Sean Connery. Russell Crowe. It's conditioning really, when you think about it. No different to the way I was conditioned to think I had to be polite. Had to smile and keep going, had to be forgiving and grateful, whatever happened.

One day I called the number the detectives investigating Barrie's murder had given me. I'd been hearing rumours – about how maybe he'd attacked your girlfriend, and that's why you did what you did. The man on the other end of the phone went quiet for a while when I asked him if this was true. He went off to check something and came back. He said, 'I can confirm that there was an attack on a woman in a flat, and I can confirm that we're no longer investigating that attack. But I can't say any more than that.'

So, I don't have any definite answers about why you did what you did. But I'm not sure it really makes any difference anyway. I can understand why you would have felt that you had to go after him if he went after your girlfriend. I can understand the impulses.

The anger. The need for a response. For consequences. Obviously. Anybody would understand those feelings. But acting on them; well, therein lies the problem for me. You didn't have to choose the way you did.

LETTER FROM DAME DIANA JOHNSON DBE, LABOUR
MEMBER OF PARLIAMENT FOR HULL NORTH
To: The Rt Hon Boris Johnson MP Prime Minister

5 February 2020

Dear Boris,

Re. Ms Vicky Foster, XXXXXXXXX, Hull, HUX XXX

I am writing to you on behalf of my above named constituent regarding Mr Steven Gallant, who tackled the terrorist on London Bridge on 29 November 2019.

Mr Gallant was imprisoned for the murder in 2005 of Mr Barrie Jackson, at the time the estranged partner of Vicky and the father of her two sons, Harry and Jack. Sadly the murder has had a lasting impact on Vicky, who suffers PTSD, and on the boys who, as they have grown, have faced significant challenges with their own mental health.

You will recall that on 8 January 2020, Karl Turner MP for Kingston upon Hull East asked if you would pay tribute to Steven Gallant for his actions on the bridge that day, to which you replied, 'It is my hope that that gallantry will in due course be recognised in the proper way.'

My constituent tells me she very much supports prisoner rehabilitation, and is pleased that Mr Gallant appears to be making good progress within the criminal justice system. She did note however the support provided to Mr Gallant to rebuild his life, compared to the lack of support her boys have ever received. Vicky tells me that at no point since the murder or it's [sic] aftermath, including the events on the bridge that day, have the family received any offer of support from statutory services, including the police or victim support.

As I am sure you will appreciate, Mr Gallant's actions led to a huge amount of media interest, the local newspaper reporting very lurid details of both Mr Jackson's history and his murder. This caused great distress to Harry and Jack. My constituent is very worried that if Steven Gallant is to be publicly rewarded for his actions, this will again lead to renewed media interest, causing further harm to her children.

Could you please tell me your intentions regarding rewarding Mr Gallant for his actions?

I would also be pleased to hear your views on the support and protections offered to victims like my constituent in situations like this?

MEMORY

Any reaction to anything I didn't like was met with the reminder that I was mad. That I'd end up with nothing and no one. Wailing in the woods. Alone. Any thought of leaving was met with the reminder that the kids would be taken from me because I was mad. Unfit to care for them. An unfit mother. That I could leave, but they would stay. And the wavering in my eyes and legs would rise up, on cue, confirming this was true. And so I stayed, over and over again. Stasis. A kind of paralysis. Because moving in any direction could tip things over.

But then something happened anyway; something I definitely wouldn't have chosen, if you'd have asked me. If you asked any mother who'd spent the last nine months reading books about birth plans and bonding. About breast is best and close body contact, and how you can breathe through just about anything. It came and I weathered it, and maybe something else was born in those days, along with my son. The seed of an idea. A tiny grain implanted that would be given plenty of time to grow, in the future: sometimes the thing you really don't want is also the thing you most need.

Not long after, came that night in bed. Me and my miraculous son together. Never more vulnerable. Never more innocent and needing love. And his heavy, loosened hands. His blank staring eyes, almost incomprehensible voice. Rough against the still-knitting fibres of my wound. Rough against my son's fontanelle – its membrane settling around the softness of his brain. And I knew it was time to go. Only I had to be careful. I could still barely stand. I could still barely lift my own child. And he was the tick-tick-ticking in the corner of the house that I had to constantly careful myself around. I had to go very, very gently because he leaked like a gas, and I couldn't afford a spark.

HOME OFFICE, DOMESTIC ABUSE STATUTORY GUIDANCE, JULY 2022

Domestic abuse is a high harm, high volume crime that remains largely hidden. The Crime Survey for England and Wales (CSEW) for the year ending March 2020 estimated that 2.3 million adults aged 16 to 74 had experienced domestic abuse in the previous year. Childhood Local Data on Risks and Needs estimated that, between 2019 and 2020, approximately 1 in 15 children under the age of 17 live in households where a parent is a victim of domestic abuse.

The police recorded over 1.5 million domestic abuse related incidents and crimes in England and Wales in the year ending March 2021. This is an increase of 6% from the previous year.

LETTER I CAN'T SEND TO BARRIE

I used to be afraid of my own periods. I was supposed to be numb as I lay on the hospital bed between operations, and mostly I was. But there were times when feeling had begun to leak through, and what I felt was blood running out of me. A steady, inexorable flow. No one was panicking. We were all trying to keep the room calm. I was explaining that I wanted them to only feed Harry milk from a teaspoon so that I'd still be able to breastfeed when I came out of theatre in an hour or so. I was asking why the bags hanging on my drip had changed from dark red to clear. I was checking every detail, making arrangements for afterwards, and I did not mention what I could feel happening below the bedclothes.

But it came back to me in the months after we split up. I was in a cycle; every four weeks, I would be reminded what it felt like to have my blood flow out of me, and I practised walking in the dark. I spoke to the police. I checked the windows and the doors and the front and back garden before I went to bed each night. I made plans. One hour at a time. One night at a time. One day at a time. I learnt how to control my body – employed my skills with spreadsheets and internet research skills – the ones I learnt at school in lessons where they said we'd need them after we left, and in my job as an admin assistant after I dropped out of college. I learnt the formulas that would trigger chemical processes, and I watched myself shrink each morning in the bathroom mirror. Fat cells released their grip on their components and slipped away into my liver and muscles. Metabolised, breathed out, released as sweat and urine. I was in control. Or so I thought. But obviously, it was never going to be that straightforward.

HULL DAILY MAIL, PAGE 4, FRIDAY 15 NOVEMBER 2002
PICKETS VOW TO STAND UNITED
FIRE DISPUTE
The first man had brought them two cases of beer and a lottery ticket.

Himself the victim of a house fire, he handed over the supplies to the picketing firefighters at the east Hull fire station only a few minutes after they had walked out to fight for more pay.

'You're worth it. I hope you win,' he told them.

Other donations followed in abundance. Food parcels, cakes and snacks have been delivered in a steady supply to keep the troops fed in Southcoates Lane.

The edible support is backed up by the reactions of passing drivers. The incessant honking of horns gives the men cause for optimism as they huddle around a makeshift bonfire. Each salute by a passing motorist is acknowledgement in return.

A caravan, donated by a generous company, provides a temporary enclave as the rain pours down. Outside, the wind rips through the plastic sheets hung up to provide some extra shelter.

Behind the clear-fronted shutters of the fire station, decked out in pay campaign stickers, all three idle fire engines. A security guard lingers around to guard the station.

The bonfire on the forecourt provides welcome warmth for the men. Branches are thrown into the cylinder, but the conditions are not enough to dampen the spirits of the men clustered together.

The pickets are still decked out in their fire jackets. Many also wear the flame-patterned baseball caps.

Underneath a corrugated roof next to the caravan, a generator powers a television. A few men crowd around to watch John Prescott speaking in Parliament.

Before long, heads shake and the simmering anger towards the Deputy Prime Minister is vented.

Few have a kind word for him. Phil Leach certainly does not. He remembers the day, 22 years ago, when he tried to go to sea while seamen were on strike.

'The head of the union was a Mr Prescott,' he remembers. 'I joined a ship and he came on board.'

'He told me to get off, took me to the Seamen's Union officer and told me never to cross a picket line. He said, "you're not going back to work until we tell you to."'

'He's now the Deputy Prime Minister.'

Now Mr Leach, 39, is part of the picket line. And not only is Mr Prescott the Deputy Prime Minister, he is also his constituency MP. So what does he think of Mr Prescott now? 'Hypocritical,' he says.

ANOTHER WOMAN
Today she has come with the scent of sea in her hair. She is carrying chalk in her chest, the wild wind of a Withernsea clifftop rides in her eyes. Her fingers are slippery with beef dripping and speckled

by toasted white breadcrumbs. Her cheeks reflect the glow from the grid-like panels of a paraffin heater, orange like a sunset, and she sits on the flocked beige flowers of a cushioned bench seat, legs crossed in faded denim, hair dark and lustrous, falling down her back.

This is before my time. I only knew her when her hair was cropped above her shoulders or ears, but all the same I can smell the paraffin, the slight damp that always sat in the caravan walls. I can feel the tremble of the floor and the furniture, hear the tinkle of her teacups. Those things I knew well.

She is talking about erosion. About intestinal permeability. About the separation between the finger-like nodules of the gut lining, which allow toxins to pass into the bloodstream. I'm not really listening. Instead, I'm letting myself remember the nights I spent tucked up on the sofa cushions in the tiny caravan living room. I don't want to hear her saying these things. She didn't believe in them when she was here. Would lift her eyes towards the ceiling when I refused her biscuits because they were loaded with gluten.

'You used to love those 2p machines,' she says now, and this slices through the fug of my memories, connects us again.

I smile. I did.

There was something mesmerising about waiting for them to drop, timing the insertion of the muddy copper discs. Watching them roll to lie over the sea of brown on the shifting shelf of the machine. The tension as the pressure built, the precariousness of those coins that hung jumbled at the edge of the ledge, the yawning metal blackness of the void below them. The slow-motion repeat and return of the mechanism.

'Your grandad always used to have to go for a walk after dinner, to let out some gas,' she says.

I remember this too. 'He did.'

Her face is soft. We both know this was something I reminded her of when I tried to justify avoiding bread and sausage rolls.

'We didn't know about gluten and all that then,' she says. 'But, you know, maybe. . .'

I recognise this as a conciliation. Close to an apology. I look up to speak, but the bench has gone, the tremble has gone, the scent and the glow and the presence of her – all gone. Just my old pink armchair, the dark walls. The carpet and the pile of books I'd been reading.

HULL DAILY MAIL, 17 NOVEMBER 2002
Police sweep red light area
Detectives hunting the attacker of prostitute Carol Ives are questioning motorists identified in a police swoop of the city's red light district.

Officers quizzed passers-by and drivers in Myton Street, Hull city centre, to gain clues as to Ms Ives' movements on the night she was battered and left for dead in a skip.

More than 100 people were spoken to – including 28 men who filled out questionnaires – during the six-hour operation on Saturday night.

Police will now sift through information on more than 100 vehicles and are promising to visit the homes of some motorists for further questioning.

Detective Superintendent Paul Davison, who is leading the investigation, described the initiative as a useful exercise.

He said: 'It gave us a very clear idea of all the circumstances around what would have happened the Saturday before, such as the number of punters and the number of prostitutes on the patch.'

During Saturday's operation, a friend of Ms Ives and fellow prostitute retraced the 63-year-old's steps through the red light district on the night she was attacked, November 9.

Police officers hoped the reconstruction would jog the memories of anyone who saw Ms Ives before the brutal assault.

And they are renewing their appeal for Ms Ives' regular clients to come forward so they can be eliminated from the inquiry and aid officers in their investigation.

'I believe in cases like this, people tell somebody about what's happened. If they have committed an offence, they tell someone,' said Det Supt Davison.

'I'm appealing to the person responsible to come forward. I'm still keeping an open mind about what happened.'

Ms Ives was rushed to Hull Royal Infirmary on Sunday November 10, suffering from major facial injuries and hypothermia.

Officers believe she may have spent the entire night in the skip where she was discovered, behind Staples Office Superstore in Myton Street.

She has undergone reconstructive surgery to rebuild the shattered bones in her face and remains in hospital, where her condition is described as 'stable and satisfactory'.

Det Supt Davison said: 'It's the worst attack I have seen in which the person has survived.

'I didn't see Carol when she was found in the skip but I'm told it was absolutely horrific.'

He added: 'I saw her in hospital and it shocked me. I know it also shocked the other detectives working on the inquiry.'

LETTER I WON'T POST TO KARL TURNER, MP

You grew up on the edge of the council estate where I lived for a while when I was a kid – only streets away – and I picture you going to Bransholme Centre. Remember the tiled floors and the covered market, the tang of fish and chips. I wonder if you ever stood with your mum in Fletchers, walked away with skinny sausages wrapped in a soft white breadcake, tomato juice dripping down your chin, like I did. I wonder if you ever gazed at the coloured lights, suspended amid tinsel and reflected in the glass atrium, as you stood and waited to see Father Christmas. I bet you did – before I was born. And later you might have passed me as I waited, laughing on your way to the pub, or finishing your Christmas shopping. It's possible that, without knowing it, I made your Christmas better one year, or you made mine. Maybe we added to each other's measure of festive spirit – your young man's high jinks, my childish wonder.

You're only eight years older than me. You would have been at secondary school when I was still at primary. You went to

Bransholme High School in the eighties, while I was at Highlands Primary, two miles away, a six-minute drive. I imagine you in shell suits and cheap trainers, like the lads I knew around there at that time. The ones that appear in old photographs – me and my mum and my brother and my dog, Rosa, in the foreground – boys like you, your age, playing football, smoking, in the background.

We have these things in common, I think, as I drive to your office, and I didn't know it at the time, but I've found out since, that we were both mature students at Hull university too. You went back in your late twenties and I found out I'd been accepted on my thirty-seventh birthday. Maybe then you, too, have sat in Larkin's library, like I did, studying late at night, rushing to finish an essay, short on time because yours had been used up on other commitments. On other responsibilities. The kind you've built up if you don't follow the usual path of school, college, uni, consecutively. The kind that creep in if you leave a gap, or get blown off-track.

There aren't many people who grew up on Bransholme and went on to become MPs. To stand in the House of Commons, at PMQs. In fact, cards on the table, I've done a bit of research on Hull MPs, and unless there's someone who grew up on Bransholme and became an MP in another place, you're the only one. This is the kind of thing that should make me hopeful. This is the kind of thing that makes me think we can expect empathy from our politicians. Representation. It should make me proud. In fact, maybe, despite everything, it does make me a little bit proud. I'm a strong believer that where you grow up helps shape you. But I've learnt from you that it's not just *where* that matters.

HULL DAILY MAIL, 21 NOVEMBER 2002
Woman anxious to track her attacker
Battered prostitute Carol Ives has told police she is desperate for people to track down her attacker before he strikes again.

The 63-year-old woman is said to be making a 'massive recovery' in hospital, but is no closer to remembering what happened on the night she was beaten and left for dead in a city centre skip.

Lying in Hull Royal Infirmary with an injured jaw, Ms Ives today struggled to talk to police.

'She's still in an awful lot of pain,' said family liaison officer Sergeant Helen Watkinson.

'But she's a very brave lady who worries more about other people than herself.'

'Carol is desperate for us to find who did this and is concerned that they are still out there.'

Ms Ives' severe head and face injuries have made it difficult for her to speak.

The bruising and swelling has gone down, and she is said to be coming to terms with the possibility of scarring.

Police do not expect her to be released from hospital for at least another week.

The investigation has also taken a downturn after it was revealed private CCTV systems in critical positions in Hull's red light district were either off or not working.

None was part of Hull City Council's city centre network which were functioning that night.

Detective Superintendent Paul Davison, leading the attempted murder inquiry, said a camera could have provided video footage of the cold-blooded act.

'The whole investigation might hinge on that information,' he said.

LETTER FROM CHLOE SMITH MP
To: Dame Diana Johnson DBE, Labour Member of Parliament for Hull North
3 July 2020
Dear Dame Diana,

Thank you for your letter of 5 February, sent on behalf of your constituent, Ms Vicky Foster of XXXXXX, Hull, HUX XXX, about Mr Steven Gallant who was involved in tackling the terrorist on London Bridge on 29 November 2019. Your letter was addressed to the Prime Minister. As the Cabinet Office is administratively responsible for the Honours and Appointments Secretariat, I am responding as Minister of State at the Cabinet Office. I was very sorry to read about the death of Ms Foster's partner, and the mental health difficulties Ms Foster and her sons have experienced as a result.

Recommendations for gallantry awards are assessed by the George Cross Committee, whose members are experienced in considering a variety of different cases, and who do so based on consideration of evidence and past precedent. The evidence comes from Police and others involved in the management of a particular incident.

We expect consideration for any cases to emerge from the incident at Fishmongers' Hall will take place in due course. However, I do hope you will appreciate that it would be inappropriate for me to comment on any individual case.

With regards to support for Ms Foster and her family, we recognise that families bereaved by murder or manslaughter have been through a traumatic experience and need effective support to cope and recover. The Homicide Service offers bereaved families access to a full range of practical and emotional support. The support is crucially based on the needs of the family and could include referrals to children and/or adults' therapy for trauma and bereavement, advocacy support and access to free legal advice.

The Homicide Service also provides access to an online forum for peer to peer support for those bereaved to share their experiences with one another. The Service continues to work with families for as long they require support, including the ability to leave and return to the Service at any stage if their needs change.

We understand that the grief of the Foster family may have been reignited by media interest around Mr Gallant following the London Bridge attack last November and so the family may now want to access support from the Homicide Service. I would therefore encourage Ms Foster to contact the Service to access the full range of support that is available to her family.

WOMAN

There are a couple, fingers linked below the table, sitting across the pub from me. She is about nineteen, twenty. Slim, wearing a top made from thin fabric. Her arms look delicate and white. He is big, chest and arms bulging in a tight-fitting T-shirt. So far, I don't think they've noticed me watching. I'm not staring; just taking more glances in their direction than is strictly necessary or normal. I have seen the way he looks at her when her eyes shift to her glass. I have seen him lean close into her neck, or her ear, to speak to her. I have seen how relaxed she is. How open. How comfortable. How soft.

Time arranges things so that a moment comes when I am sitting alone, and she is also sitting alone. He is at the bar, getting more drinks. I look up again, catch her eye, smile. She smiles back. She looks so happy. My body is urging me to stand, take the seven steps between us, and ask if she's OK.

Are you really OK? I want to say. *Is this as good as it looks, or does he sometimes tell you you're a little slag? Does he sometimes tell you he'll drag you out of the house by your fucking hair? Are those soft white arms unmarked all the way to the top?*

She looks fine, I tell myself. *She does look fine. Don't be a weirdo. Get your shit in check.* What if someone had asked me that when I was nineteen? What would I have said? I remember bumping into all my old friends in a bar once, after Jack was born. I was with Barrie. I was so pleased to see them. It was only when they all appeared at once that I realised how much I'd missed them. I didn't ask myself why it had been such a long time since I'd seen them. Your brain can be good like that, building in partitions. They seem so sturdy, but they're just clay. OK in dry conditions, but any rush of water will dissolve them. This was not a rush, though. It was a trickle. And only warm feelings trickled through. They asked me how I was doing, and I remember my bluster – nice house, nice car, new baby. I didn't say 'happy'.

I don't know whether Barrie heard. I don't remember where he was while we talked. Only that he appeared suddenly, throwing punches, and I was dragged away. We hadn't got far before the punches were being thrown at me. I was pinned against a fence, my white arms useless in the face of his fury. I knew it was my fault. I'd deviated. I wasn't sure how, but I knew I wasn't to be trusted. I knew I couldn't trust myself.

Her boyfriend comes back from the bar, and I return to my phone, to my night.

LETTER I WOULD LIKE TO SEND TO PRIME MINISTER BORIS JOHNSON

I spent this afternoon reading your old *Telegraph* columns. Not all of them – that would have taken far longer than an afternoon. You've been quite prolific over the years, haven't you? All those column inches, all that spooling out your words, your thoughts, the intricate little workings of your brain across white space. It's quite damning, really, when you see it all together. The *Telegraph* have grouped them in what they call the *Boris Archive*.

I was Googling you, too; re-reading things I knew you'd said and discovering things I didn't know – like the time a woman questioned you on the way you spoke about single mothers, and you said something like, 'Well, if you ferret around in all my old columns, you're going to find something offensive,' like it's not your fault. Like you can't be held responsible for what comes out of your mouth or your head or your typing fingers. Like you weren't being paid £275,000 per year for doing it.

Two hundred and seventy-five thousand pounds every year. I've been trying to make sense of that amount of money, and it hasn't been an easy task. I started off thinking about the physical size of it. I thought if you stacked fifty twenty-pound notes together, you'd have a thousand pounds. One twenty-pound note is about fourteen centimetres wide. If you laid out those one-thousand-pound stacks, end to end, all two hundred and seventy-five of them, you'd have one-thousand-pound stacks stretching nearly forty metres – one hundred and thirty-one feet. That's the length of four double-decker buses. That's how much money you earned in one year. Four double-decker buses' worth of thousand-pound stacks.

I tried to think about what that amount of money would be like to have. I spend quite a lot of time on mortgage calculator sites online. I've got the one I use the most saved to my favourites. I'm forty-two years old, and so far I've lived in twenty-one different houses, but I haven't owned any of them. I dream about being able to do it – having a little patch of earth that's all my own, where I can sink seeds deep in the dark soil and be around long enough to see them bloom. But I have to tell you, Boris, the results I get when I type in my digits have not, to date, been encouraging. I currently can't afford to buy a house around here with enough bedrooms for me and my children to live in, and the house prices in my city are among the cheapest in the country. I decided I'd see what I could afford if I was earning two hundred and seventy-five thousand pounds each year. You won't be surprised to hear that it came out much, much better than when I put my own numbers in. The future (or at least the living accommodation) looks far, far brighter for you, Boris, than it does for me. Apparently, on that salary, you could get a mortgage of up to one million, two hundred and thirty-eight thousand pounds. Wow, you could be living it up. But what am I saying? What do I mean you 'could be'? I've been reading your columns all afternoon, so I know that you have been living it up for a long time. A long, long time. All your life, in fact.

There's no wonder people want to pay you lots of money for your really expensive views on everything. They're so valuable, aren't they? And why should you remember everything you wrote or said about other people's lives, about their life choices (or lack of them), about whole races of people, whole segments of society? Of course, their thoughts and feelings aren't nearly as important as yours are. That's why you're on the big bucks, isn't it? Obviously. If other people can't afford to have the kinds of views you're entitled to, well that's not your fault, is it?

But look, I'm waffling. I'm almost ranting. I need to calm down. I need to rein my neck in. Nobody wants to listen to a whingeing woman, do they? I should stop frowning. I'm going to make those upright lines in the centre of my forehead even more pronounced, and I really can't afford Botox. Plus, given my body's unpredictable reactions to things like foods and medication, it's probably not advisable anyway. Nobody wants a woman with a forehead like a Klingon knocking about, do they? I'll have to stop reading about you. It's not good for my forehead.

HULL DAILY MAIL, FRIDAY 22 NOVEMBER 2002
Attack on prostitute: man held
Detectives investigating a brutal attack on a city prostitute today arrested a 28-year-old man on suspicion of attempted murder.

The man, of no fixed address, was arrested today and being held at Priory Road Police Station, west Hull.

[. . .]

Officers must decide whether to charge the arrested man within 24 hours of arrest or apply for an extension.

HULL DAILY MAIL, FRIDAY 22 NOVEMBER 2002
Photograph shows a crowd of men, some dressed in full uniform, some dressed in firefighting coats and jeans, filing out of a fire station, in front of the clear glass doors, behind which sit the fire engines.

The caption reads: *BACK ON STRIKE: Firefighters walk out from Central Fire Station in Hull.*

This was Barrie's fire station. He was arrested the same day the photo was taken, as he arrived for work. That night, police came and knocked on my door.

TOMLUFC, *HULL LIVE* COMMENTER
She doesn't mention that her late partner was a violent man just condemns Gallant. . A fireman is supposed to be a hero not a violent thug that Jackson was.

TOMMY14, *HULL LIVE* COMMENTER

Didn't the ex fireman leave someone for dead behind Staples.

Pity she doesn't think what her ex partner did to other families

ERINHENNLEY, *DAILY MAIL* COMMENTER

I find several points in this article disturbing. As a disclaimer, I feel no one, man or woman, has the right to knowingly do physical harm to another human. True, it can sometimes be understood, but not necessarily condoned. Mr Jackson was hardly a fine, upstanding individual. Have we all forgotten what he did? Certainly, our attacker had no more right to damage him, than Jackson had to damage the woman. I am sad to say that his attackers are at least understood, right or wrong. And the wife is acting as if they are releasing her late husband's attacker far before they should. He has little time left. He has served most of his prescribed term. His act of valour saved lives. No one can question that. Seems to me a few months off of his sentence is justified. He cannot erase his crime, but he has gone far in repaying a debt to society. The wife is painting her late husband as a fine, upstanding citizen. This is beyond the pale.

WOMAN

I knew, because I felt it in my bones, that he was going to get worse if I left him, and I've carried so much guilt about that. For twenty years. In July 2002 I packed my things and the boys' things into black bin bags and left in the night. In November 2002, Carol Ives was nearly killed. When the police came and knocked on my door, told me he'd been arrested, I didn't doubt that he was responsible. I felt that he'd almost done to Carol Ives what he had told me, over and over again, he would 'one of these days' do to me. And it seemed to me like I was somehow responsible for what had happened.

Would things have been different if I'd stayed? Obviously. But how they would have been different is impossible to say. Do I feel sometimes like other people have paid a terrible price so that I can live this life I'm living? Yes. It's one of those things I have to fight off – along with the thought that I should have stayed. Should have continued putting my body between him and wherever his fists were aiming.

But I remember my three-year-old son crying for his daddy to let go of his mummy. I remember the softness of my newborn baby's skull. And I know I couldn't do that any more. It shouldn't have been my job.

Part Three

Salt

The figure of a woman is moving on the ground, writhing and distressed, trying to pull herself up, reaching out a hand for some support. There is a man, standing over her, watching, not moving, until he reaches his own hand down inside his deep pocket, tears open a paper sachet, sprinkles white powder over her where she lies. She sizzles and pops. There's a faint smell of saline-scented smoke.

WOMAN

People talk about bravery like it's a binary notion. Something clear and obvious: act or do not act. Something spur-of-the-moment, physical and certain. But for me, that's not what bravery is; sometimes, but not always. What about bravery that happens alone in the dark, night after night? The bravery of closing your eyes to sleep, not knowing what might happen in the blackness? The bravery of getting up, morning after morning, to face the un-face-able? What about those braveries? What about the bravery of walking around with labels you don't deserve? Of being judged and maligned and disadvantaged and disabled and disregarded? What about those braveries? It's easier, surely, to be brave in the brightness, with people watching. What about the bravery that happens every day behind closed doors? The choice between a short sharp burst of energy and a long, painful stretch.

HOME OFFICE, DOMESTIC ABUSE STATUTORY GUIDANCE, JULY 2022

Abuse can continue or intensify when a relationship has ended or is in the process of ending. This can be a very dangerous time for a victim including an increased risk to their physical safety. It is a highly critical period for ensuring support for victims, as they may consider returning to perpetrators during the period immediately after fleeing or ending the relationship. Separation can raise both the likelihood and consequences of risk because of the perpetrator's perceived lack of control.

Post-separation abuse may involve a range of abusive behaviour. It may be facilitated by technology and without effective intervention it can be ongoing and may escalate. In the year ending March 2021, 57 women and 10 men were recorded as being victims of homicide by a current or ex-partner. According to the Femicide Census, 38% of the women killed by their ex-partner or ex-spouse from 2009 to 2018 were killed within the first month of separation and 89% in the first year.

FIVE THINGS I KNOW ABOUT SALT

1. Salt can be found in naturally occurring sources, such as sea water or the vast beds of dried-out lakes. Mining salt is an ancient practice, but modern techniques have made it much quicker and easier to do.

2. Salt is corrosive. Water could wear cliff faces away on its own, but it would take a long time. Add salt to the water, and you'll speed things up. Move things along. Wear down what appears to be solid much, much quicker.

3. There is salt in almost all of our bodily fluids – blood, sweat, tears, urine, saliva. When you break them down, many of their components are the same: just mixed up differently, in different proportions.

4. You need salt to live – it's essential for all your bodily functions. But if you get too much of it, it becomes dangerous, causing dehydration, raised blood pressure, headaches – and these are just the short-term effects. Too much salt for a long period of time can increase the risk of stomach cancer, trigger chemical processes that cause mineral deposits to form in your kidneys, even weaken your bones.

5. The phrase 'rubbing salt in the wound' is widely used to mean making something worse, exacerbating the pain. Anyone who's ever eaten chips with a cut finger will understand why, but imagine that scaled up. Imagine a wide, bleeding wound and an ocean full of salt to tip over it.

MEMORY

After the busyness of police interviews and visitors and watching what the news was saying, there came quiet – when everyone else had gone home and the kids were in bed. Just me, and the windows without locks; their brittle, ready-to-crackness; and the door with no bar. All openings without sensors, with no warning system. Just me.

I lit lamps and candles, and watched the jumping red and green bars of the baby monitor in the corner of the room. I turned down the volume on the telly to listen. To check. Weighing the sound of my sons' small bodies breathing against anything that could be someone else, any shift or movement. It's hard to think about it, even now. My body braces. For what? Impact? Assault? I didn't know. I don't know.

Nights like that are long, measured out in units – the space of a TV programme, a long phone call with a friend, a film. All of them counting down to the moment when I had to stand, move through rooms and darken them, flicking switches. I made myself do it slowly. Made myself breathe and pace out the spaces. Let my eyes grow accustomed to not seeing, or to seeing gradually, in the pale orange glow breaking through the thin slats of the blinds.

I took the stairs, my back to the front door, the blank space of the landing wall before me, at a snail's pace, making myself not look back. Breathing slowly. Checked on the boys, peering through the bars of the cot and the mesh of the bed-guard in the rooms he'd painted only months before. Saw tiny toes that had wriggled out from below blankets or duvets, tucked them in, made them warm again. Then moved into the gaping black space of my own bedroom, not letting myself flick the switch beside the door. Waiting until my bum rested on the new duvet at the edge of my bed. Then fumbling in the dark for the switch of the lamp, pausing if I felt panic begin to rise, eventually warming the room with the yellow glow of a bedside bulb, letting it take form around me, finding him not there.

His physical body never appeared in the light, but he'd already done enough. He was always there in the darkness. He knew what it would be like for me. He was clever at things like that. I made a plan. What I'd do if he did get in. It was part of the reason for walking in the dark. I could find my bedside table drawer by touch, where the red button would be, and something sharp. But it was all a pretence: if he'd have come in while I was sleeping, there was nothing I could have done. The thickness of his arms and thighs, the breadth of his chest. Those things I'd once loved would be weapons, and I'd heard what they could do. But I had to find a way of getting through the night.

HULL DAILY MAIL, FRONT PAGE, MONDAY 13 OCTOBER 2003
HULL: Firefighter pleads not guilty to prostitute's vicious beating
   COURT HEARS OF ATTACK
   [. . .]
The defendant pleaded 'an emphatic not guilty' to an additional alternative charge of causing grievous bodily harm, put to him this morning.

Prosecutor Andrew Dallas opened his case by telling the jury how Gary Robinson found Ms Ives on the morning of November 10 last year.
   [. . .]
Mr Dallas said Ms Ives was propped up against the inside of the skip.

She was taken to hospital where her core body temperature was measured at 'a fraction over 25 degrees centigrade'. Mr Dallas said people usually die if their body temperature falls to 25 degrees.
   [. . .]
The jury was shown photographs of Ms Ives taken 10 days after the operation.

Mr Dallas said forensic pathologists who examined the injuries concluded they were most likely caused by someone in shoes stamping on her head.

He said the injuries to her lips and chin were consistent with someone having kicked or punched her.
   [. . .]
'The most likely case of events is that Ms Ives had been punched to the ground while standing near the skip, and either her face had been stamped on or thrust against the floor of the yard.'

(Proceeding)

LETTER I CAN'T SEND TO BARRIE
You used to tell me, every time you lost your temper, that it was my fault. When you got arrested, you said it was my fault. As your

life slowly unwound itself, you told me, every step of the way, that it was my fault, and, though I didn't accept it at the time, the words stayed with me. Revisited me in the dark and the quiet. A small, hidden part of me always believed you.

My logical brain knows I can't trust anything you said. Lie after lie after lie after lie, looping and swirling in knots. It knows I never unravelled or ruined you. You did that to yourself. But the trouble is, we are not purely logical beings, and so many of your words, despite all my best efforts, still, somehow, have life.

You can't exorcise something still living. The idea in itself is a contradiction. Logically I know this too, but what choice do I have but to keep trying to do it? I have said, rolling the words on my tongue like a prayer, that you can wean yourself off anything, even your own feelings, in the same way you can wean yourself off cigarettes. It gets easier as time passes. You take it day by day. When I said these things, I forgot about the way a passing stranger can blow out smoke and make my stomach clench. But you've got to play the long game: a few moments of stomach-clenching uncertainty versus giving in; a lifetime of deterioration, of abnormality that tightens and buckles into malignancy.

MAN AT A PARTY
I'm not being funny, but you must have done something for him to have gone off smashing stuff up like that.

MAN IN A CAFÉ
How's your sex life? Maybe you're not having sex with him enough.

WOMAN IN CAFÉ
You can't just have sex with him whenever he wants, you know. He won't respect you.

MAN IN A TAXI

Women can drive men nuts. They won't admit it, but they know what they're doing. Manipulative, that's what they are. Winding them up and then crying when it all gets out of hand and they don't like it any more.

HULL DAILY MAIL, FRONT PAGE, LATE EDITION, MONDAY 13 OCTOBER 2003

HULL: Firefighter pleads not guilty to prostitute's vicious beating

DNA LINK TO FIREMAN

Forensic DNA evidence has linked a city firefighter to a brutal and sustained attack against a 63-year-old prostitute who was dumped in a skip, a court was told today.

[. . .]

The jury was told how a pair of shoes belonging to Mr Jackson were found to have DNA belonging to Ms Ives.

The shoes were recovered from his brother Jamie's house in Field Street, east Hull, shortly after his arrest.

Scientists said there was a one in 60,000 chance the DNA did not come from Ms Ives.

Prosecutor Andrew Dallas said: 'There was a link between the defendant and her. This is a lady who he's repeatedly said he had never "seen" or had anything to do with in his life.'

[. . .]

Mr Dallas told the jury it may never be known why Ms Ives was by the skip in Myton Road on the night she was attacked, as the pensioner can remember 'little or nothing'.

But they heard how Ms Ives was a street prostitute who often took her clients to that spot.

She was seen by two prostitutes at 1am and 1.50am in the same area, and it is believed she sustained her horrific injuries shortly afterwards.

The court heard how Mr Jackson had been wearing the Timberland moccasins, where the DNA evidence had been obtained, at a wedding reception at the Cornmill Hotel in Mount Pleasant on the night of Saturday, November 9.

Mr Jackson then left there with a friend to go to Silhouette nightclub before they went their separate ways just before 2am.

Mr Jackson was next seen in Hessle Road, west Hull, where he was involved in an argument with the parents of a girl he was interested in.

The prosecution said that he was seen by a friend of these parents.

The jury heard how he later went to a friend's house in Shannon Road, Longhill at 3.30am.

And Mr Dallas said there is a question mark over what he did during the intervening period.

He added: 'Whoever inflicted these grievous and extensive injuries to this 63-year-old must have intended to kill her.'

(Proceeding)

MEMORY

I was supposed to be at college on the day the trial began, and I did start the day there. 'I'm not going to go,' I told everyone – even myself – and my new boyfriend had made it clear that I was not allowed to go. But Hull College is 0.2 miles from Hull Crown Court.

I think I was trying to do an English A Level. Just one. Just one A Level, seeing as I'd not finished any of them after leaving school. It would be a start. I had dreams. I told myself I could do what I liked now that he was locked up. Now that he was going to stay locked up for a long time. But I couldn't concentrate, as much as I wanted to. I needed to know. I knew there would come a time when the kids would want to know, too, and I wanted to be able to tell them myself. I wanted to hear with my own ears. Facts. Evidence. DNA proof – they told me they had it. I remember the phone call when they rang to tell me they had it. They'd re-arrested him. He was going to be charged. He was going to be locked up for a long time, because they'd found her blood on his shoe.

So, I rose from my seat. I made an excuse. I walked across the road, in through the double doors and up the stairs, and I sat in the foyer. It was filled with people in suits – journalists, solicitors, police and Barrie's family. I was wearing old jeans, old trainers, an old cardigan, carrying a worn-out grubby bag with my college folder inside. I began to sweat. My hands began to shake. The room was getting smaller and smaller, and I decided I needed a fag, reached down into the pocket of that scruffy old bag and pulled out the worn, faded, misshapen tin of rolling tobacco. I'd never smoked rollies before, but let me tell you, whatever people might say, you can't afford to buy Embassy Number 1 on income support. I wished I didn't smoke. Every lungful, I felt guilty about the money spent on this and not spent on the kids. But I didn't know what else to do with the stress. Smoking seemed the thing, so I bought tobacco and I rolled, because it was the cheapest way. It was windy outside, so I decided I'd make a roll here on the bench seat first.

I don't know how everyone heard it, but they all turned to look. Maybe I exclaimed. Maybe it made a popping noise as it opened. Maybe the tin clattered on a hard wooden floor. I don't know; I don't remember whether there was carpet. I just remember the looks on the faces of the people who turned, the straggly dark strands scattered over my legs and the floor, and how it felt sitting there, with all those eyes on me, in that moment. My brain flashing up what I thought they might be thinking: 'Ah, there she is, the one whose fault this all is. The one who drove him to it.' Or worse, '. . .the one whose fault it is that an innocent fireman is here in court, his life ruined.'

Could they tell by looking at me what was happening in my house again now? Could they see that already, in the time since Barrie had been on remand, a new man had moved in and was now abusing me? Did they nod their heads and say to themselves, 'Some women just make men act that way.'?

HULL DAILY MAIL, FRONT PAGE, TUESDAY 14 OCTOBER 2003
I have no memory of attack, says prostitute
A 63-year-old prostitute has blacked out memories of an alleged attack sustained before she was dumped in a skip, a court heard.

Carol Ives took the stand at Hull Crown Court to explain how her life had changed since she was allegedly attacked and left for dead last November.

But the only thing she said she could remember was making a desperate 999 call for help as she lay in a skip at the back of Staples Office Supplies, in Myton Street.

Ms Ives told the court: 'I can't remember anything. I had a mobile in my pocket and I must have dialled 999. They kept asking me where I was but I didn't know where I was.'

She was eventually found by scrap-metal collector Gary Robinson, hours later.

The court heard Ms Ives had worked as a prostitute in the Myton Street area for more than 20 years, after divorcing her husband in 1976.

As she gave evidence, she said she was still having treatment for her injuries, including a ragged zigzag cut to her forehead.

She told the court: 'I'm waiting to have my nose operation. I cannot chew because of my jaw and I've got to have plastic surgery on my head.'

'I'm not as strong as I was.'

The court heard how Ms Ives remembered boarding the 9.40pm bus near her west Hull home on Saturday November 9 – the night of the alleged attack – and arrived by the former Tower cinema, in Anlaby Road, at around 10pm.

She said she was planning to go to Napoleon's Casino, in George Street.

[. . .]

Asked by prosecutor Andrew Dallas whether she took clients to the skip, Ms Ives bowed her head.

'I'm so ashamed of that part of my life,' she said.

Gripping the edge of the witness stand, she then revealed how she had been throttled by a punter and beaten by an ex-husband.

HULL DAILY MAIL, TUESDAY 14 OCTOBER 2003
HULL: DNA CLUE LINKS ACCUSED TO SAVAGE ASSAULT
'I can't recall brutal attack'
[. . .]
When questioned by prosecutor Andrew Dallas, Ms Ives said she had no idea why she was in the area.

'I quite regularly went there,' she told the court.

But she later added: 'I never walked through town after 11pm. I was frightened of people who drink.'

[. . .]

Some 11 pairs of shoes were seized by police from the Field Street home of Mr Jackson's brother Jamie in east Hull after the arrest.

Detectives felt shoes were the best way to check for evidence after the pathologist concluded the attacker had possibly stamped on Ms Ives' head.

The items were sent off to a laboratory, where scientists discovered a tiny speck of DNA material on the right shoe of a pair of Timberland moccasins which were owned by Mr Jackson.

When they analysed the material further they found it to be a speck of blood belonging to Mr Jackson layered on top of a second DNA sample.

The court heard how this sample could have come from any body fluid belonging to Ms Ives.

ANOTHER WOMAN

She is lying on the beach, a thin, rough cotton towel spread out over the shingle. She might be in Thornwick Bay, where she had her last caravan. The place where she and I used to scramble down the steep cliffs with my kids, to pick out shells and admire the swimmers as they struck out towards the caves. But it's hard to tell. I can see only the small section of white stones on which she is lying. She doesn't seem to feel them at all. She is stretching out comfortably. She could be on a chaise longue in a swanky hotel. She is young. Limbs limber. Vague white smudges of drying saltwater on her skin. Hair with the crunchy thickness brought about by sea-swimming and sunbathing.

'The problem is that all the frameworks have been constructed by the patriarchy,' she says. 'That's the main problem we're facing. Well, that you're facing. It doesn't matter so much over here.'

She pauses, and I consider my first question: patriarchal frameworks or the concept of over there? I've hesitated too long, and she speaks again before I decide.

'For example, a man says you're over-reacting, and you get upset. You explain that you're upset, and he says that's an overreaction. You're so busy trying to process the upset feelings whilst also trying to pin down what exactly it is about what he's said that has upset you, that it's difficult to defend yourself. You start to waver. Maybe your voice raises slightly in pitch. He lifts an eyebrow, as if to say, *See, you're proving me right, right now.*

'The upset is compounded. In fact, it's becoming distress. You try and calm yourself. You say, it's the word *over-reacting* that you object to, and he half-smiles, moves his head in what appears to be a very slight shake. You say, 'Don't shake your head,' and he says, 'I'm not shaking my head,' which is technically true. He didn't quite do it. You stumble again, doubting yourself, and before you know it, he's walking away, feeing justified in his original comment, and you're unable to defend yourself or set out your objections fully. Sound familiar?'

Yes, very.

I realise I haven't said it out loud. This conversation is unexpectedly heavy.

She nods. She isn't angry. In fact, she looks quite serene. It's a serenity I understand. A point well articulated, the space in which to make it, unchallenged and unjudged. It's a precious thing. I'm glad she's savouring it, enjoying it. I'm about to respond when she begins to fade, leaving behind the impression of her chin jutting forward, one eye closed in a wink, a knowing smile playing over her lips.

HULL DAILY MAIL, WEDNESDAY 15 OCTOBER 2003
HULL: Officer took sample from defendant and victim

DNA evidence 'contaminated'

Doubts have been cast over DNA evidence linking prostitute Carol Ives to the man accused of beating her and leaving her for dead in a city centre skip.

Hull Crown Court heard how the same scenes of crime officer investigated the skip where the pensioner was discovered – and also tested defendant Barrie Jackson's belongings.

They included the pair of moccasins on which the DNA of 63-year-old Ms Ives was later found.

A jury at Hull Crown Court was told this should never happen in an 'ideal world' because of the risk evidence could be contaminated.

Mr Jackson shook his head repeatedly as he listened to civilian police officer Colin Jordan assuring the court he had taken all necessary precautions when touching the shoes.

[. . .]

Mr Jordan told the jury of seven women and five men how he was called to the scene on Monday, the day after the attack.

He had climbed into the skip where Ms Ives, now 64, had been buried and removed her red shoe.

Some 11 days later, on November 22, he was then sent to screen Mr Jackson's belongings, which were at his brother Jamie's house in Field Street, east Hull.

He was the first officer to touch the moccasins on which the police later discovered two DNA profiles – one from a speck of blood belonging to Mr Jackson, and a second from an unidentified body fluid belonging to Ms Ives.

When asked by Tony Stevenson, defending, if an officer who went to one crime scene should then go to another scene which may prove significant, Mr Jordan said: 'Not in an ideal world.'

Mr Stevenson then asked if there was a risk of transferring DNA from one site to another.

But Mr Jordan said: 'It is always a theoretical risk.'

He said he had worn disposable protective clothing, rubber gloves, coverings over his shoes on all occasions.

(Proceeding)

HULL DAILY MAIL, WEDNESDAY 15 OCTOBER 2003
HULL: Claims defendant told about using prostitutes

Accused's vice confession

The man accused of the attempted murder of 63-year-old prostitute Carol Ives has admitted to using street girls, a jury was told today.

Hull Crown Court heard today how Barrie Jackson, 29, spoke to his work colleagues about sleeping with prostitutes.

[...]

Today he sat in the dock staring straight ahead as work mate Andrew Martin told the jury about a conversation he'd had with Mr Jackson about prostitutes.

He said: 'He said that he has used a prostitute and when he uses them they are usually of a younger age.'

Tony Stevenson, for the defence, said: 'Barrie Jackson does not remember saying that to you but he said it to someone else at work.'

[...]

Today [Carol Ives] sat in the public gallery and listened as witness Graham Parish told the court how he had had an argument with Mr Jackson at around 2.30am that night.

Mr Parish said how he had been out with friends John and Pat Simmons to Tam Tam's nightclub in Anlaby Road, west Hull.

He said the group left the club some time before 2am and were having a cup of coffee at Mr Simmons' home in Hessle Road, west Hull, when Mr Jackson unexpectedly arrived.

Mr Parish believes the defendant had come to visit the Simmons' daughter, Emily, who is in her 20s.

He said Emily was not home and that Mr Simmons asked the defendant to leave.

The court then heard Mr Parish then went outside with Mr Jackson.

Mr Parish said: 'I had an argument with him about something totally different.

'I saw him get into his car. It was probably about 2.30am.'

He said he saw Mr Jackson drive back towards Hull city centre.

(Proceeding)

LETTER I CAN'T SEND TO BARRIE

I've been thinking about Biscuit Island, and wondering if anyone in the world, apart from the two of us, ever heard that phrase. Someone must have. You must have learnt it from somewhere. Or maybe not. Maybe you made it up. You were good with words, twisting them together in unexpected ways.

I only ever heard you say it twice, during a conversation we had while we were stuck in traffic on the ring road. We'd made the mistake of coming out at rush hour, and were stopped at lights, caught between two traffic islands that had trees and bushes growing thick along them. You were agitated. You said you hated getting stuck next to Biscuit Island.

'What are you talking about?' I asked.

'This place,' you said. 'I hate it. Sometimes when you get stuck here, you can see the prostitutes and their punters in the bushes.'

'What?' I said. 'What are you on about?'

And you nodded towards the car park on our left that I knew was part of the red-light district. The car park that in the not-too-distant future would be in the newspapers. Everyone knew what happened there after dark, but I'd never heard anything about these traffic islands before. Never heard this phrase before.

'Everyone knows about Biscuit Island,' you said.

But they didn't, and I didn't ask how you did. I never forgot it though. Never forgot how you had a strange little name, that made no sense to me, for a spot used by sex workers, that I didn't even know existed. Biscuit Island was where my driving problems started. I used to have to pass it on my way to work at the shipping office every morning.

After you were gone and I could walk around properly again, I took the first job I could get – at a breaker's yard, straightening out their accounts and setting up filing systems. But after a year or so, I got sick of the oily surfaces and the constant disorder, and applied for a better job in the forwarding department of a big, old shipping company close to the river. I didn't think I'd get it, but

I did. Better money, better conditions. All I had to do was turn up every morning and work until lunch.

But to get there every morning, I had to wait at those same traffic lights. A few feet from Biscuit Island. A few feet from that car park. And the panic attacks would come on so quick and so hard that by the time I got to work, I could barely get through the door. Gradually, I started to have panic attacks everywhere I tried to drive. But traffic was the worst. The pent-up feeling. The claustrophobic feeling. The need to get out.

The same thing happened in supermarket queues, and busy pubs or gigs. I had to hang about by the door, be able to see a clear way out. School concerts, business meetings, weddings, funerals – any place where I felt closed in, where the bodies of other people blocked my way, panic attacks would come. Or in any place where a bright light, like the one on that operating table, shone in my eyes. It's surprising how many places have those lights. You wouldn't notice unless they'd taken on a strange significance, like they seemed to have done for me. Shops, the dentist, the benefit office, court buildings, colleges, and, as I discovered much later, any kind of stage where you might step out to give a performance.

HULL DAILY MAIL, THURSDAY 16 OCTOBER 2003
HULL: Forensic scientist throws new light on vital evidence
Mystery DNA may be from Carol's relative
DNA found on the shoe of a man accused of beating a 63-year-old prostitute and dumping her in a skip, could have come from her sister, a court heard.

Forensic expert Zoe Burgess said there was a one in 70 chance that DNA discovered on the side of a Timberland shoe belonging to Barrie Jackson may have come from Carol Ives's sister or another sibling.

[. . .]

However, Dr Burgess, of the Forensic Science Centre in Wetherby, analysed the partial profile and said there was a chance it could have come from her sister.

She said: 'The closer the relative is, the more likely they will share the same components.'

[...]

Dr Burgess told the jury normal DNA samples contain 20 'numbers' or 'peaks,' but the profile found on the shoe only contained eight and was mixed with Mr Jackson's profile.

This meant it was more difficult to confirm precisely who it had come from.

She said the faint DNA profile, which did not belong to Mr Jackson, could have been left on the shoe in three ways.

She said it could have been on the shoe before Mr Jackson's blood dripped on top of it at a later date, it could have been deposited at the same time as Mr Jackson's blood, or the DNA profiles could have been mixed elsewhere and rubbed onto the shoe.

The mystery DNA profile could have come from numerous sources, including mucus, blood, saliva or urine.

Earlier, her colleague Dr Samantha Wanakulusuriya explained how she had analysed 41 items connected with the case, including a blue jumper, jeans, cords and cigarette butts.

She discovered no suspect DNA on anything other than the brown moccasin shoe.

Mr Stevenson asked where the blood would have splattered if Ms Ives had already been bleeding when she was punched and kicked.

Dr Wanakulusuriya said it would most likely have been on the cuff of the jumper or on the seam between the shoe and the sole, but she found nothing.

Mr Stevenson said: 'You looked for all of these things on your examination and found nothing – is that right?' She said: 'That's correct.'

However, she agreed with the prosecution that if the attacker had stamped on Ms Ives' head, as the pathologist had already suggested, the blood would have been on the sole, which she said would have been 'easier to remove'.

(Proceeding)

HULL: Question marks hangs over forensic evidence found on suspect's shoes

Police in dock over DNA

Police have been accused of wrongly telling the man suspected of savagely beating a 63-year-old prostitute they had found her blood on his shoe, a court heard.

Sergeant Albert Johnson told Barrie Jackson the blood of Carol Ives had been discovered on his moccasin when details of the type of DNA trace had not been fully established.

Hull Crown Court heard yesterday a fax from Dr Zoe Burgess at the Forensic Science Centre in Willerby to Sgt Johnson did not specify whether Ms Ives' DNA on the footwear was from any particular source at all.

Earlier in the case, Dr Burgess said the DNA could have come from numerous sources, including Ms Ives' mucus, saliva, urine or blood.

It was also stressed that the profile could have come from Ms Ives' sister or another close relative.

[…]

Tony Stevenson, defending, told Sgt Johnson he had repeatedly hit Mr Jackson with the claim which was 'wrong'.

Sgt Johnson replied: 'I did not mean to say "blood" to deceive anyone.'

Mr Stevenson said: 'The result was that questions were being put with a misleading bias.'

Sgt Johnson's reference to blood as the source of the DNA came in a February interview when Mr Jackson denied ever knowing Ms Ives.

The court also heard transcripts from the interview Mr Jackson gave to police in February after his arrest.

At the time he said: 'I have never seen or met this female in my life.

'This is the biggest stitch-up this side of Marrakech.'

However, Mr Jackson later told police he 'may have' bought the Timberland moccasin shoes before the attack.

LETTER I WON'T POST TO KARL TURNER, MP

It's funny, the impact the words we choose can have on people, situations, outcomes. I have words all kinds of people have said to me imprinted on my brain. Like they've been etched there. I'd quite like to forget a lot of them, but I've come to accept that it's impossible to make yourself forget. You either do, or you don't.

Although we've been in the same places on quite a few occasions, we've only ever had one conversation, but some of the words you said to me are among those I haven't been able to forget. The first of these words is 'freemans'. It's a word I've heard before, but there'd been a long gap between those other times and the day I came to see you in your office. I'm excluding the times I've heard people talking about what they've ordered from their Freemans catalogue, because the version of the word you used has all the same letters, but not the same meaning. No capital F. Adjective, not noun. It's probably about twenty years since I heard someone use it the way you did that day. It's one of those words that was in fashion when I was in my late teens and early twenties, and I was surprised to hear it again in 2020. That's the first, minor point I want to make about this word.

The second, more important point, is the context in which you used it. The context is what upgraded the surprise to shock. I was trying to explain the way my experience, the experiences of my children, the experiences of millions of victims and co-victims of crime, contrast starkly, in so many ways, with Steven Gallant's experiences. I was talking about a lack of support – financial, emotional, social, physical. I was telling you that I didn't disagree that offenders should have access to support, but I did feel that victims and co-victims of crime should have the same levels of support available to them.

The example I zeroed in on, in an attempt to illustrate this, was university. I told you about my son, who had been studying away in Manchester – an A and A* grade student in his GCSEs and A Levels. His first time living away from home. How all of this stuff in the media had affected him so badly that he'd had to leave. Come home. Give up his studies. How I'd read in the newspaper that Gallant had gained a degree while he'd been in prison, and how that opportunity had now, at least for the time being, been taken away from my son. You thought about it for a beat, and then you said, 'Well, that's prison for you, innit? Freemans. Everything's freemans. Go to university? Freemans. Go to the dentist? Me and you would have to pay, but for them it's all freemans.'

Google doesn't know about this meaning of this word, but you knew I would. I don't know if you knew anything at all about me before I knocked on your door that day, but my accent gives me away as someone who grew up not far from you. My face gives me away as being not far from the same age as you. I suppose this is why you chose to use that word that day. Google thinks it means: 'A person who is free; a person who enjoys personal, civil, or political liberty.' It also suggests: 'A person that will not be ruled or enslaved. A self-sufficient, independent person of any sex . . . that is self-directed, self-disciplined and self-governed.' You and I also know it to mean getting something for free, probably undeservingly — almost like a con.

I think you chose that word to try and promote empathy between us — or maybe more accurately, for me to have sympathy for your point of view. A shorthand way of saying: 'Look, we come from the same place, we have the same ideas about things, just trust me on this one, yeah?'

It's interesting, isn't it, the way our word choices can affect things? Your use of this one on this day in this context told me so much. Words can be very revealing.

HULL DAILY MAIL, FRIDAY 17 OCTOBER 2003
Suspect 'mixed up' over dates
HULL: A jury has been told how attack suspect Barrie Jackson called to be interviewed by police again after realising the account of his whereabouts he had given to police was for a different day.

Mr Jackson, who at this stage was already charged with attempted murder and grievous bodily harm with intent, said he wanted to give more information.

The 29-year-old told police he had got his days 'mixed up' after drinking alcohol.

In an early interview with detectives Mr Jackson said he had spent November 9 and the early hours of the following day – when Ms Ives was attacked – with his father in Great Thornton Street.

But he later told senior investigating officer Detective John Harding he had instead been at a wedding at the Cornmill Hotel, Holderness Road, and at the Silhouette nightclub in the city.

In an interview read out to court, Mr Jackson said: 'For me to specify accurately on this particular matter was difficult.

'After I was with my sister, I was told about the wedding we went to and this was on November 9.'

Mr Jackson said he left the wedding reception around 10.30pm before going to the nightclub.

It was there Mr Jackson said he met friends from his school days before leaving between 2.30am and 2.45am.

He said he then went to a friend's home on the Longhill estate and returned to the home of his brother, in Field Street.

HULL DAILY MAIL, SATURDAY 18 OCTOBER 2003
HULL: DNA on prostitute's alleged attacker 'not contaminated'

Police: 'Forensic evidence is safe'

Police have rejected fears DNA evidence found on the shoe of the man accused of attacking Carol Ives could be contaminated.

Forensic expert Joanne Ashworth told Hull Crown Court the chance of a police officer transferring Ms Ives' DNA evidence was 'nil'.

The development came on day five of the trial where DNA evidence was closely scrutinised.

[...]

[Mr Jackson's] defence counsel Tony Stevenson cross-examined Mrs Ashworth.

[...]

But when he asked Mrs Ashworth about the chance of the DNA evidence being cross-contaminated, she said: 'In this specific incident, I think the chance is nil.'

She also stressed the 'passage of time' between the different visits would also eliminate the chance of contamination.

Previously Mr Jordan said the same officers would not be sent to the crime scene and to a suspect's address in 'an ideal world'.

However, supervisor Trevor Laugley said Mr Jordan's views were old-fashioned.

He said: 'That opinion has changed. Our protocols have evolved.

'Providing full protective clothing is worn, there is no question of any secondary contamination.'

Mr Laugley said it was his procedure to wear a full body disposable suit, two pairs of disposable overshoes and two pairs of latex gloves when investigating serious incidents.

Both he and Mrs Ashworth told the jurors these procedures were followed at all times.

The case was adjourned until Monday.

ANOTHER WOMAN

'Paradox one,' she says. 'Being subjected to one form of trauma, often, unsurprisingly, leads to another. It's fairly obvious how it happens, once you focus your attention on it. The paradox is that the more trauma you experience, the less people want to hear about it, and the less likely they are to believe you, even if they do listen. This is especially true if the trauma takes the form of a man having done something to you that was extremely unpleasant / frightening / painful / distressing. In order to be able to speak about more than one of these experiences, and in order to feel like you stand a chance of being heard, you may begin assessing: you might start calculating whether your cultural capital, level of popularity, current rate and method of sharing things that you claim are true-life occurrences, allow for the sharing of one more thing. What is the severity of this thing? Is it something that is currently gaining public attention and therefore more likely to be believed? Has there been a recent universal outpouring about it on Twitter; was this outpouring on Twitter too recent / not recent enough for you to be sharing details now? If you share it now, will it appear too contrived; if you share it now, has it, in fact, become contrived? Is it now, in this form, still the same experience that you intended to share in the first place? Is it still true? What is truth anyway? Why did you start doing this? Bin.'

'I thought you didn't know what Twitter was.'

'I told you I can see everything.'

'But . . .'

'But nothing. You need to start listening better. Is that all you've got to say? What about the rest of it?'

'It's like you've read my mind.'

'Correct,' she says. 'I did, and I have to tell you I'm getting a bit pissed off with what I'm seeing when I do it.'

'Well, thanks a lot.'

'Don't get defensive. Someone needs to say it.'

'Well, I'm not wrong, am I?'

'I don't know whether you're wrong or not. Either way, it's not doing you much good.'

'You sound like my therapist.'

'I know. I like him. I wish I'd have had a therapist.'

There's no way I can *not* laugh at this. I think she's going to be mad, but when I look up, she's smiling.

'You and a therapist?'

'I don't see why it's funny.'

I don't even answer. I only have to raise my eyebrows.

'Well, you didn't need therapists in my day. Twenty fags, a game of darts, a few pints, and two paracetamol before bed. Sorted.'

'OK,' I say. 'Sorted.'

MAN IN THE STREET
Don't get all fucking la-di-dah on me. You know you love it. Literally the only reason women dress like that is so men will shout stuff at them.

MAN IN A BAR
You can't take a compliment. You're wired up wrong.

MAN ON THE PHONE
There's no wonder your ex did what he did. You're a fucking nutter.

HULL DAILY MAIL, TUESDAY 21 OCTOBER 2003 (PAGE 11)
HULL: Firefighter claims he would not commit 'cowardly' attack
'I've never seen this woman before'
A firefighter accused of battering 63-year-old prostitute Carol Ives has claimed he would never commit such a 'cowardly, spineless' attack.

Barrie Jackson, 29, took the stand at Hull Crown Court to repeatedly deny beating Ms Ives and leaving her for dead in a skip behind Staples Office Supplies, Myton Street, on November 10 last year.

Mr Jackson said he had never seen Ms Ives, now 64, and could not explain how a speck of her DNA came to be on shoes he was seen wearing that night.

[. . .]

Under cross-examination from prosecutor Andrew Dallas, ex-Royal Navy man Mr Jackson told the court: 'Not only did I not carry out this cowardly, spineless and toe-rag attack on Carol Ives, I've never seen this lady before in my life.'

Mr Dallas said Mr Jackson had backtracked on much of what he said during police interviews, first claiming to be with his father on the night of Ms Ives' attack but later saying he had been at a wedding reception.

The jury also heard how Mr Jackson said the only nightclub he had been to in the past two years was Tam-Tams, Anlaby Road, west Hull, but later admitted he went to Silhouette, west Hull, on November 10 and left around 2am.

Yesterday, Mr Jackson told the court he left the club for ex-girlfriend Emily Simmons' house in Hessle High Road to see if his father was at a party there.

He then said he drove to friend Michaela Lines' house in Shannon Road, Longhill, and slept on a settee with girlfriend of 10 days Sue Kuskor.

He could not say what time he arrived.

The jury had earlier heard how the last sighting of Ms Ives was at 1.50am.

Mr Dallas suggested Mr Jackson was lying and had really gone to Ms Ives that night because he was 'desperate for a woman'.

He said: 'You were running out of options. Having drawn a blank at Emily Simmons you decided to find a girl, and in your drunkenness, something went horribly wrong.'

When Mr Dallas suggested he had no 'reliable recollection' of the night, Mr Jackson said: 'If you are asking me if my mind was so absent that I could have carried out this attack then no, that's not true.

'I have never deliberately misled the police.'

Mr Jackson had told the court he had been drinking too much after splitting up with a long-term girlfriend and mother of his children the previous June.

He said he was 'devastated' after she stopped him seeing his sons, aged one and four, and was out drinking most nights.

This, he said, had become worse after his arrest because people began 'pointing the finger' at him.

He also defended initially telling police he had bought the contaminated shoes after the attack.

'The shoes cost £130,' Mr Jackson told the court. 'Generally speaking, fire brigade wages would not have permitted me to go and buy these shoes.'

He said he had mistakenly assumed he bought them after receiving £20,000 later that month from the sale of his house.

Mr Jackson admitted using prostitutes in the Myton Street area and said he may have had sex by the skip where Carol was found. He initially said he may have visited the area in November but later denied this.

(Proceeding)

HULL: Man, 29, cleared, but jailed for unrelated assault

Firefighter not guilty of attack

A city firefighter was today cleared of attacking 63-year-old prostitute Carol Ives – and leaving her for dead in a skip.

Barrie Jackson, 29, remained impassive as the jury found him not guilty of attempted murder, and the lesser charge of grievous bodily harm with intent, after four hours of deliberations.

However the jury was then told Jackson would be going back behind bars after it emerged he had pleaded guilty to knocking another woman unconscious in an unrelated case just weeks before Ms Ives' attack last November.

Judge Michael Mettyear sentenced the ex-Navy man for two years in prison.

Jackson had admitted to assaulting Rosaleena Capell, 43, when she dialled 999 after watching him beat his father in the street.

A member of the jury held her hand over her mouth as the court heard how Jackson had been seen by Mrs Capell punching his father Leonard Gibson on the floor in Albert Avenue, west Hull, at 11.45pm on October 18 last year.

She had been out with her husband and sister when they saw Jackson punching Mr Gibson repeatedly in the street.

Mrs Capell tried to ring 999 but Jackson stood up and punched her hard in the face knocking her unconscious and leaving her scarred for life.

Judge Mettyear, in passing sentence, told Jackson: 'It's disgraceful. Punching a woman full and hard in the face is unacceptable conduct – only custody can be justified.'

[. . .]

During the trial, defence barrister Tony Stevenson argued that the DNA – which could have come from any body fluid – could have been transferred onto the shoe by simply brushing against a cigarette butt or used condom in the street, or by police unintentionally contaminating the evidence.

In his closing speech, Mr Stevenson said: 'How on earth can you possibly convict a man on the basis of a microscopic speck of who knows what on the side of his shoe?'

Today Ms Ives sat with her head bowed as the verdict was read and left the court moments later.

And Detective Superintendent Paul Davison, who headed the inquiry, said his officers were disappointed with the verdicts but respected the jury's decision.

Mr Davison said Jackson had been the only suspect in the Carol Ives inquiry and officers would wait to hear if there was any more information from the public before deciding how to proceed.

WOMAN

Closure can be an elusive thing, especially when all you have are blurred facts. The erosion of anything certain. Your only hope then is distance — not look at it all for a bit. But you can't make things disappear. You can't make them un-happen. So you try to make some space where they aren't the only things that happened. You swallow all the difficult stuff. Then hold yourself tight enough to keep it in. Hold back the flow of the vicious, corrosive, saltiness of it. Try to carry the uncomfortable swishing and swelling all by yourself, so the people you love don't have to deal with it.

For a long time, I carried it. Learnt to walk with the added weight. The extra burden. Carried it in the dark pit of my belly, hoping my boys wouldn't see it. But I might as well not have bothered, because here it all is anyway, spewing out across the Sunday papers and the internet and the national news, flooding our lives, carrying us in its wake: not only is that thing real, but this one too, and here's a new one. My kids are not little any more, so I can't distract them with songs and games and trips to the park. I can't stretch myself out across the noticeboards outside the corner shop or just turn the telly off. It was all a waste, and that's a lot to accept, you know? And it's like the structures that have been holding me together suddenly begin to break down. Like years of corrosion kick in, all of a sudden, working on the substance between ligaments and bone joints. Like the action of salt on limestone or brick. I can't stand up straight any more, so I think I'll just lie down here now, let my body crumple into the shape of a soft brown cliff that slides into the sea, and people can do whatever it is that people do nowadays. Let them flit and wave and say things that flutter and die on the tongue. I'll be like the dark earth in stillness, moving as slowly as the burgeoning roots of grass.

MAN IN THE PUB
Why do women have small feet? So they can get nearer to the kitchen sink.

No, no, I've got a better one: After my wife died, I didn't look at another woman for ten years, but now I'm out of jail, I can definitely say it was worth it.

ANOTHER MAN IN THE PUB
What is it with women – they can't take a joke nowadays. No sense of humour. Fucking feminists.

MAN IN THE PUB
There's no wonder some women get themselves slapped about a bit, is there?

MEMORY
After the day I leave for court, I never go back to my A Level course, because the outcome of the trial makes my life suddenly shrink in on itself again. I was expecting fifteen years – space to spread out in, bring my kids up in, build a life in, free from him. A not-guilty verdict means that won't happen. But he is definitely guilty of assaulting another woman – so badly she needed plastic surgery.

I think for a while that I might get two years, at least. But it turns out that a two-year sentence doesn't mean two years in prison. It means one year in prison, and a year on licence, so he's served most of his sentence while on remand, and within a few months, he's a free man. He starts turning up at my house again, so I decide the best thing to do is move house. Again. Give up the beautiful old building I'd made into a home over the last eighteen months or so. Never mind the new carpets I'd bought, the hours scrubbing and painting and making good. The new curtains. The garden I'd tended 'til it bloomed. It wasn't safe any more. That was clear.

So I moved. To the only other place I could afford. A council estate where I didn't know anyone. Despite everything I'd heard about it, I decided that home is what you make it. I hired a removal van and booked family to help, but it was still a few days' work. On the third day, I arrived at my old house to pack up the garden, and found Barrie there, taking down the boys' climbing frame with some other men. I kept on driving, and rang him, told him he couldn't be there. That he needed to go. He laughed and said my landlord was a pal of his, had told him I was moving. He'd come to help, had brought his trailer. I told him to go, called my solicitor. But the damage was done. The next morning, as I walked Jack to school, I saw him drive past my new house in someone else's car, wearing sunglasses, like I wouldn't know it was him.

HOME OFFICE, DOMESTIC ABUSE STATUTORY GUIDANCE, JULY 2022
Impact of Domestic Abuse
   This chapter covers:

1. The impact of domestic abuse on victims – including on physical and mental health, stability and livelihood, which can be interlinked and cumulative.
2. The impact of domestic abuse on children, highlighting different aspects of the experience of young people and how the

statutory definition of domestic abuse is to operate alongside measures that address the safeguarding of children.

MEMORY

Once he's located where I live, his visits start up again. Letters through the door. Presents on the path. Nobody seems to be able to stop him. When I don't bow to his pressure and just hand over my kids to go with him where he likes, he resumes taking me to court for access.

I never got a chance to contradict him when, during the trial, he said one of the reasons he'd been drinking so heavily at the time of the attack on Carol Ives was that he was 'devastated' I'd stopped him seeing the kids. But it wasn't true. I only stopped him taking them out on his own *after* he was arrested, and then he was still allowed supervised contact while he was out on bail, until that broke down too. I even took them to visit him in prison once, because Jack was having nightmares about the place where his daddy was locked up, and I decided that the reality couldn't be worse than what his little head was dreaming up. It worked. He began to sleep again. But now Barrie wants me to just hand my boys, two and four years old, over to him, despite everything that's happened, and the court seems to agree. My solicitor argues for a psychologist's report to be made first.

The report concludes that he is positive, outgoing and optimistic. He's completed his anger management training in prison and he's good to go. No reason at all why he should not be allowed to see the kids.

LETTER FROM CHLOE SMITH MP

To: Dame Diana Johnson DBE, Labour Member of Parliament for Hull North

12 August 2020

Dear Dame Diana,

Thank you for your letter of 10 July addressed to the Chancellor of the Duchy of Lancaster, and for your clarification email of 4 August, on behalf of your constituent, Ms Vicky Foster of XXX XXXX, Hull HUX XXX, about Mr Steven Gallant who was involved in tackling the terrorist on London Bridge on 29 November 2019. I am sorry to hear you felt my previous reply failed to appreciate the issues you raised and the specific concerns of your constituent.

I hope some further explanation as to how gallantry is handled might explain the stance taken in my previous response. With a major incident such as Fishmongers' Hall, potential nominees for awards will be considered after the police investigation into the matter has been completed. Any nominations thought to meet the criteria for national recognition would then be submitted to the George Cross Committee (GCC) for assessment. The Committee makes independent assessments based on the evidence, probity, propriety and other factors available – and this may indeed include the consideration of the type of moral questions that Ms Foster asks – and makes recommendations to the Prime Minister and HM The Queen.

Should the Committee be asked to consider nominations related to Fishmongers' Hall, the Honours and Appointments Secretariat will ensure that Ms Foster's concerns are drawn to its attention.

May I, again, convey my condolences to Ms Foster for all the loss she and her sons have suffered.

MEMORY

Before Barrie's contact with the kids is agreed, there has to be a report made for the court by CAFCASS – the Children and Families Court Advisory and Support Service. So I go to the office, in a village on the outskirts of Hull. Sit in the friendly little room. It has a sofa. Not really like an office at all. I've thought a lot about this appointment before I get here. I've been making myself remember the details of things he did before we split up. The things he's done since. Things I know for a fact are true because I saw them with my own eyes and felt them with my own skin. But they don't ask for specifics. I don't get a chance to tell them about the time he pinned his uncle against the wall by the throat and I had to slide my eight-month-pregnant self between them; unprise his fingers. No space in the conversation for the fight in my front garden with my brother after Barrie tried to force his way into my house again. No space for him holding me by the throat; no space for his banging on the windows, the threatening phone calls, the abusive language. No space for the long list of things that I have coughed up from my stomach and that now lie, curling away down my throat.

I don't remember all the questions, just the feeling of being locked in. Like all the things I've been remembering, have summoned to the surface, that are brimming behind my lips, waiting to spill out, are suddenly checked. I remember only one of the questions they asked me that day: Leaving everything else aside, just focusing on his relationship with the children, do you think he's done his best at trying to be a good dad?

I had to pause at this. I thought about all the things I knew about him, the things he'd told me about when he was a kid, the way his eyes glaze over sometimes, how he doesn't always seem to know what he's doing, especially when bad things happen. The way he likes to play with the kids, how desperate he's been to see them. I say, 'Yes, yes, I think he's done his best,' because I do actually think that this is probably the best he can manage. And these are the words that are written in the CAFCASS report. There must have been others too, but those are the ones I remember. He is doing his best, and they can see no reason why he shouldn't see the kids.

HOME OFFICE, DOMESTIC ABUSE STATUTORY GUIDANCE,
JULY 2022
Impact on Victims - Psychological

Not all domestic abuse begins with or results in physical abuse.
Domestic abuse and associated trauma can have a significant impact
on a victim's emotional, psychological and mental wellbeing. This may
involve feelings of isolation, worthlessness and dependency on the
perpetrator. It can also include depression, anxiety, post-traumatic
stress disorder, and sleeping and eating disorders.

A victim's day to day life can be affected by trying to manage the
abuse, leading to increased anxiety and a focus on adapting their
behaviour to appease the perpetrator. This can subsequently lead
to a victim adopting the perspective of the perpetrator and starting
to blame themselves for the abuse and may result in the victim
questioning or doubting their own experiences and developing low
self-esteem.

ANOTHER WOMAN

'I'm sorry,' she says, 'about what I said last time.'

'Are you?'

'Yes,' she says. 'It's just I'd been thinking about Trigger and his
sweeping brush.'

'OK . . .'

'You remember,' she says, 'that episode where he gets the medal,
and he says he's had the same broom for twenty years.'

'Oh yeah,' I say.

I do remember. *Only Fools and Horses* was a staple in our house.

'I suppose I'm just struggling to understand what that's got to
do with you saying you didn't need therapists in your day, though.'

'Well, it's the same thing, isn't it? Trigger says he's had the same
broom for twenty years, but it turns out it's had loads of new heads
and loads of new handles, so it's not the same broom at all, is it?'

'No, it's not,' I say, 'but I'm still not making the connection.'

'Well, how many times can you change yourself and still be you?'

MEMORY

There's a little police station at the top of the street that gives away free dog-poo bags. I pop in one day to collect some, cos every little helps, and the man behind the desk asks for my address. I tell him and he goes off for a bit. Comes back.

'There's a man across the street from you that we're interested in,' he says. 'Drug-dealer. Nasty piece of work. I wonder if you might think about whether we could install some cameras in your upstairs windows to keep an eye on him?'

'There are already cameras in my upstairs windows,' I say. 'I've already got detectives coming round every week, to pick up the footage of a man who's not supposed to come anywhere near me but still does it anyway. I think I've got enough on for now, thanks.'

LETTER I WILL NEVER SEND TO SG

I've received the ministrations on your behalf from the Restorative Justice Service, and I'm sure you know by now that I've had to get a bit bolshy and ask the National Homicide Service to request they leave me alone. But you should be reassured; they tried very hard to be persuasive. Their first email was something between a sales pitch and fan mail. They'd heard my Radio 4 show. They'd been looking for me for a long time. They wanted to talk to me about something they thought would be of interest to me.

I'll be honest, it nearly worked. I felt like I had no choice but to call the number below the email signature as soon as I'd read it, even though it was supposed to be a holiday; even though I was supposed to be resting, and eating mince pies and watching old films, and doing all the other things that normal people do on those hazy, befuddled days between Christmas and New Year. I was wearing my red flannel pyjamas and my new Christmas dressing gown when she told me who she was. Told me how many times she'd sat down and spoken with you; how very desperate you were to talk to me; how very helpful she thought I might find it.

It took me ages afterwards to stop crying enough so that I could tell Simon what had happened. He found me – cinnamon-candle burning, Christmas tree lights glowing, Judy Garland paused on the telly mid-song – crying uncontrollably with the phone in my hand. At first, when I told him, I thought he was angry with me. I saw anger fold down over his face, and it's a common thing for women who've been domestically abused to be conditioned to be afraid when they see anger in a man.

But he's gentle. He explained to me why he was angry, and if I'm honest, I couldn't see it at first. I was fighting the overpowering urge to say I would come and talk to you. That was the only thing in my head. This dread. That I was obliged, morally, to do it. That I was obliged, morally, to get straight on the blower to my kids, on these days between Christmas and New Year, and tell them that the man who had murdered their dad sixteen years ago, and then turned up to tip our lives upside down again nearly a year ago, had been in touch, and he wanted to talk to us, and so we really should, in the name of all that's good, get our shoes on and pop along down for a mince pie. Or something like that. It wasn't clear to me how it would work. Only that we should all do it. As soon as possible. Because this nice woman, who I didn't know from Adam, had made me feel like it was our moral obligation.

It was days before the anger kicked in, but when it came, it came with a vengeance.

WOMAN IN CAFÉ
You know what men are like. You've got to make allowances. Plan around them. Be smarter.

WOMAN IN THE PUB
Don't be so nice to them, then they'll leave you alone.

ANOTHER WOMAN IN THE PUB
You can't be rude to them, cos they're just gonna turn nasty.

MAN IN MY HOUSE
It's about time you learnt when to keep your mouth shut.

MEMORY
I pay a subscription for Jack to do mixed martial arts classes. I can afford it because I've planned well. I work part-time as a cleaner while Harry is at nursery. I shop cheap, and cook fresh. I plan activities around all the free stuff – museums, library events, parks. I budget for everything. Lay it all out neatly in lists on notepads. We can't afford holidays, but we can afford this.

The gym where he trains is cool – an old warehouse with thick mats, punchbags, mirrored walls and white concrete pillars. It's not traditional training. It's a mix of judo and boxing. Kind of freestyle. I've decided it will help build his confidence. One day, while I'm sat watching with the other mums and dads, I see a poster for women's classes – self-defence – and decide that's probably a really good idea. The first one is free, so the next week I find myself sitting in Lycra and trainers one night, in the middle of the mats, instead of in my everyday clothes on the benches at the side.

I love it, right from the start. I haven't told anyone I'm coming, but I've been fantasising all week about what it will feel like. Moving through air to land well-placed kicks. Spinning free from grasping arms. Throwing punches. I'm competent quite quickly. I always had good aim in cricket and netball. I'm fit. All that running around after the kids and the physical labour of cleaning pubs and offices for a living. *This is it*, I'm thinking, all the way through that first class. *This is how I keep myself safe.*

The woman who runs things is fierce and firm and agile and strong. She holds everyone's attention when she demos moves, snapping out fists and feet, throwing her male helper to the ground. But before we leave, there's a pep-talk on the mats. She explains slowly that while it's good to learn all this stuff, we all need to remember that if a man were to grab us on the street it's unlikely we'd get a chance to do any of it. They're always going to be bigger and stronger than us, no matter how much we've learnt. If it happened in real life, we'd need to just remember the basics. Use your nails. Go for the eyes, the balls. Shout, scream, keep your keys handy. All the same stuff I've been told since I was twelve.

HOME OFFICE, DOMESTIC ABUSE STATUTORY GUIDANCE, JULY 2022

We recognise that more women than men are affected by domestic abuse. Statistics from the last ONS bulletin showed that in the previous year, women were around twice as likely to have experienced domestic abuse than men.

In the CSEW data for the year ending March 2020, women were significantly more likely than men to be victims of each type of abuse asked about, with the exception of sexual assault by a family member where, although higher, the difference between males and females was not significant. From the year ending March 2018 to the year ending March 2020, the majority of victims aged 16 and over of domestic homicides were female (76%). This contrasts with non-domestic homicides where the majority of victims were male (86%). When looking at perpetrators of female domestic homicide, 78% were a partner or ex-partner, 16% a parent and 7% a child or other family relative, such as a brother or sister.

MEMORY

It is dusk, in summer. The street has begun to quieten down, though the distant shouts of children still echo off the concrete paths and house fronts. The light is running away. The boys are asleep, and I have turned on a lamp, turned on the TV and sat on the sofa. I have poured a glass of wine, and I am going to try to unwind.

But as I sit down I realise there's some sort of kerfuffle going on outside; there are shouts that don't sound like children, and they are close by. I'm on high alert immediately. I creep up to the window to check what's happening, and see the drug dealer from across the road. He is coming towards my house, walking backwards. In his hand is a machete. Facing him is another man. In his hand is a hammer. They are moving at a steady pace, tensed, the way cats circle each other, hackles raised, ready.

I can see that Drug-dealer Man is heading straight towards my car, which is parked on the road outside my window. He is probably three steps away from it when he realises something is coming up behind him. He spins and jumps, straight onto the bonnet, and the other man, triggered by his movement, runs after him. Drug-dealer Man is on the roof and off the boot, Hammer Man chasing. They circle my car, slowing and speeding up, on and off the bonnet, roof, boot, before one of them makes a break for it, leaps straight from the boot while the other is just leaping up to the bonnet again, and runs headlong away towards the high street, in the middle of the road, machete swinging madly backwards and forwards. Hammer Man chasing.

I am still looking out from behind my curtains when I see what must be Drug-dealer Man's girlfriend or wife step out of their open front door and look in the direction the men have run. She pauses for two beats, her ponytail swinging slightly, her slim body still in a light summer dress and flip-flops, her face expressionless. Then she turns, walks back through the front door and closes it behind her. I've never seen her before, and I never see her again.

WOMAN

It's the weight of them that's the problem. The sheer weight of them – all their words, all their actions, the physical mass of them in crowds or lying over you or blocking you in a corner. Almost every man who passes me in the street is physically stronger than me, and some of them will be going home, opening up Google and typing in *rough sex*, or *violent sex*, or even *rape porn*. I could do it myself if I wanted to. Type it in and see what comes up. But I won't. I don't want to know. I'm employed full-time now in trying to convince myself that there's nothing to worry about any more. Trying to soothe my body back into a normal state; lessen the tensing, the headaches, the stomach cramps, the aches. I'm trying not to think about it all right now.

WOMAN ON THE PHONE
You can't let it get to you. You're best off not thinking about it. Just don't be going out at night on your own.

MAN ON THE PHONE
You shouldn't be doing that at night on your own. You'll get yourself in trouble. Either find a man to go with you or stay in.

MAN ON FACEBOOK
All this shit about putting men on a curfew is pissing me off. Angry feminists could start an argument in an empty room. Stop the world. I wanna get off.

MEMORY
I am sitting at a table: a long, narrow table. Beside me is my solicitor. There are other people there too: some sitting at this table, some off at other tables in the room, but they are blurry. Everything is blurry, except the fact that Barrie is sitting opposite me. He must be only five feet away, or less. Probably less. Probably more than an arm's length away, but not much more. Not so far away that he can't reach me, if he wants to, and I can't see anyone in this room who looks like they're going to stop him if he decides to do it.

Last time we had a contact hearing, he was behind glass screens, at the other end of a long courtroom, in what looked like a dock. There was at least one custody officer visible, and Barrie was handcuffed to the rail in front of him. Very little chance of him making it across the whole length of the courtroom to where I stood behind another wooden barrier, being cross-examined.

But there's none of that today.

I'm not concentrating – at least, not on what's going on in the room around me. I'm concentrating on how badly I feel like I need to pee, on controlling my breathing – three breaths in, five out – to avoid hyperventilating.

My solicitor is saying, 'Having to be in contact with Mr Jackson would be detrimental to my client's health, and therefore to the welfare of the children. She suffers panic attacks when she has to be around him.'

The judge is saying, 'Mr Jackson does not have to dress as a superhero and climb to the roof of a building to prove to me that he has a right to see his children. There is no evidence of domestic abuse, and if your client is not capable of looking after her children, then maybe we should consider whether they should go to live with their father.'

Mr Jackson is smiling at me from across the table. I am being walked out into a holding room. My solicitor asks me to wait for a moment so he can speak to someone and come back, then asks where my car is parked.

He is saying, 'I will walk you to your car.' As we are walking, he tells me, 'Mr Jackson was shouting in the other room that he wanted to kill you. He was shouting that if it was the only way for him to see his kids, he was going to fucking kill you. It's a shame the judge didn't see that.'

I am getting into my car. I am driving. I am arriving home, and my children are there. They are small and they want their mum, and they need their dinner, but their mum can't breathe. She is struggling to breathe. She is struggling to be in this room, and suddenly she begins to feel that she is in the wrong place, these are not her children, this is not where she's meant to be, and she goes upstairs, and she lies down for a bit – for just a few minutes. She closes her eyes, and when I open them again, I know I am back in the room, back in my bedroom, back in my house, and my children are downstairs. But I don't know what I am going to do.

HOME OFFICE, DOMESTIC ABUSE STATUTORY GUIDANCE, JULY 2022

Long-term trauma may not always be recognised in victims, who may be facing multiple disadvantages, such as, but not limited to, disabled victims, those with cognitive issues, mental ill health and/or issues with substance misuse. The impact of trauma may similarly be overlooked in children and young people. Prior experiences of physical or psychological trauma, because of bullying, discrimination and hate crime, may make victims of domestic abuse less likely to seek help. Adopting a trauma-informed approach to responding to domestic abuse is therefore essential, recognising the signs and symptoms of trauma and, in acknowledging this, providing appropriate support seeking not to re-traumatise.

MEMORY

One night, things in my house get worse than usual. The new man who is now living in my house and abusing me really won't stop again. He's taken my phone again. He's taken my front door keys again. I know I can't press the panic alarm, but my bag is by the back door, and I manage to make a break for it, bag in hand, car keys in bag, out into the back garden. I get as far as the front garden before he catches me, holds me by the arm, and we enter a strange kind of stalemate. I am tugging, pointlessly, trying to get away, even though I know I can't. He is just holding me, every now and then tugging in the opposite direction. I am shouting for him to get off, but it has no effect. His grip doesn't loosen, the closed curtains of the other houses don't twitch. There are no cars passing. Then a man, a stranger, turns the corner and begins to walk on the pavement beyond our front garden fence. Two feet away.

''Scuse me,' I say. 'Can you help me?'

The stranger doesn't look at me. He looks at the pavement. Keeps walking. Doesn't speak. The man holding my arm doesn't let go. His grip tightens. He holds my gaze. Then he speaks.

'All right, mate,' he says.

The man walking past lifts his eyes. Nods his head towards him. Glances briefly towards me. I try to look how I think it would be best to look, in order for him to help me. I don't want to look mad, that's the main thing. Or hysterical. Or angry. I can't look angry. I aim for something pleading and helpless – these are the two predominant emotions that I am feeling. The seconds draw out. He doesn't look back. He is about to round the corner, so I try again.

'Please,' I say, 'he won't get off me.'

This time the stranger looks straight at me, a half-smirk stretching his face in the shadow of the street.

'None of my business,' he says, as he quickens his pace and walks away into the night.

My arm goes limp. I stop struggling.

He pulls me back inside.

The women's centre is at the top of the street. I've been there once before. Walked inside. Said I thought maybe I needed to speak to someone, then had a massive panic attack on the sofa. A kind woman taught me some breathing exercises, but I didn't stay. I was too scared of what would happen. I said I had to go. That I'd come back. But I haven't been, and now I don't see how I can.

The realisation settles on me that I will just have to brace myself for whatever is coming next, unaided. This man, calling me vile names every night, withholding money, refusing to pay bills, holding my head under the duvet to punch me so it leaves no marks. Sneering at me. Every day. And the letters, from Barrie and his supporters and his solicitor and the courts. The people who shout at me in the street or in shops, the heavy gaze of people in the playground, the knowing looks. Because I am now suddenly terrified of something worse than the physical violence, the shame, the seemingly endless days and nights when I don't know what Barrie is going to do. The prospect that I might actually lose my kids has become real. And also, that I might lose my liberty into the bargain.

That passer-by – shrugging his shoulders, walking away, saying it's none of his business – has clarified exactly where I stand.

WOMAN
It's so subtle, the way you can become trapped. Tiny, tiny, featherlight threads winding around you, until suddenly you find you can't move. And when you can't name the thing that's trapping you, can't see it clearly, can't pick out a segment of one strand and look at it closely enough to identify it, how can you begin to fix the problem?

The little things that happen in your own life don't come with names or explanations attached. They evolve and dissolve and they've gone before anyone, sometimes not even you, can notice.

HOME OFFICE, DOMESTIC ABUSE STATUTORY GUIDANCE, JULY 2022
Victims may not recognise the abuse they face as domestic abuse or underrate their experience or the experience of forms of abuse that are not physical. They may be unclear on how to seek help, therefore continued efforts are required to help ensure that resources and services are accessible and that communications about what help is available give consideration to how to reach people within local areas including minority groups and communities.

MEMORY
The next time I go to court, my solicitor meets me at the door, takes me aside.

'Mr Jackson's not here,' he says. 'He's been accused of assaulting a minor. Arrested. The proceedings are adjourned, *sine die*.'

'And what does that mean?' I say.

'It's over,' he says.

I feel a moment's relief at these words. It's over. It's over, and I need it to be over. But the relief doesn't last long. I know he's only talking about the court case. The court case is over, that is all, and there will be plenty more of everything else still to come.

HOME OFFICE, DOMESTIC ABUSE STATUTORY GUIDANCE, JULY 2022

Impact on Victims - Physical

Domestic abuse can cause serious and devastating long and short term physical and mental, emotional, and psychological health impacts on adults and children.

For victims who suffer physical health issues, injuries can include bruises and welts, lacerations and abrasions, abdominal or thoracic injuries; fractures and broken bones or teeth; sight and hearing damage and head injuries. Victims can be seriously physically injured as a result of domestic abuse and experience long-term injuries.

Victims may suffer from functional disorders or stress-related conditions such as irritable bowel syndrome, gastrointestinal symptoms, fibromyalgia, chronic pain syndromes and exacerbation of asthma. Psychological harms can be associated with poorer physical health and this can include psychosomatic symptoms such as numbness and thrombosis, shaking and nervous twitching, cramps and paralysis.

WOMAN

I remember trying to sleep in my nanna's caravan at Withernsea, feet from the clifftop with the sea attacking the land mass, the wind rocking the sky. I imagined the caravan lifting, the cold plunge. The thin shell that we lay behind always felt too flimsy for me, but my nanna said it would be fine. And it was. I remember a trip on the ferries from Hull to Rotterdam. The way I didn't sleep. The toilets swimming with sick as the ship rocked. I sat alone by the captain's cabin, thinking this was the best place to be if an emergency happened. Thinking that knowing soonest might mitigate for the odds of welded steel against all that wide expanse of angry water. They said it would be fine, and it was.

All that time I was worrying about the sea, I was worrying what would happen if it were to meet my body, the impact, the sudden frozen shock. And all along, I was the cliff face; the soft, slowly eroding clay, being taken in the night while nobody heard.

I remember the squat glass beakers in the school science lab. The butane blue flame of Bunsen burners. The way the salt disappeared into the water. The cloudiness. Then clarity. I remember the dusty saline mess when the water disappeared. The tight smudges along the inner sides and rim. I remember that the salt in the glass after evaporation will be the same weight as the salt added to the glass at the start of the experiment. Conservation of mass. Nothing will be lost. But tell that to the glittering sharp crystals as they slide from the lip of the steel. Maybe it depends on your perspective. Are you the one in the white coat with the spatula, or are you the salt?

Part Four

Air

Here stands a woman, hollowed out. At her core, she holds empty space, like an excavation has taken place. A drilling or bombing. A brutal erosion. She knows that energy applied to molecules will cause them to vibrate, faster and faster, until they fly apart. She feels a tremor run over her surface, lifts a hand to her face to check if she's really there.

WOMAN

I was so brave when it all started. But the thing I've learnt about being brave is that it's OK to do it for a short time. It's manageable. Enjoyable, even. Doing it for a long time, though, is a different matter. Then it starts to have effects. *Worn down.* That's what happens. As much as you try not to, you get worn down. And I never understood what that meant when I was younger. Not really. I used to hear people in my family saying it, but it didn't really mean anything. Now I know it's an actual physical process. *Worn down.* Like someone has taken sandpaper to your edges. Like you're being ground away.

FIVE THINGS I KNOW ABOUT AIR

1. It's difficult to measure the volume of air – it all depends on the container it's in, and the amount of pressure applied to it. Its molecules will expand or contract depending on these things.

2. Air seems weightless, but even though it has no apparent physical form, and you usually can't see it, it's still exerting pressure on you. If the level of pressure being exerted on you suddenly shifts, it's going to affect you.

3. Air is one of those things you don't really notice until something goes wrong with it; it becomes polluted, is contaminated by smoke or allergens, or you can't get enough of it in through your lungs. All of a sudden, it becomes very important to understand what's going on in the air you're breathing and the apparatus you're using to get it where it needs to be.

4. If the air where you're living does become polluted, there are probably things you can do to sort it out. You're going to need an expert, though, and it might not be a quick fix. You might have to be prepared to put a lot of effort in, over a long period of time. You'll need to get to the source of the contamination, and in the meantime you're going to need to find a safe way to breathe.

5. Humidity levels describe the amount of water in the air. Relative humidity tells us how much water is already in the air, in comparison to the maximum it can hold, because even air has a breaking point, a spilling-over point, before it disintegrates into drizzle, or worse.

WOMAN

I think there was about a year between Barrie being released from prison and his murder, but it's hard to say for sure. It's all a bit of a blur. It's been misted out. Every now and then, the fog will spontaneously clear on some small part of it, and I won't know why. I won't know what's triggered it, so I won't know how to avoid it happening again. A kind of Russian roulette of everyday experiences.

A few months ago, I met someone I hadn't seen for sixteen years, and she started talking about things that had happened to me during that time. It was almost like she was talking about someone else. Someone who had my name, who looked a bit like me, who lived in my old house, with my kids, and police cameras installed on her windowsills. Someone whose feelings still lived in my belly. We were eating lunch as she talked, in the trendy little café where my son works Saturdays, but I didn't feel like I was there at all. I felt far away. Disembodied. Out of time.

I can't avoid unknown triggers, but I decided I would have to avoid this woman in the future. The next time she texted me, asking to meet up, I didn't reply. I think that's called ghosting. I know people would say it's not a nice thing to do. But I didn't see any other option, and after all, the person she wants to talk to does feel like a kind of ghost to me.

HULL DAILY MAIL, MONDAY 25 APRIL 2005 (PAGE 3)
Murder inquiry after man dies outside a pub
HULL: Detectives have launched a murder inquiry after the death of a 30-year-old man outside an east Hull pub.

The victim was allegedly beaten with a hammer during an 'altercation' with three men at 10.30pm yesterday.

Forensic teams were this morning searching the scene of the attack around the Dolphin pub in Greenwich Avenue, off Holderness Road.

Police received an anonymous emergency call that a man was being assaulted at 10.37pm.

As part of the investigation, two white vans have been recovered by police.

'Investigators know there was a celebration in the Dolphin on Sunday evening by a football club who had a successful season and there would have been a number of people in the area who would have witnessed the assault or events leading up to it,' said a police spokesman.

Anyone with information is asked to contact the incident room at Tower Grange Police Station on (01482) 796275.

A 27-year-old man has been arrested on suspicion of murder.

MEMORY

It's not even 7 a.m. when my phone rings. Instant anxiety. Either something's happened or it'll be the man who's currently abusing me. Either way I don't want to answer. It's Monday morning. I need to get the kids ready for school and nursery. I've sat them in front of the telly to watch cartoons for ten minutes while I have a fag on the back doorstep because I wake aching every morning. I need to try to bring myself round.

I glance down. It's the man currently abusing me. I'm half-relieved. Nothing new has happened. Just his usual checking up on me. I answer.

'Barrie's dead,' he says.

A hit of adrenaline.

'He's what?'

'He's dead. Everyone was talking about it when I got into work this morning. On Greenwich Ave. Last night. He's dead.'

'What do you mean? Dead? What do you mean?'

'I mean he's dead. Somebody's killed him.'

'Somebody's killed him? He's dead?'

I can't focus. I can't hear him. The walls of the back yard have closed in. I'm hovering outside of myself, but I can still hear my heart beating. The blood in my ears. Everything blurs. I'm far away. I'm far away, but I'm still here. The back yard is closing in.

'Are you there?' he says.

'Yeah, but I've got to go. I'll ring the police.'

I put the phone down. Try to think.

'Fuck,' I say. 'Fuck, fuck, fuck.'

I pace the few steps to the gate and back. I close the back door.

'Fuck, fuck, fuck.'

Cartoon theme tunes begin to sing out through the kitchen, through the glass, and I know that means little feet will soon follow, looking for me, and a hug, and a uniform, and a packed book bag, and a signed reading record, and so I pull myself together a bit and I call the number I have for the detectives.

I say, 'I'm calling about Barrie Jackson.'

They say, 'What about him?'

I say, 'Well, is he dead?'

They ask who it is, and I tell them.

They confirm it's true. He died last night. They tell me they'll be coming to speak to me later in the day.

I can hear the kids shouting for me, wanting their breakfast, so I lay my hand on my chest, take three slow breaths. Then I go inside and feed my kids and dress them and take them to school and nursery. Buy myself some time to figure out what to do.

HULL DAILY MAIL, TUESDAY 26 APRIL 2005 (FRONT PAGE)

HULL: Former firefighter was tried for attempted murder and jailed for assault

VIOLENT END FOR A VIOLENT MAN

A man bludgeoned to death with a hammer outside a city pub had a history of violence and was due to appear in court next week charged with intimidation.

Former firefighter Barrie Jackson, 30, was today described by police as a 'violent man who met a violent death'.

Mr Jackson was found bleeding to death outside the Dolphin pub in Greenwich Avenue, east Hull, on Sunday night.

He had been due to appear at Hull Crown Court next Tuesday for intimidating a witness during a previous court case.

He was also due to appear at Hull Magistrates' Court next month charged with attacking a man on September 18 last year.

[. . .]

Today, Humberside Police Chief Superintendent Paul Davison, who investigated Mr Jackson as part of his attempted murder trial, described him as a 'violent man who met a violent death'.

It is believed Mr Jackson was attacked by three men on Sunday night.

He was found dying in a pool of blood. A 27-year-old man is in custody after being arrested on suspicion of murder.

A team of detectives, headed by Detective Superintendent Ray Higgins, today vowed to leave no stone unturned.

Mr Jackson, who was believed to have been living at Middleham Close in east Hull, had spent Sunday evening at the Dolphin pub.

Police believe he left the pub at 10.30pm, fearing he was in danger. Within an hour, Mr Jackson was declared dead at Hull Royal Infirmary in Anlaby Road.

A post mortem has concluded Mr Jackson died from severe head injuries.

A police spokesman said: 'He was met by three men who expected to find him.

'Mr Jackson was allegedly sprayed with CS spray by one of the men and then chased from outside the Dolphin pub and towards the roundabout with Staveley Road.

'He was then subjected to a physical attack and a hammer was used to assault him. A CS spray canister has been recovered at the scene.'

WOMAN

I used to laugh when I told people Barrie had been murdered. It broke the awkwardness of the statement. It was a thing I never wanted to say, but I kept ending up in situations where I had to say it. You meet some other mums at a kid's party and the conversation eventually turns to where your kids' dad is. You meet a man in a bar, you go on a couple of dates, and the conversation eventually turns to where your kids' dad is.

'We split up,' I'd say, hoping that would be enough. But other people don't know when to push and when to stop — it's a thing I've noticed — so they'd say, 'Do they see much of him?' and I'd say, 'No, he died when they were small.' Then — even though I'd used all my best body language skills, even though I'd tried distraction and paralinguistics, and moderated my use of eye contact to try and send the message that I didn't really want to talk about this any more — they'd ask: 'How?'

And I would end up laughing as I said it, to lighten the load for them. Because nobody wants to talk about murdered dads at kids' birthday parties or on dates.

HULL DAILY MAIL, TUESDAY 26 APRIL 2005 (PAGE 3)
HULL: Cleared of attempted murder but jailed for beating woman
Victim was a bully with a brutal history
[...]

Many believed Mr Jackson got off lightly when he was jailed for just two years for the attack on Ms Capell.

But detectives yesterday opened an investigation into the murder of the 30-year-old himself.

And they urged potential witnesses not to let Mr Jackson's history stop them from coming forward.

Inspector Steve Page said: 'Despite the high profile nature and result of the case involving Carol Ives, it is vital that this should not colour anyone's judgement about the victim.

'The case against Mr Jackson in that incident has long since closed.

'Our absolute priority is to bring to justice those who have killed Barrie Jackson.'

[...]

However, no one else has faced charges relating to the brutal attack on Ms Ives.

Ms Ives was told of Mr Jackson's death yesterday but declined to comment.

LETTER I WILL NEVER SEND TO SG

Your motives have become like the shadow or echo of my every thought this last year or so. I try to drown them out, the constant loop, the constant guessing and second-guessing; be loud enough or busy enough; create a distraction. But like all things that rumble about in our heads under the noise and brightness of the everyday, I see and hear them clearly when I lie in bed at night. What if you just want to help people? What if you really have learnt from what you've done? Am I wrong for feeling this way about you? Is there something wrong with me for feeling this way?

I don't want you shadowing my thoughts. I don't want all the potential echoes of what your motives might be reverberating back off my own plans and ideas. I want to be free of you. Want to cut you away from me. I don't want this attachment. This weird link.

I've decided to use some of my daytimes to try and lean into what it is about you that's affecting me. But every time I picture you, things get shaky. The rage comes back, wavering before my eyes like a wall of heat, and I have to lie down. It makes me dizzy. I don't trust myself when it comes on like that. I put in headphones. Run a bath. My body aches. I picture what it would look like if a bomb had gone off inside of me. I can see it clearly; the space opening up, the way my skin moulds and bends to absorb it. It makes me feel better. Like I've contained something toxic.

I remember lying on a treatment bed in someone's back room, feathers and strange-shaped pieces of wood hang on the wall. I have closed my eyes and she is standing over me. I feel her moving sometimes at the sides of the bed, hands outstretched. There is warmth spreading over me and suddenly I want to cry. She says, 'Your aura is very tattered in places, like it's been stretched too thin,' and I know there's a thick knobbly root of something sitting in my stomach.

MAN, TWITTER
If people can't afford to feed their kids, they shouldn't have had them in the first place.

WOMAN, TWITTER
Half the women at the school gate are single mums. It's a fucking disgrace. Smoking their heads off. Mobile phones. Whingeing that they don't get enough on their benefits. This country needs to sort itself out.

WOMAN ON THE BUS
Them kids are little shits. I know their Dad's not around, but that's no excuse. She needs to man up a bit. Get a grip on them. Doesn't take a rocket scientist to work that out.

MAN ON THE BUS
It's just boys doing what boys do. Testosterone, innit? You can't blame them.

ANOTHER WOMAN
'Too much turning the other cheek will make you dizzy,' she says.
   Her hair is moving briskly about her face, like she's caught in strong wind. I can smell the fresh air on her. See the sharp, clear, sea-tinged sky of a bright winter's day in the distance.

'That's one of mine,' I say.

'I know. You posted it on Facebook once. You were pleased with it. It got a lot of likes, and you've got a point. I mean, who wants to keep getting hit across the face anyway?'

She throws her arms wide as she speaks and adjusts her feet forwards. I look down, notice how close to the cliff edge she is standing.

'Careful,' I say, and she shakes her head. Half-laughs. Carries on speaking.

'I'm afraid I have to disagree with Jesus on that one,' she says. 'We'll have to agree to differ with him there. And while I'm on the subject, "bend don't break" is bollocks as well. There's no OR. You keep bending, you will eventually break. We all have a point. A snapping point. A breaking place. It's not one or the other. And if you think about it, spending all your time bending and then breaking anyway means you're getting the shitty end of the stick and the pointy end of the stick, doesn't it? Just stop bending so much. People are always talking about picking your battles. Pick your bends, I say.'

She's getting excited. She doesn't look steady. I can sense the strength of the wind she's standing in, and again I say, 'Be careful.'

She steps forward again, half a pace, so that the toes of her muddy old white trainers are just overhanging the cliff edge, and suddenly my perspective shifts: a vertiginous, sweeping view of all the empty space falling out and away from the clifftop. The wide, open, empty air that cascades away endlessly into the blur between water and sky.

LETTER I WON'T POST TO KARL TURNER, MP

I don't think I told you when I came to see you that I'm a member of the Labour Party. That I spent hours in the rain and snow knocking on doors with my local MP during the run-up to the last election. That I've dialled in to the funny telephone canvassing software and made calls on Saturday afternoons. That I've been to meetings, subscribed to the emails; that I pay my membership money every month. I didn't think it mattered. It somehow didn't seem fair. I didn't want that to influence the conversation we had. In short, I trusted you. Just to hear me. To understand the weight of the situation and act appropriately. That was the spirit in which I set out.

But you don't look me in the eye when you speak. That's the first thing I notice. As I try to tell you what it's been like for me and my children over the last fifteen years, I search your face for some understanding of what I'm saying. But I don't find it. Then when you reply, it's Simon you look at. Simon, whose eyes, as far as either of us know, never processed a real-life image of Barrie. Whose lips never exchanged words or kisses with his. Whose hands never knew what his skin felt like beneath them. Never knew the curve of his hands, the roughness of fingers that sanded and screwed washing-machine parts, lifted a small child from a burning wardrobe, laid bricks, built fences from rough-hewn wood.

My face, my hands, that could have linked you back to all of these things and more, you turn away from. It doesn't make me angry when you do this. I don't consider it deeply at first. It's the same thing the man in the car showroom does when I take Simon with me to look at a new car I'm thinking about buying. The same thing the man with the tape measure does as he explains the layout for a kitchen that I've provided all the specifications for. The same sort of disappearing that happens to women in all sorts of situations.

I've never been a fan of Lady Macbeth, for what I hope, by now, are obvious reasons. But I feel some of her frustrations as I see you do this. If I could be unsexed, maybe you would hear me. Maybe you could see me. Maybe my words would be lent some substance. But I have no spirits to call on. I'd thought I only needed to call on the understanding I'd felt sure I'd be able to find in you; the connection that flares up between people when they're able to lift away guards and pretence. The thing I like to think all people are capable of doing, deep down. But I see now that's not going to happen here today.

WOMAN

I reckon I got about five fairly normal years after Barrie died, if I don't count the panic attacks. And I don't count them. I can't count them.

They were years of relative peace. I appreciated my new freedom. I got on with things. Enjoyed small pleasures like being able to put the bin out without feeling scared. Stopped checking and rechecking to see who was behind me when I walked, stopped checking my rear-view mirror obsessively.

I progressed from cleaning pub toilets to being an admin assistant, office manager, shipping clerk, then changed career and became a teaching assistant. I moved house a few more times. Got the kids to school every day. Brought them up. Cracked on. Knuckled down. Decided that I could do the work of two parents, no problem. Decided if I tried hard enough, carried out enough after-school activities, cheered them on at touchlines, helped them with their homework, cuddled them enough, I could make it all right.

In the middle of all of that, I didn't really stop and think much about the other court case that would now be happening. I didn't think about the people who would be on trial or why they'd done what they'd done, or how they'd done it. I decided it was absolutely nothing at all to do with me. That chapter of my life was over.

In short, I put on a grand act of kidding myself. But I didn't realise it then, and I didn't have a whole lot of other options on offer.

ANOTHER WOMAN

'It just feels like people have stopped being interested,' I say. 'Like we're supposed to have won now. Like we need to shut up. It's frustrating, you know?'

She has her face turned away from me, twirling a cigarette between two fingers. Her hair is immaculately shaped into a beehive front with a long, brown ringlet over one shoulder. Her dress is A-line, printed with big green-and-yellow daisies. She doesn't look like she's going to speak, so I carry on.

'You know, you must have seen it,' I say.

I pause, and she still doesn't look at me.

'I suppose what I'm saying is, the thing that's frustrating is the job is half-done. I'm not denying that there has been progress, but when you read about what was happening in the eighties, it all seemed so positive. If you read books about the sixties, it did. You wouldn't believe we could still be where we are now after all the strides women made in the last century. It's like they did all the colourful, loud hard work, and we're left with this constant unpicking of knots in tongues and words – it feels like you're going round in circles sometimes, wrapping yourself in twine.'

This time, she does look up. Looks me straight in the eye. Raises a perfectly arched eyebrow.

'From here,' she says, 'I can see everything, and what I see is thousands of women with their fingers in the dam. Thousands of women with their arms stretched high, holding up the sky. And yes, some do spend their days unpicking the knots in tongues, the knots in stomachs. I see a battle being fought on a thousand tiny fronts. The colourful, loud hard work isn't over at all. It's just that it's not one small group of women singing on their own now – thousands, millions, of them are singing together – some are whispering, some have developed a deep bass, a soaring soprano, but every single one raises the volume.'

'OK then,' I say, 'but what if no one is listening? What happens then?'

'You mean, what if men aren't listening?'

I think about it. I suppose I do. But. . .

'Not just men,' I say. 'Lots of women still aren't listening either. You see them all the time, arguing about how empowering it is to dance round a pole, or work in porn. Lapping up all the stories in the *Hull Daily Mail* about how great it is when you give up your job as a doctor or a solicitor and set up an Only Fans site instead.'

'What's "Only Fans"?'

'You don't want to know,' I say.

'Maybe *you* shouldn't know.'

'Well, I do know.'

She closes her eyes, takes a deep breath, then speaks.

'I thought you didn't go in for victim-blaming,' she says.

'What do you mean?'

'Don't blame the women who decide that posting pictures or videos on the internet is better than standing on a line somewhere like I did, or cleaning up puke in pub toilets like you did. Good for them if they can get away with it.'

'I thought you didn't know what it was,' I say.

'All knowledge in the blink of an eye,' she says, suddenly stern. Then she disappears abruptly, and the air she leaves behind is chilly with disapproval.

WOMAN

It is possible to come apart slowly. So gradually that nobody notices. One day you can be walking around, cooking the tea, hoovering, going to work, getting your nails done, and another day you can be lying on the sofa saying you can't walk. It won't make sense to anyone when it happens. It didn't make sense to me.

But now, it seems like the strange thing was that I kept walking around doing all those things for as long as I did, like a chicken after its head's been cut off, or those mackerel in the bottom of the rowing boats at Bridlington, where we used to holiday with my dad; the slow rocking of the little wooden vessel, the shimmering surprise of silver and blue; then the thwack of a heavy knife, the salty, bloody mess; the slick shock of its still-jumping body at our feet.

THE ME ASSOCIATION WEBSITE
GENERAL INFORMATION
Recognise that people with ME/CFS may have:

- experienced prejudice and disbelief and could feel stigmatised by people (including family, friends, health and social care professionals, and teachers) who do not understand their illness.

MEMORY

One morning in 2011, I wake to find I'm pinned by Hollowfibre, which seems somehow appropriate. Forces I don't understand seem to be exerting control over my body. I feel like a kind of nothing. There's nothing in the tank. There's nothing going on upstairs, and there's nothing going on downstairs either. There's just nothing. I am a hollow space beneath the duvet. Limp and placid.

My eyes are closed, heavy, as though someone has stitched tiny weights along the lids. Tiny, but heavy. They will not open, and the rest of my body isn't helping. There's no go. No give. I can hear, distantly, the sound of my alarm; know I should snooze it. Know I should, right now, be dragging myself upright, spinning my legs to place myself at a ninety-degree angle to the bed, feet on the floor; feet sliding into slippers, and then striding across the landing to the boys' room, waking them, singing them my morning song: 'Good morning, good morning, you've slept the whole night through!' I should be making my way downstairs, opening the blinds, letting sunlight stream in, turning on the news, turning on the coffee machine, letting it heat, turning on the grill, unfurling silver foil and laying it over the grill pan, peeling thick-cut back bacon, pink and promising, from the pack in the fridge; slipping the slices evenly onto the grill, forming three neat pairs. Opening coffee beans, pouring milk to warm and froth, scrambling eggs and buttering hot toast. Then the pleasure of their faces, healthy and happy, as they sit around the table, eating, drinking; rich maroon sweatshirts with little blue polo-shirt collars lying neatly at the neck. Neatly ironed grey trousers, shined black leather shoes, book bags stashed with neat homework. The chatter on the walk to the bus stop, and as we wait in line with the other kids and mums, before I make my way off to my own school, up the road, royal blue polo shirt, neat black trousers. Kids and parents know my name – 'Morning, Mrs Foster' – and one kid in particular will be especially pleased to see me when I get there. He's the one I'm paid to look after every day.

I can see all this, like a distant dream, but my eyes don't open. Maybe today someone else will do it. Maybe this is someone else's life I'm remembering. Far away, my brain registers that the beeping of the alarm has quieted, and my eyes stop struggling to open, settle back into full sleep.

When they do work themselves fully open again in the quiet room, I fumble for my phone on the bedside table. 9.05. What the fuck? How has that happened? I try to pull myself up, groggy. The room spins. Everything hurts. Feet, legs, stomach, ribs, chest, arms – they all throb dully. The glands in my neck pulse, as they have for days now, in time with my armpits – they've been swollen and inflamed, and I never knew that armpits could be so painful. The sinus pain and headache I'm accustomed to – they've been hanging about for years – apparently some sort of allergy, but no one knows what to. The blood-smeared snotty tissues that accumulate in my pocket throughout the day are normal. I've bought a little watering-can contraption that I use to flush my nostrils each morning and night, and that helps the congestion, but not the pain in my cheeks and forehead. When I lay the breakfast table in the morning, the boys each have a vitamin tablet on their placemat, and it's standard procedure to place two small white ibuprofen pills next to my knife and fork.

I should be rushing, but I haven't got it in me. I feel rooted to the bed, like the fibres have woven themselves under my skin while I was sleeping. I can't separate. I'm useless under the weight of the duvet. I slip my phone back into my hand, thumb through phone numbers until I find my school. Thank God I'll go through to the office, to the kind lady on reception, who'll be busy fielding these kind of phone calls at this time; and not to my own area, where the head of foundation, or the teacher from my class, or any of the other teaching assistants who will have to pick up the slack my absence creates, won't be able to keep the disappointment from their voices. It's not their fault. They're stretched. Everyone knows they're stretched. But seeing it, being inside it, is a different matter. I'm paid to look after one boy with special educational needs, but in fact I look after two all day – one of them has not been awarded the statement that would win him his own one-to-one support. So,

I look after them both. They can't manage in the classroom without that. And the class teachers will struggle to teach the other kids anything at all without someone supporting them. I know this. I love my job. But still my body won't move.

Once the phone call's made — redundant, really, cos they must know I'm not coming by now: school started half an hour ago — I turn my attention to my own kids. They're still sleeping, tucked up in their lovely bedroom, in twin beds. Newly painted walls, clothes tidy and smelling of Lenor in the fitted wardrobes, plush new carpet beneath their feet when they wake, new curtains that match the new bedding, transfers they've chosen above their beds. But Jack won't be happy when I finally wake him, and he realises he's late for school. He's fastidious. He hates being late. But still no sign of movement from me. My head has not yet left the pillow, and the throbbing is still happening, lying still.

If I don't ring the kids' school, they'll ring me — and they'll have that accusatory tone they adopt when you haven't informed them why your child isn't in school, and they have to go to the trouble of ringing you and asking. How do I explain them both not being in? I can't say they're both ill with the same bug on the same day — and anyway, they're not. They're absolutely fine. So, what do I say?

Sorry, but this morning, I just don't work. My body's packed in, and my brain's not far behind, so there you go. Toodle-pip.

It's not like a heart attack or a stroke. It's not a car accident. Not an emergency. What's the protocol for just can't get out of bed? What will they think if I say I've got some sort of bug and I've slept in and now I can't move to get them to school? Maybe that's it. It must be some sort of bug, and I've slept in. That's it. I scroll through my contacts again, click on their number.

'OK. Well, will you be able to bring them in shortly, then?'

Maybe I will. Maybe after lying here for a while, I'll be able to pull myself out of bed, into their room, and into the car. It's only a five-minute drive. How hard can it be?

'Yes, I'll get them there as soon as I can.'

And that's the truth. I just don't know when that might be.

Turns out I can't get them there at all. Turns out that the walk to the toilet in the en-suite bathroom is enough to set my head spinning. I flush the chain and sit on the seat for – I don't know how long – until the spinning stops. Then drag myself back to bed.

My friend rings. 'What do you mean you can't get up?'

'I don't know. What I say.'

'But why?'

'I don't know why.'

I ring the doctor's.

'Is it an emergency?'

'Well, I don't know.'

'Do you need to see someone today?'

There's no way I'm going anywhere today, and I'm not dying, am I? I don't think so. It's scary, but it's not a heart attack, is it?

'No.'

'OK, well, the next appointment to see the doctor is two weeks on Wednesday.'

ANOTHER WOMAN

She doesn't come back for weeks, and I wonder if I can write her a note and leave it on my desk – whether she'll see it. Like when I used to leave letters in the chimney for Father Christmas. What would I write though? Where do I start?

I want to ask her if she saw *A Taste of Honey* when the film came out. If she ever knew any of the Headscarf Revolutionaries when they were marching on the docks or petitioning Downing Street, or before they did that, or after. Did she drink with them in the pubs on Hessle Road or in her social clubs? I want to know what she felt like when the sexual revolution was happening in the sixties – did she go and get the pill when it came out? I want to know why we never talked about this when she was here, and in response to that, I hear her voice.

'Do you really think that in-between the two 'til ten, or the ten 'til six or the six 'til two, and the cooking and the cleaning and the washing and raising my own kids and then picking you up from school, and cooking your tea, so your mum could go to work, that I had time for chit-chatting about any of that?'

WOMAN IN HER LIVING ROOM
You can't be weak with men. You've got to stand up to them. You can't let them get away with shit.

WOMAN IN CAFÉ
He's a lovely bloke. No way she's not doing something to wind him up.

WOMAN IN CAR
I'd be out of there like a shot.

WOMAN IN CAFÉ
She should have left him years ago. Not being funny, but if she gets her kids taken away it's her own fault.

LETTER I WON'T POST TO KARL TURNER, MP
I'm trying to be kind here. I'm mitigating on your behalf. You weren't expecting me. You didn't know what I was thinking. Maybe you thought I'd come baying for blood, but I hadn't. I'd come with a genuine question. I wanted to know why you were doing this – what was so compelling that you either hadn't thought about what this might be like for us before you did it, or you'd thought about it and decided it was worth our sacrifice?

Looking back, I see you just hadn't considered it. Looking back, and maybe I'm being too kind, but you surely wouldn't have gone for the blustering route if you could have seen how I was really feeling. It's true that I must have looked a sight. I must have looked half-wild. I was half-wild by that point, I admit it. I'm not ashamed to admit it. But only half wild. Only half raging mother. The other half of me is reasonable, intelligent, balanced – though you accused me of lacking balance. You actually said that. Do you remember? I do. It's one of those words that's etched on my brain. You told me I was incapable of balance on the subject. But you were wrong. It was you who was lacking balance. I wonder if you've found it now. I understand it was probably a shock for you, me turning up that day. I could see it in your eyes. The slight panic. *Gorylocks, Gorylocks, somebody's been sitting in my constituency office and she's still here.* But there really was no need for panic. Not if you had genuine answers for me.

WOMAN

Memories aren't solid. Or fixed. They don't seem like the kind of thing you can rely on. They don't end or begin anywhere. They don't have physical substance. They're air. The transmission of faded images over empty space. I wish I could hold them in my hand and look at them properly. I feel like I need proof. I want to check all the details. I wish I had 4K Ultra HD digital copies of the things that flit like dodgy old VHS tapes across the screen of my brain. Something to show someone, check their response, get their feedback. Have I read it wrong? Was there something I missed? Have I laid my own faulty functioning, like a filter, a distorting mesh, over the facts of what happened? I wish I still had all the documentation so that I could at least prove some things. It used to sit in a huge pile in the cupboard under the stairs of every house I lived in. Solicitor's letters, court documents, newspaper cuttings. Evidence. There as a backup, a line of defence. But after Barrie died, I tore each sheet into tiny, tiny pieces and put them all out with the rubbish.

THE ME ASSOCIATION WEBSITE
GENERAL INFORMATION
Explain that ME/CFS:

- is a fluctuating medical condition that affects everyone differently, in which symptoms and their severity can change over a day, week or longer,
- varies in long-term outlook from person to person – although a proportion of people recover or have a long period of remission, many will need to adapt to living with ME/CFS,
- varies widely in its impact on people's lives, and can affect their daily activities, family and social life, and work or education (these impacts may be severe),
- can be worsened by particular triggers – these can be known or new triggers or in some cases there is no clear trigger,
- can be self-managed with support and advice (see the section on energy management),
- can involve flare-ups and relapses even if symptoms are well managed, so planning for these should be part of the energy management plan.

MEMORY

In the period between 2007 and 2011, I've been going to see this doctor fairly regularly; every few months or so. Being knackered is normal for me. I'm mum to two young boys, work is tiring, and I study at night for the Open University course I've started – a sociology degree. All mums are knackered. I know because we all tell each other all the time. But when the pain in my face gets too bad, or the swelling in my throat, or the swelling in my stomach, or the aching in my legs that keeps me awake half the night, or when the staying awake half the night is happening for no good reason, and I toss and turn until 4 a.m. and then get a few hours' rest before the day starts – when any of these things feel like they're tipping me over – I'll ring and have the same conversation with the doctor's receptionist. I'll dutifully wait the two weeks for my appointment, and invariably be told by the doctor that I'm just run down, I'm just tired. I should eat an apple and an orange every day.

Six weeks after not being able to get out of bed, I'm still not back at work, still struggling to get up each day, still not able to move from the sofa all day. Our morning routine has changed; now Harry makes me a poached egg on toast every day, before they both walk together to the bus stop, on their own. Jack resents this, and I don't blame him, but Harry is full of optimism and excitement, like this is a new adventure where he gets to do stuff he couldn't before.

When they've gone, I get ready, waiting for 8 a.m., with my finger poised over *Doctor* in my contacts list. Six weeks was the magic number; he said a virus could last six weeks, and if I wasn't better by then, I could go and see him again. I've spent those six weeks flitting between optimism that it would pass and any day now I'll wake up back to normal; and a skulking fear that he knows that's not going to happen but this is the drill. A box we have to tick before we can move on to the next stage.

He told me that if I'm not better in six weeks, he'd have to start running some tests, so today I'm going to make an appointment that will tell me exactly what's going on. Except it doesn't work like that. It works like this: scores of blood tests, which all come back negative, nothing wrong, then allergy testing, which all comes back negative, nothing wrong (not surprising, given I've purged every known allergen from my diet and am currently eating only gluten-free, dairy-free foods that I've successfully reintroduced after an exclusion period). Followed by waiting varying periods of time, repeating the tests, being told nothing's wrong. But something *is* wrong. Something is very wrong, because I'm a thirty-one-year-old woman who can't stand up long enough for the kettle to boil.

I'm not surprised when they eventually tell me that they think it's chronic fatigue syndrome. My dad had it years ago – mostly during the period when we didn't really speak – and he's told me what it was like. It was just like this; how I am now. It's not a thing that shows up on blood tests, it's a thing they diagnose by absence; if you tick enough boxes and nothing shows up in blood tests, it's probably that. Probably, but not definitely. First, they have to do a brain scan, because my symptoms are very similar to multiple sclerosis, too, and only the absence or presence of scarring on the brain will tell them for sure. I'm bloody petrified. I've been Googling 'chronic fatigue' for weeks, and throwing up words such as 'bedbound', 'difficulty swallowing', 'lifelong', but these have been tempered by stories from people I know, including my dad, who have recovered and are managing along mostly normally now.

The waiting list for the MRI scan is long. By the time it comes around, I'm at the stage where the only few times I've left the house in the last six months have been on short journeys to break my monotony, places where people could drive me and where a wheelchair was available. I've been pushed in the free wheelchairs at The Range, because I can't walk round and I just wanted to do something normal. I've been pushed in a wheelchair that I hired from a shop in town, up into the disabled viewing area at City Hall to watch the boys sing in a school concert, because I felt like the worst mum in the world if I wasn't able to go.

Eventually though, I get an appointment to ride through the giant polo of an MRI machine, which should be simple, but it's not. Being in an enclosed space, having to keep still, gives me flashbacks to being locked in tight spaces with abusive men – the survival reflex of needing to get out. The panic. The nurse is kind. Says people have this kind of reaction sometimes. She holds my hand, strokes my fingers. Gets me through it.

The results, when they come, are clear. No scarring on the brain. I've got chronic fatigue syndrome or ME, as some people call it. I spend a lot of time on the ME Association and Action for ME websites, learning what I can do to make myself better.

There are no cures. No medication. It's probably lifelong, so you have to try and manage it, and the main way in which you can do this is by using pacing. This means tracking and planning all your activity, staggering any activity with periods of rest, finding out what you can manage without having crashes. The first main priority is to find your baseline – what you can do consistently without being completely knocked out again.

Five minutes of activity followed by two hours of rest is my baseline. I have to build from there.

WOMAN

There are no such things as big sadnesses. I realise there are things that people can point out, and say, 'Oh, yeah, that's a BIG one.' Like murder, chronic illness, domestic abuse. But they're not one big thing either. They're made up of lots of tiny little sadnesses clustered together. A missed school assembly because you're too anxious to be crowded into a room with all those people; your kids dropping out of the rugby team because they can see how difficult it is for you to get them there on a Sunday morning in the way the other parents do; not being able to afford for them to go to Spain on a school trip with their friends in their year; not having the energy to keep the house as clean as you'd like; a Christmas without presents. The effect is cumulative. You can look at a hunk of limestone or a church or a castle and admire its solidity. But we know that's just a fallacy. It's quivering below the surface. Millions of molecules vibrating together.

LETTER I WILL NEVER SEND TO SG

Part of the problem for you is that you found me at the wrong time. Ten years ago, I'd probably have been more than willing to come and speak with you. I'd probably have felt like I owed you something. Accepted the idea that it was somehow my responsibility to help you move on. That I should maybe even be grateful to you. I can't say for sure, of course, but I think I can make a fairly accurate guess, based on the other shit I was putting up with at the time, the people who were around me, and the attitudes I held. Also, based on the way I reacted when I first posted on social media after finding out about what had happened, and when the Restorative Justice service got in touch. I did, briefly, revert to type, and I have since then had lots of moments of having to fight off that neat little package of thoughts and feelings. Maybe, under pressure, they're still my default setting. Only difference is that now I'm better at reasoning them out. Unpicking them.

I've been annoyed at myself about how they can still sneak in, but I don't actually think it's my fault. I mean, there's been some pretty stringent pressure applied to me. But when I meet these thoughts with logic, I find I'm just not willing to accept them any more. I've learnt too much. I know too much. I'm too aware of just how much I've put up with in the past, to my detriment and my kids' detriment, and the detriment of everyone around me who cares about me. I've come to value my health and wellbeing like these are prizes. Because they are. I've invested a lot of time and energy in them. I've worked hard to get them, retain them, and I'm fighting again for them now. If you think for one minute I trust you enough to enter into any sort of communication with you and risk them, then you are very much mistaken.

I have become a very watchful person over the course of my life. I pay attention. I weigh the implications of people's words and actions. I don't always do it consciously, but I do it constantly. The people who are in my life now are there because I have decided that they are trustworthy. Not infallible. Not 'good' – whatever that means. But trustworthy. I know they usually operate within a certain spectrum of behaviour, dictated by what I have come to know as their personal beliefs, their integrity, their desires, their actions. And I feel safe when I'm with them. Safe to let go of analysing. To relax, have a drink, sing, share words, get undressed, close my eyes, sleep, share my time, space, thoughts and feelings. To be vulnerable.

I've often said, over the course of my life, that those people who had found a new way of being, of living their lives – those people who have had to overcome massive setbacks, really dig deep and change the way they are – are my favourite kind of people. But you've made me question that. Because you would not make it onto my list of favourite people. Sometimes I wonder if I'm a hypocrite. If I only apply this rule when it's convenient for me, when it fits my worldview and lies within the boundaries of my experience. But I don't think I am a hypocrite. I think the problem is that I've got absolutely no evidence that you've changed at all. In fact, I know virtually nothing about you. All I have to go on, in essence, is maybe half an hour's worth of your actions seventeen years ago, and another half an hour's worth from two years ago. How can I possibly be expected to trust you or know if you've changed?

I do know that when it comes to making amends, you haven't learnt the most important part: that you don't have the right to inflict pain on anyone else in order to facilitate your own public 'redemption'. I don't know what they taught you about rehabilitation, but if they didn't teach you that, they missed out the most important part. You have already taken these last two years from me, in the form of a relapse triggered by your desire to be in the papers and on the TV. I've spent much of that time watching my small slice of the world pass by from my window, my time marked out in cells on spreadsheets. The suggestion that I should give you more of my time, more of my energy, risk more pain for myself and everyone around me at your instigation? No. No, I do not accept that. So, if you think I will sit down in a room with you and open myself up, you are very much mistaken.

THE ME ASSOCIATION WEBSITE
GENERAL INFORMATION
Awareness and Impact
Be aware that ME/CFS:

- is a complex, chronic medical condition affecting multiple body systems. The pathophysiology is still being investigated.
- affects everyone differently – for some people symptoms still allow them to carry out some activities, whereas for others they cause substantial incapacity.

- can affect different aspects of the lives of both people with ME/CFS and their families and carers, including activities of daily living, family life, social life, emotional wellbeing, work, and education.

MEMORY

When I am forced to stop, lie still, it is as though things begin to settle in me. Everything that has been churned up by movement also lies down, like sediment. This feels like a kind of relief at first. A quieting. A sudden silence after a constantly loud room. But it doesn't take long before the relief changes to something else. As the clouds begin to dissipate, it starts to feel like maybe there are things inside of me that I hadn't noticed, or had chosen not to notice.

I travel to a hospital in another city where a specialist works – a man who is an expert on chronic fatigue. From behind his desk, he says that I seem to be doing a really good job of managing my physical and mental energy.

'But,' he says, 'don't forget – because this is a thing that a lot of people don't think about – don't forget the impact of emotional energy too. You need to consider whether there's anything in your life that causes you stress – a lot of people who come to me here have experienced really difficult things in the past. That can drain your energy too. It's something you need to consider.'

And ha! This is really funny, because now I can no longer pretend that I'm just being silly or over-reacting or being too sensitive. All the things I've been trying not to feel really are catching up with me. They begin to take form, an endless open void before me, a pit filled with oppressive air swelling out in front of me. I teeter at its edge and try not to wonder when the ground will disappear from beneath my feet.

WOMAN

Sometimes I wake in the bedrooms of houses I don't live in any more, the sound of a man nearby making me clench myself. I listen in the half-light for a baby crying, then realise my babies are full-grown men now.

Time is not a one-way street. It plays tricks on you. It's hard to measure in the tiny segments allotted to it. It is unruly. It leaks out. I kid myself that I can make it go where I decide, make it lie down, be obedient, like a well-trained dog, and most of the time it's true. But sometimes it bares its teeth at me. Sometimes it shits on the carpet while I'm out, and I've got no choice but to clean up, do my best to get rid of the smell.

LETTER FROM DAME DIANA JOHNSON DBE, LABOUR
MEMBER OF PARLIAMENT FOR HULL NORTH
To: The Rt Hon Boris Johnson MP Prime Minister
  26 October 2020
  Dear Prime Minister,
  Re: Ms Vicky Foster, x xxx xxxxx, Hull HUx xxx

I wrote to you on 5th February 2020 about my constituent Ms Vicky Foster whose estranged partner, Mr Barrie Jackson, was murdered by Mr Steve Gallant, who in recent months has received publicity for his actions during the terrorist attack at Fishmongers Hall. I finally received a reply from the Cabinet Office Minister Chloe Smith MP on 3rd July 2020 and there was a further exchange of correspondence between the Cabinet Office and myself on 10th July, 4th August and 12th August 2020. Copies are attached to this letter for ease of reference.

As you will be aware, I raised with you, my constituent's concerns about the distress and hurt caused to her family by the actions of Mr Gallant and the lack of support and consideration that they had received over the years, as the victim's family. This is set against the call by some for an award to be made to Mr Gallant for his recent actions.

On Saturday 17th October 2020 I received an email from my constituent to say that a journalist had been in touch with her son Jack to ask what he thought about Steven Gallant receiving a pardon from the Queen. There had been absolutely no contact with the family to prewarn them of what was about to happen. As I had set out in previous correspondence the family have felt abandoned by the state and not supported at all in dealing with what had happened to them.

In the *Sunday Mirror* on Sunday 18th October an article appeared and quoted Jack. This again has caused a huge amount of distress to the family.

I am simply flabbergasted that having been in correspondence with Ministers that no one thought it appropriate to take the action of forewarning me or my constituent of what was to be announced. It is highly disrespectful to a family that have gone through so much over the years.

I therefore spoke to your PPS Alex Burghart MP on Sunday 18th October 2020 and relayed my constituent's concerns about the whole way this information had come to light. As I have pointed out in earlier correspondence my constituent believes in the rehabilitative nature of prison and acknowledges what Mr Gallant did in the middle of a vicious attack, but that has to be set against his earlier actions of murdering a man.

I would welcome hearing from you about what has happened and whether you feel this has been handled appropriately and sensitively.

ANOTHER WOMAN

'Of course,' I say, 'there was a time when they used to burn clever old ladies – in fact, clever ladies of any age. At least they weren't discriminatory in that respect. Actually, I don't think it was even necessarily particularly clever ladies. They used to burn any woman who knew something a man didn't know, or had a feeling a man didn't have, or brewed up a funny-smelling tea, or retreated to a little shack in the woods. You, up on your clifftop in your caravan, going on contemplative walks by yourself – you'd have been in big trouble.'

'Burning,' she says.

'Yeah,' I say. 'They'd have called you a witch. For definite.'

'No need to be bloody rude,' she says.

I laugh and carry on. 'If you told them that stuff about knowing you were going to bump into someone while you were doing your shopping, because you'd thought about them as you were waking up, that would have been it. Kaput. A bloody big bonfire for you. And answering back would definitely have been out. And saying you saw red mist sometimes? Devil in you. Spirit in you. Flames, rope and a big bit of two by four for you.'

'Two by four wouldn't have been thick enough,' she says, 'not to hold me.'

'See what I mean?' I say.

This time, she laughs. 'How do you know I'm not a witch?' she says.

'Oh, you'd never catch me saying you weren't.'

'Exactly,' she says. 'Imagine the shock they'd have got when I lit my fag from the flames and then hovered up, out of the fire, to blow smoke in their faces.'

'They didn't have fags then,' I say.

'Imagine the shock they'd have got when I produced the biggest Rizla you'd ever seen, spread it out like a carpet, rolled them up in it, and then lit the tip from the fire they tried to burn me in.'

'You don't smoke rollies.'

'I'd have made an exception for them, and stop picking holes in my plan. Get on board. This is how we defeat the patriarchy. Roll 'em up in Rizlas and smoke 'em.'

I smile, and she smiles, and, even though I've been wanting her to come back, I find myself now, for the first time, willing her to fade away. If I hold her gaze for too long, she'll know that something's wrong, and how can I tell her that once again I have begun to fear the smell of smoke? That I begin to feel myself carried up in the curve of its nothingness, carried along by its little-seeming substance, that I am weightless, that I can't feel my own feet, am not capable of standing straight, let alone defeating anyone or anything.

MAN IN MY INBOX
You've got a lovely smile
  And lovely tits
  Why aren't you replying? Think you're too good for me stuck up cow.

MAN IN A LETTER PASSED ON TO ME BY SOMEONE I KNOW
I know you don't know me, but you rejected my friend request and I haven't got your phone number, so thought I'd write. I really think we should get together some time.

MAN ON MY DOORSTEP
If you don't answer my calls, and block me on social media, what am I supposed to do? I only want to know if you got my flowers.

MAN ON THE PHONE
I wouldn't have to call from a withheld number if you hadn't blocked my number would I? Blocking me is weird. You don't block people like me. I'm the normal one.

THE ME ASSOCIATION WEBSITE
Diagnosis
All of the following 4 symptoms should be present:

  · Debilitating fatigue that is worsened by activity,
  · Post exertional malaise/symptom exacerbation,
  · Unrefreshing sleep and/or sleep disturbance,
  · Cognitive dysfunction.

Other symptoms that may be present include:

- orthostatic intolerance and autonomic dysfunction, including dizziness, palpitations, fainting, nausea on standing or sitting upright from a reclining position.
- temperature hypersensitivity resulting in profuse sweating, chills, hot flushes, or feeling very cold.
- neuromuscular symptoms, including twitching and myoclonic jerks.
- flu-like symptoms, including sore throat, tender glands, nausea, chills, or muscle aches.
- intolerance to alcohol, or to certain foods and chemicals.
- heightened sensory sensitivities, including to light, sound, touch, taste, and smell.
- pain, including pain on touch, myalgia, headaches, eye pain, abdominal pain, or joint pain without acute redness, swelling or effusion.

MEMORY

There is a woman in a suit sitting on the sofa in my living room. Not the living room where I was laid out, ill, newly diagnosed with chronic fatigue, for about three years. Not the living room where police detectives used to come regularly to sit and drink my tea. Not the living room where my kids stood for photos on their first day at secondary school. Not the living room where, in a few years' time, the figures of three bloody men will appear. This is a living room in another house, during another period of what should be relative calm. I have gradually (oh, so gradually) got myself strong again. I have begun to feel normal again. I have begun to feel like the past is shuttered firmly away again, behind me. But just as this has been happening for me, the ground has begun falling away for my children.

They have reached the ages where they have questions. Where they are beginning to need to know what happened when they were small. I try to dispense the details in the best way I can. Make them manageable. Easier to hold. But they are not easy to hold, however

I try and dress them up. They are heavy. They are uncomfortable. They are strange shapes and strange sizes and they don't fit anywhere easily. One of my boys has been just about managing to swallow them, letting them quake and shake in the pit of his belly. One of my boys finds, when he tries to absorb them, that they don't stay put. That they rage through him. Mobilise him. Need an outlet.

The woman in the suit on my sofa is reading to us. A report she's written. It's the summary of the information we shared in the interviews she did with us a few weeks ago, where she asked us all about everything that had ever happened to us since my son was small. He's seventeen now. There's a lot of stuff to remember. It's not the first of these kinds of things we've done. In fact, we've done quite a lot of it by now. You'd think it would get easier, the more you do it. But it doesn't. It's not easy saying it all, and it's not easy listening to it being read back to you either. So I'm sort of blanking out a bit. Not on purpose. I'm trying to pay attention, but my brain does this thing sometimes where it just goes far away.

Suddenly though, I'm pulled back, firmly, into the room, because she's just said the word *neglect*.

THE ME ASSOCIATION WEBSITE
ME/CFS Illness Severity Definitions
Definitions of severity are not clear cut because individual symptoms vary widely in severity and people may have some symptoms more severely than others. The definitions below provide a guide to the level of impact of symptoms on everyday functioning.

MILD
People with mild ME/CFS care for themselves and do some light domestic tasks (sometimes needing support) but may have difficulties with mobility. Most are still working or in education, but to do this they have probably stopped all leisure and social pursuits. They often have reduced hours, take days off and use the weekend to cope with the rest of the week.

MODERATE

People with moderate ME/CFS have reduced mobility and are restricted in all activities of daily living, although they may have peaks and troughs in their level of symptoms and ability to do activities. They have usually stopped work or education, and need rest periods, often resting in the afternoon for 1 or 2 hours. Their sleep at night is generally poor quality and disturbed.

SEVERE

People with severe ME/CFS are unable to do any activity for themselves or can carry out minimal daily tasks only (such as face washing or cleaning teeth). They have severe cognitive difficulties and may depend on a wheelchair for mobility. They are often unable to leave the house or have a severe and prolonged after-effect if they do so. They may also spend most of their time in bed and are often extremely sensitive to light and sound.

VERY SEVERE

People with very severe ME/CFS are in bed all day and dependent on care. They need help with personal hygiene and eating and are very sensitive to sensory stimuli. Some people may not be able to swallow and may need to be tube fed.

WOMAN

Some days it seems impossible, or at least, highly improbable to me that we still live in a world where almost all of our history and law and literature has been written by rich, white, able-bodied men.

It is true. I know that. But the probability of it seems so fragile to me; it shakes and moves like a ghost at the edge of my mind, wavering, like a cloud of steam blown out by a kettle. Visible only for a short time. About to fade away into nothing.

They have been such flawed repositories and fonts, but don't ever seem to have noticed this about themselves. They have been writing about what they might call facts. And that's quite funny, because the idea of facts shakes and wobbles even more precariously at the edge of my mind.

But I shouldn't laugh really, because the roots of all our words must live in those so-called facts. And that probably explains why words can betray you if you're not careful. Why they might not mean what you think they mean, or they might turn up in places you don't expect to find them. Why they might turn on you when you're not expecting it. Why they might work well for some people, and really not at all well for others. Words written down in guidelines and rulebooks. Words placed there by people who have no way of knowing anything at all about the people to whose lives they're going to be applied.

MEMORY

The woman on my sofa doesn't pause. She's carried on reading her report like nothing unusual just happened. So I have to interrupt.

'Sorry,' I say, 'did you just say, *neglect?*'

'Yes,' she says, 'that's right. He experienced neglect when he was a child.'

'So,' I say, 'that means by me, then? He was neglected by me?'

'We're not saying he was neglected by anyone, just that there was neglect.'

I can't speak. She goes back to her piece of paper, begins reading again.

'Sorry,' I say, 'but can we just . . . for one minute. Why are you saying he was neglected? I don't think I did neglect him. Things were difficult, obviously, but I don't think . . . neglect?'

There's a beat. Two beats. I can't hold her gaze. My eyes drift off, looking up to my left. I am thinking about the way he was bathed and put to bed with soft, clean skin and soft shiny hair every night, whatever was happening. About the books and toys and games I always made sure he had. About my meal planning and shopping, about the books I read on nutrition, and how always talking to your kids made them clever. About the woman in the fruit shop on Holderness Road who used to say to me, as I loaded apples and bananas and kale and carrots onto the back of the pram, 'It's so nice to hear you talking like that to him. You don't hear that very often.' About my nanna telling me that she and my grandad had been saying to each other how smart my boys always looked, even though I didn't have much money. About the bedtime stories and careful explanations of maths and how to form letters. About those freezing mornings at school gates; the afternoons when people would stare at me, knowing all about me, their eyes creeping over me, weighing up what they'd read in the paper against what they saw at the gates. About how I was still always there. How it was always me. How I always smiled when he came out, and was cheerful, and asked what he'd been doing and took him home and made a snack and washed his uniform. How I planned and saved for new school shoes and coats every autumn. How I set up and ran a toddler group with my friend. How we planned activities and trips.

'Neglect?' I say.

'It's nothing against you,' she repeats. 'It's just a fact that when there has been domestic abuse in a house where a child is present, then that child has, by definition, been neglected.'

All very crisp and logical. She smiles half-apologetically, and I can see there's no point in asking any more questions on the subject, so I sit and smile politely, listen to the rest of her report and say goodbye at the door when she's finished. But I don't forget it. I can't shake that word out of my head, because it is now written down in an official document. My child experienced neglect. My children were neglected.

The online dictionary tells me: *neglect (verb) fail to care for properly; neglect (noun) the state of being uncared for.* The NSPCC website tells me: *Neglect is the ongoing failure to meet a child's basic needs and the most common form of child abuse.* Seeing as I'm the only person with parental responsibility for my children, I've got to assume I'm the person guilty of this failure. I must be the person guilty of neglecting my kids.

WOMAN

There are voices that live in my belly. All the things people have said. All the things I've let snake their way down, down, to crawl in the dark there. Did I let them? Maybe I had no choice. Some of them were forced there; teeth jammed apart; throat pinned open. Some of them were laid on me and kind of seeped in, gradually, over time. Repeating and repeating against my flesh. A kind of permeation. A kind of osmosis.

A lot of the time they live quietly in the dark, but sometimes they are roused. I think they eat away at the lining of my stomach, peep their little heads out, listening, waiting for someone to say their name, or to catch a breeze that calls them; yes, little snakey, it's time for you to rear up now, because someone is saying Vicky is a bad mum again. Someone is saying Vicky does not deserve anything good again. Someone is saying she can't expect better than men who are violent. Someone is saying that everything that has ever gone wrong is all her fault. Someone is saying this is just the way things are. Suck it up, bitch.

Hiss, little snakey, come and hiss now. Come and churn her stomach over and laugh at the little pills and the torrents of thick white liquid she pours over you to try and quiet you.

THE ME ASSOCIATION WEBSITE
Management
Be aware that ME/CFS symptoms can be managed but there is currently no cure (non-pharmacological or pharmacological) for ME/CFS.

Energy and activity management
Health professionals should discuss the principles of energy management, the potential benefits and risks and what people with ME/CFS should expect. Explain that this:

- is a self-management strategy led by the person themselves with support from a healthcare professional in an ME/CFS specialist team.
- includes all types of activity (cognitive, physical, emotional, and social) and takes into account overall level of activity.

- helps people learn to use the amount of energy they have while reducing their risk of post-exertional malaise or worsening their symptoms by exceeding their limit.
- recognises that each person has a different and fluctuating energy limit and they are experts in judging their own limits.
- can include help from a healthcare professional to recognise when they are approaching their limit – children and young people in particular may find it harder to judge their limits and can overreach them.
- uses a flexible, tailored approach so that activity is never automatically increased but is maintained or adjusted – upwards after a period of stability or downwards when symptoms are worse.
- is a long-term approach – it can take weeks, months or sometimes even years to reach stabilisation or to increase tolerance or activity.

MEMORY

I can't leave this neglect thing alone. I can't stop thinking about it. Months after the woman writing the report came to see us, I'm still trying to work it out. I have never, to my knowledge, been reported to the police or social services. Have never been investigated, charged or brought to trial. It is now acknowledged in this report and other official documents that there has been domestic abuse, and because of that there has also been neglect. But see, here's the other strange thing: I did make reports to the police about some of the incidents that are now, in this report, classed as domestic abuse, but in relation to each of them, despite police attending my house and me telling them what had happened, no charges of domestic abuse were ever brought against anyone. There were no trials, no penalties, no restrictions placed against anyone. Nobody was questioned or interviewed in a formal setting, as far as I'm aware. There were no fines, no repercussions at work or in social settings. No reprimands were given by anyone, ever, to the men involved.

A number of people did tell me it must have been my fault though, so I suppose I was reprimanded, in a fashion. But nobody ever told me I was being, or had ever been, domestically abused. It took me years to work it out for myself. And well, forgive me, but it all seems a bit rich. I don't think it's my fault that I'm struggling to get my head around all of this. I'm not only guilty of my own abuse, but also guilty of neglecting my children while I was experiencing the abuse. It seems a lot. It seems quite big. I'm just one person, after all, and I seem to be guilty of a lot of stuff.

LETTER I WOULD LIKE TO SEND TO PRIME MINISTER BORIS JOHNSON

I don't know if you've ever had a laptop or a mobile phone that's been getting old. I'm not sure you have. You probably get a new one every two years, or even every year, when the next slick, up-to-date model comes out. Come to think of it, that probably is what you do, so the way I'm about to describe things probably won't work on you. But I'll persist, in the spirit that, even if you do have the most expensive, most up to date of all things at all times, sometimes something will still go wrong. Maybe there's a chance we can find some common ground.

So, here we go. I'm going to let you into a little secret about why I'm a writer. I've done a lot of interviews where people ask me, and I give them what has now become a fairly sanitised, slips-off-the-tongue version of an answer. I say it all very cheerfully, because, on the whole, I'm pretty chuffed that I get to be a writer.

I say: 'When I was little, and a teenager, up to about the age of nineteen, I used to write all the time, then I got busy having kids and working and I stopped, for about thirteen years, until I got ill in about 2011, and suddenly I was at home a lot, with nowhere to go. Someone told me I should start keeping a journal, and when I began to write in it, stories and poems started to come out.'

That's it. The cleaned-up version. I do mention being ill, but it's not where the focus lies. The focus is on stopping because I was busy and starting again because I was not. And really, if I was going to be one hundred per cent truthful, the whole focus should be on being ill. I would be a liar if I didn't say that sometimes I long for an office job, or to work in the community, to be a local councillor or a youth worker, a social worker or a shop worker. To have that feeling again, every day, of getting up and having somewhere to be, of knowing that people are waiting for me, needing me to do something, expecting to see my face, and that they would see it. That I would rise predictably at the same time, shower, eat breakfast, dress, leave the house while the air is still chilly, the light is still new, catch a bus or walk, or bike, or drive my car, then spend the day doing something useful, that people couldn't get by without. Being part of a system; a predictable, reliable part of it. But I can't do that.

Have you ever picked up your mobile phone, expecting to see the clearly picked-out, crisp white numbers telling you the time, the date; expecting the little boxes – green and blue flashes – of notifications, signalling someone is communicating with you, the backdrop of planets or your favourite photo of you on holiday; expecting it to recognise your face and fall open; the whole world, your whole contact book, an array of communication methods at your fingertips – and instead, nothing? Blank, black dullness. Unresponsive. You might get mad. You might search out a laptop or a tablet, Google ways to turn it back on again, to make it do what you need it to do, and it might work, but in the meantime, you are cut off. Unable to do what you usually would. Inconvenienced.

I mean, I'm sure you're never inconvenienced for long, because you can probably, in the worst-case scenario, go into a shop, or send someone else into a shop, to buy you a new one. Back up and running in a period that can most easily be measured in minutes. But in the spirit of trying to find common ground, I'm going to focus on that feeling of something not working like it should. The being cut off, that temporary lost feeling, that falling feeling, because I'm sure you must have felt it, and I'm trying to find a way of explaining to you, that if you could scale that feeling up, you'd start to get an idea of what it's like for me on the days when I wake up and my body just doesn't work.

WOMAN
I fantasise sometimes that there's a place I can visit with candles, incantations, someone stamping their feet and chanting. Somewhere where someone can cast me a spell. Something like that. Something dark, earthy. Something that could dig deep, dig this out of me, these creeping things, these keep-me-up-at-night things. Some sort of ritual with heavy sticks sunk into the earth. With fire. With red and orange. Dancing. Something loud.

   I Google and Google it. I can't find this place. I look up pictures of Chalice Well and stone circles. I dust off my tarot. Meditate. Imagine I'm a horse. A bird. A mythical creature. When none of this works, I visit the doctor. Modern magic. Watch as he conjures up words like fluoxetine, citalopram, mirtazapine – take it at night to help you sleep. I pray as I pop the pills from their tiny, metallic sheets, the sharp edges cutting into my hands.

MAN IN PUB
Don't be losing any more weight – your arse isn't as nice and grabbable when you're skinny.

MAN IN PUB
You've piled it on, haven't you? You used to be real fit.

MAN IN PUB
Come here, son . . . Which of these barmaids do you think has got the nicest arse?

MEMORY

During the Covid lockdowns, I do some online training with the women's centre — it's manageable; exercises I can research and fill out online as and when I've got the energy. Short Zoom calls with trainers and other volunteers. I earn a certificate, so I can be a volunteer, but I have to wait a while for social-distancing restrictions to be fully lifted, before I can do my first shift. I finally pull into the car park in November 2021. The old building has been knocked down, and this new one is further up the road. I relearn how to use a franking machine, learn where all the different departments are, how to work their phone system, what to do when someone buzzes at the secure door, who's allowed in, who's not. Volunteers come and go, sorting bags of stuff for the charity shop, the queue outside of which started to form at 8 a.m. — all women. The shop doesn't open until 10, but it's only fifty pence an item, and that's a bargain, even by charity shop standards.

There are boxes and bags of stuff everywhere, waiting to be sorted or dropped off or collected. But at some point in the afternoon, my new friend, who is training me, nods towards one big pile that's sitting by the front entrance. She tells me that a woman is fleeing tomorrow, and these are her things, to take with her when she goes. Amongst them are quilts and pillows wound tight in plastic. Suffocated. Waiting to spring out on a bed somewhere and stretch out their corners, let everything inside them fluff up, be dressed in soft, many-times-washed cotton.

On one of our trips outside for a vape, I see there's a building site across the road. I ask what it is, and my new friend tells me it's new houses. There are lots of new houses being built round here. And I remember that I know this. Remember the time, a few years back, when I made myself drive down my old street to see what it looked like now, and found the front doors and windows neatly shuttered by brown metal, the houses somehow still appearing to gape open, despite this. I ask if my old street is still here, and she tells me, 'Yes, it's still here — it's there.' She nods across the road, and it is so close I can read the road sign. But the houses are almost all gone. A few still stand, grey pebbledashed, waiting. Very close to the site where the piles of sand and gravel are laid out.

Good, I think. *Good. Good.*

But I still wake in the night, and this is what I'm thinking of. The houses almost gone. The piles of sand and gravel. And once awake, I wonder how that other woman is sleeping tonight. The fleeing woman. I hope that sometime in the next ten hours, she'll be ripping open plastic wrapping. Sliding a knife or the ragged edges of a fingernail in where the tightness is, and letting it all spread out, somewhere new.

WOMAN

I'm trying to anchor myself. Tracking sleep hours, glasses of water and exercise calories in the neat little squares of apps on my phone. Confining activity in the cells of spreadsheets. I will organise my way into normality. Plan my way into normal health. But planning takes energy. Everything takes energy. Energy applied to molecules causes them to fly apart, and I feel myself beginning to fly apart. Again. Again. I want to stay together, but the pull of particles away from each other feels irresistible.

You can't go backwards, can you? You can't be the same person you were eleven or fifteen or sixteen years ago. You can't fall through time. Positive mental attitude. Don't panic. Think your way out of this, I tell myself. You're having a blip, you won't go back to how you were before. It's different now. It's different now.

But it doesn't feel different. I'm locked in the house with the men in my living room and my body, yes, whether I like it or not, my body feels like it's giving up again. Tightening, tightening into nothingness. Irresistibly flying apart. No safe container in which it can be held.

THE ME ASSOCIATION WEBSITE
GENERAL INFORMATION
Be aware that people with ME/CFS are unlikely to be seen at their worst because:

- debilitating symptoms or the risk that their symptoms will worsen may prevent people from leaving their home
- cognitive difficulties may often mean people wait until they feel they can speak and explain clearly before contacting services.

LETTER I WILL NEVER SEND TO SG

It's 10.32 a.m., and today is already a hard day. I didn't want it to be. I wanted to get up, drink coffee, eat breakfast, meditate, journal, go for a walk, clean the house, go shopping for groceries – something nice for tea with no meat, no gluten or dairy, that was within my calorie intake for the day. I'm trying to lose weight. I've gained twenty-one pounds in the last eighteen months. That's what stress of this kind always does to me. I don't use drugs or alcohol to escape from what's happening, but I eat a lot of Chinese takeaways and cake – the fat and sugar, the bursts of flavour, are a reminder that there is still good in the world. *There is still good in the world.* But I can't do any of the things I've planned yet because I've woken with this heavy, dragging feeling in my body again. This heavy, dragging feeling in my mind.

It's because you were on the telly last night. I haven't watched it yet, though I suppose I will at some point. I've seen a clip on Twitter though, with the sound off. You walking in the bright daylight on London Bridge with Jon Snow. He has tweeted it, calling you 'the hero of the hour', which feels like a betrayal. I like Jon Snow. Simon and I watch Channel 4 News because they tell the stories that other shows shy away from. We admire Jon's ties. Talk about how good he is. How full of compassion. How wise. I didn't watch it last night. I'm steeling myself. I've never heard your voice. I don't want to. Could have quite happily lived the rest of my life never knowing what your voice sounded like. But now I feel like I have to find out.

I don't know if you've ever heard of the Hippocratic oath that doctors take before they begin practising. I've always believed it included the line, 'First, do no harm.' I've thought about that a lot since all this started. Everyone going on about how much good you've done, while me and my boys suffered here at home. But actually, it turns out that 'first, do no harm' is not part of the Hippocratic oath. I've just been reading an article about it from Harvard Medical School. It asks if it's even possible to do no harm when you want to heal someone. Operations involve cutting people open, the risks from anaesthetic, post-operative infections, blood loss. All drugs have side effects, the risk of allergic reactions. Blood tests cause pain and bruising (and in my case, extreme anxiety and faintness).

But all the patients who are subjected to these harms first give their consent. They do that for their own benefit. Short-term risk or pain for long-term gain. I have not given my consent to any of this. Have not even been asked if I would like to give it. Was not consulted at any point. And I can't really see how this is doing me any good.

I am now informed, in advance, of any media appearances you might be making, but honestly, I haven't decided yet if that makes it better or worse. Trading the short, sharp shock of unexpectedly seeing you on a screen somewhere, for the slow-burn build-up of knowing it's coming. Theoretically having the option to avoid it – although that never feels like an actual possibility for me.

I resent how well you look in the short clip I've seen. Lean and muscled. Your skin clear. Your eyes clear. The cut of your coat and clothes. What have you done to earn those things? You only left prison four months ago. I can't help thinking about my Jack. Struggling. Not sleeping. Missing uni because of anxiety. Or Harry. The way he looked when I dropped him off at the recovery centre in Liverpool last year. Skinny. Pinched face. Dark circles below the eyes. My own face when I looked in the mirror this morning – bloated, like the rest of me. Lined. Spots standing out purple or dark pink against the rest of my pale skin. What did we do to deserve those things?

Have we failed some test we didn't know was coming? Have we failed to take our medicine? Act for the greater good? Why don't we just submit to what everyone else seems to so clearly agree on? Bow down before the heavy, pressing knowledge that you should be forgiven? Be thanked, even? Just admit that you've earned the right to all good things and to speak on public platforms and receive praise from MPs, the Queen, the papers, and now Jon Snow?

I'll tell you why. It's because we know better. Whatever the combined qualifications of all these people are, they do not have ours. We've lived through the consequences of your actions, and the actions of other men like you. We know, intricately, what happens. It is not short-term pain for long-term gain. It is harm upon harm upon harm. It grows exponentially, and it is our job to mitigate against it every single day of our lives. To build foundations of therapy and meditation and exercise and journalling and self-management and self-regulation, before we even do anything else. Before anything more constructive than self-destruction or any other kind of destruction can happen.

But we do make those other things happen. I'm going to meditate now, and journal, and then I'll have a hot bath to try and stop the aching in all of my limbs that comes back with a vengeance every time you pop up in the news. But after that, I'll get in my car and drive to the women's centre. Like I have been doing for the last few weeks. I'll answer the phone to women trying to flee violent men. I'll pass their details to the duty worker. I'll pass on food parcels to the women who've been referred by their workers – social workers, domestic abuse workers, healthcare workers. I'll frank the mail. Update the signing-in-and-out sheets – a constant job because there are so many women coming and going all the time. I'll chat to the other volunteers and staff, vape outside with them in the smoking area, share cups of tea and stories, and then we'll all get back to what we were doing. They will have been sorting donated clothes to sell in the charity shop, or offering reduced-rate legal advice to women in abusive situations, or writing policy documents, or working in the nursery, or delivering or receiving training on how to build confidence, how to apply for a job, how to write a CV, how to spot domestic abuse. None of us will be on the news tonight. Not one.

MAN IN A NIGHTCLUB
I'm only offering to buy you a drink. Trying to be nice, you know? No need to be a snotty cow about it.

MAN IN A NIGHTCLUB
So you're just gonna drink the drink I bought you and not speak to me then?

MAN IN PUB
Doesn't speak. Just gives me a look before he disappears into the crowd – to let me know it was him who just grabbed a handful of my breasts.

WOMAN
Sometimes I fall out of time completely. Become Victorian, lounging around, pallid and weak, waiting for someone to stride in, opening windows, carrying a bowl of warm water and a thick, rough, cotton cloth to dip in it. Send me away for sea air. Let the stiff breeze revive me. I want to stay there when it happens. I watch period dramas on repeat. Eat afternoon tea.

In this day and age, people don't behave that way, do they? Had a shock or a bug? Early night. Shot of hot whisky. Get back to it the next day. The pharmacy is full of pills and free helpful advice so you can sort yourself out. You should be able to sort yourself out. Lazy, layabout, shirker, malingerer. Doctor's appointments require being functional at 8.a.m, and capable of sitting on the phone, listening to muzak for fifty minutes, in a bid to win the daily competition for appointments. Hospital visit? Lift your feet over the signs on the corridor floor that ask: *Do you really need to be here?* Or that inform you: *Nine out of ten people who visit A&E should have stayed at home.* Still not sorted yourself out? Can you fill in this form explaining over the course of fifty-odd pages why you aren't at work, please? And then, five months later, can you spend an hour on the phone being interrogated by someone you've never met about the worst you've ever felt, what it's like getting a bath, whether you can lift a kettle, how often in a week you get dressed, if you've ever thought about hurting yourself, and if so, why you didn't do it? Answer all our questions correctly, score enough points, and maybe we'll send you some money. For essentials.

ANOTHER WOMAN

'You're a forty-one-year-old woman, locked in your own office, crying,' she says.

There's no point in arguing. She's summed things up quite nicely. I *am* crying. I can't stop. It just keeps coming out. I imagine myself laughing, tossing my head dismissively, telling her I've decided to just let it run its course. But I can't speak, and the truth is, the decision is out of my hands. It's happening whether I like it or not. But I don't know how to start explaining this to her.

I get a sudden flashback to just after my grandad died, when she was having chemo for her second lot of cancer, and I was telling her off for getting the bus to the hospital instead of letting me give her a lift. She was standing eye-to-eye with me, exactly the same height, in her crisp black trousers and flowing, glittery top.

'There's no need to fuss over me,' she'd said. 'I'm strong, Vicky, you should know that by now.'

I try to raise my head but can't look her in the eye, so instead I speak to my knees, apologetically.

'Simon and Jack have been popping their heads in periodically to see how I'm doing,' I say, 'but I don't know what to tell them. I can barely string a sentence together.'

'I know,' she says. 'They don't seem to be able to do much good, so I thought I'd have a go. I've been hanging on, hoping if I waited a while, you might tidy yourself up a bit.'

She is glamorous today. Wearing one of her soft black scarves dotted with shimmering dark sequins. Skin stretched tight over high cheekbones. I'm wearing sloppy pyjamas, a huge jumper, fluffy socks. I'm bloated and baggy, like someone has pumped me full of hot air and then punctured me.

I'm huddled in the old armchair I bought from a second-hand shop, with my laptop perched on the arm, binge-watching *The Haunting of Bly Manor*. Occasionally I pause it to cry again or write something in my journal. I'm hungry, but imagining myself walking upstairs, assembling the ingredients of a meal and actually cooking it — feels about as possible as cleaning the house: not very. There's just no go in me. No give. No energy. The battery is dead, the bank is empty.

'You shouldn't be spying on people when they're not fit for visitors,' I say.

'Oh, get over yourself,' she says.

This is like my worst nightmare. Her seeing me like this. Knowing what the house looks like. Seeing how incapable I am. I wait for her to speak again. I want to know if she ever had days like this. Did she ever fall apart behind closed doors? But I can't ask her. If she wants me to know, she'll tell me, I think.

'I've got this image in my head that keeps repeating,' I say, to fill the silence. 'It's a little wooden boat, bobbing along on the tide. Someone's painted it in jolly colours. It's not much, but it belongs to someone. Somebody cares about it. Somebody lives there; you know from the gentle puffs of white smoke that are drifting up from the chimney.'

I pause to look at her.

'I don't know if real-life wooden boats have chimneys,' she says, 'but this one is in your head, so fair enough. Carry on.'

I do as I'm told. Resume my story. 'Maybe the person in there is cosy, reading a book in front of a fire,' I say. 'Maybe they're cooking a meal, or just making a cup of tea. But then suddenly, the image changes. No blue sky, no pleasant bobbing. The boat is smashing against rocks, against a sheer cliff face, relentlessly. Over and over.'

'Interesting,' she says. 'Not very comforting. Realistic though, I'll give you that. Nobody ever gets calm seas all the time, do they?'

I can feel the tears coming again, the constriction in my throat. Words are coming too. Words that I don't want to say to her, but I can't stop them. They're irrepressible. They drift out of me.

'It probably goes without saying that I'm not well. Haven't been well for some time now. Someone from the trauma therapy service, which I've been referred to by the National Homicide Service, told me I've got high clinical indicators for depression, extreme anxiety and PTSD, which is sort of a relief, to be honest. Until he told me that, I'd just been worried that I was mad. Or extremely lazy. Or a malingerer. At least now it has a name, I suppose.'

'Well, there you go then,' she says. 'That's better, isn't it?'

'Is it?' I say.

'Don't be dramatic,' she says. 'You know it is. You've got to let the dog see the rabbit. At least now you know what you're dealing with.'

THE ME ASSOCIATION WEBSITE
Advice for people with suspected ME/CFS
When ME/CFS is suspected, give people personalised advice about managing their symptoms. Also advise them:

- not to use more energy than they perceive they have – they should manage their daily activity and not 'push through' their symptoms,
- to rest and convalesce as needed – this might mean making changes to their daily routine, including work, school, and other activities.

WOMAN
Sometimes I am almost air. Spirit-like. Waif-like. Feeble. About to be carried off by the breeze. Trying to weigh myself down with things to do, with sugar and fat. Watch the numbers on the scales rise higher. But I don't come back. I go further away. Look in the mirror and can't find my face. Sometimes I want to be air and can't

quite make it. Stay stubbornly solid, the mass of me taking up space that I wish was empty instead.

MEMORY

One day, mid-lockdown, when the only place we're allowed to visit is the supermarket, Simon and I go shopping. As we pull up in the car park, I slip my phone down into the compartment in the door, slide out of the car and walk away, quickly, across the road and into the park. There is a field there; and in the field, I find a big rock. There is a group of boys a way off, playing football, who stop to look at me for a while. I must look strange, sitting in this field, on my own, on a rock.

Once I sit, I find I can't move, and the sentiment, the feeling, the one recurring thought that I've been trying to shake off for months now, falls on me full force. I can't go on. I can't do this any more. I can't take any more. I have a vague memory of being a person with energy and life about them, who wore a pretty, yellow dress and rode a pink bike and wrote poems and sang, but she has gone now. This person is broken, and she can't move from this spot. Not just yet.

But I will move. I'm planning in my head what will be the best way to do it, and I've decided, like at every other time in my life when I've reached this point, that the Humber Bridge will be the thing. I'm beginning to work out how I will get there, when I become aware that Barrie is standing at the other end of the field, looking at me and smiling.

'See,' he says, 'I told you it would have been better if you'd have died.'

And I say, 'Yes, you're right, it would have been better if I'd have died, and you'd have lived. You're right.'

I know he's right because I can't see how my shot at doing something with my life, at being a parent to our kids, could have gone more wrong. I have one son in the throes of addiction, risking his life every day, another struggling with anxiety, and me, in this state, with no energy, no money, no current means of getting any money, and no signs of anything improving at any time in the future. How much more wrong could it have gone?

And yet, there is another voice, tiny, distant, elsewhere in my head, that is saying, 'You will get through this, Vicky. You have not walked out on all this before, and you will not do it now.'

I stand up, and I begin to walk, and I haven't got my phone or any money, and I haven't got the energy to get very far. But I think if I make for the main road, Simon will find me. He'll be looking for me. I walk and I wait, and eventually Simon does find me. He picks me up and drives me home in the car. He tells me to go upstairs and get into bed, but I don't get past the bedroom door. I have to lie down on the floor. Simon finds me again, tries to help me into bed, but I tell him I can't do it. I tell him I can't take any more, I can't do any more, I've had enough now. He tells me I just have to get through this next minute. This next thing. Just get into bed now.

I do, and he brings me food and I put my headphones in and listen to stories – other people's stories – and eventually I sleep. And when I wake the next day, I find I can do a little bit more. I can take a little bit more. I can do this day. This one, and then we'll see how we go from there.

Part Five

Water

There is a narwhal. Swimming somewhere out in the far north Arctic
Sea. The tang of saltwater plays around his twisted tusk as he moves.
He may look like he is charging, poised to attack as he approaches
another male. But his tusk is not only a weapon. Ten million nerve
endings are pulsing inside it. Maybe, if he runs it very gently along
the tusk of this approaching other, they can communicate.

WOMAN

I used to have this vision when I was a teenager and a young mum. It was of a huge swimming pool. Cool, clean water tinted blue by the ceramic tiles at the bottom. I think in my mind it was based on the swimming pool where my dad used to take us when we were small. But in this vision, there's something funny happening.

I'm just learning to swim – my head bobbing precariously at surface level, sometimes dipping under. At those points I'm gulping in water. It's in my stomach. It's in my eyes. It stings a bit. It doesn't taste good. But it's clean and clear, thick with chlorine. And then I look up and see a woman getting in – I don't see her until she's already half submerged, up to her calves. And I see that she is totally covered in shit. Some of it's wet, some dry, but already it's beginning to colour the water around her. Little soggy lumps and flakes are hanging suspended between the surface and the blue tiles and they're spreading out towards me. I know what's going to happen the next time my head bobs below the surface. Even if I could get out right now, which I can't, I would still be tainted by it. It would still be on my skin, in my hair. But I can't get out. I'm in it, and I'm gonna stay in it until I'm big enough to be able to heave myself out and find another place to swim.

That's what sent me into therapy after Barrie died. That vision. It's why I spent my tax credits on cognitive behavioural therapy and graded exposure therapy, and whatever else I thought might work, instead of on holidays or day trips or expensive Christmas presents. I didn't do it just for me. It was for my kids too. Whatever is in my pool, I thought, they are gonna swallow down. You've got no choice where your home is, what your water is like, when you're little. You've got to be there. Clean water at home all the time is more important than anything else, I thought. But, of course, I was already too late. It wasn't just my pool. It never is. There were already seven kinds of shit in there before I spent a penny on therapy.

FIVE THINGS I KNOW ABOUT WATER:

1. Condensation is the process of gas turning back into liquid, usually as it cools, and the energy in the molecules is dissipated. You see it happening every time you look up at cloud formations and trace out patterns and shapes in the misted movement. Or when you boil the kettle, steam spreading out to fill the shape of your kitchen as you stand poised, teabag in cup. Or when you run a bath and it clouds the windows. I always imagine it as the dispersed water molecules coming back to themselves, remembering what they are.

2. When enough water vapour molecules are gathered together, they begin to form droplets. They fall as rain, or run in rivulets down over glass, or pool in shallow dishes, or are collected in huge water-gathering warehouses and are used to water crops.

3. Some bodies of water begin really small: tiny streams or springs that trickle, often underground, unnoticed, but almost always running towards the sea or some huge lake. There would be no lakes or oceans without the gathered drops of vapour, without the tiny springs, without the small rivers hurdling boulders and strange courses.

4. When salt is dissolved in water, the sodium and chlorine atoms separate, allowing them to move around freely and separately in the water. Saltwater is a good conductor of electricity because, once this separation has occurred, the two ions contained within it will be opposites – one positive, one negative. But if you were to place a drop of saltwater on your tongue, you wouldn't be able to tell this had happened. It would all taste the same.

5. You can't defeat water. You can't disappear it. It might change form for a while, but it persists. It keeps coming back, one way or another.

WOMAN

Bravery is so close to recklessness, isn't it? Like two roads that run parallel for a while and suddenly veer off, colliding, so you find that now you're travelling along one road and not the other. I've often wondered whether the majority of brave acts might mostly arise from just a few separate sources.

The first is just not thinking things through properly. You start off doing one small thing that sort of feels right, and before you know it, you're on a course you can't change. One thing happening after another so quickly that you're just reacting.

The second is not really wanting to be here any more. Maybe, in that case, a dangerous situation just becomes an opportunity – a potential way of escaping that can't be criticised after you're gone. A way out.

The third is thinking you're not worth very much. You think you're a tatty old five-pound note, dog-eared and grubby – something someone might find tucked away at the bottom of a pocket and not be too impressed with. Worth a flutter. Worth the chance to try and turn it into something better. Not much to lose if it doesn't come off, but what a story to tell if it does. What an elevation.

The fourth, and maybe the rarest source of bravery, is love. When someone is thinking clearly, can see the potential consequences, has thought it through, knows the risks and the sacrifices. And then does the thing that needs to be done anyway, because they can see the suffering that will be caused to someone else if they don't.

ANOTHER WOMAN

Her face has hardened. She is staring out of the window, at the birdbath I brought from her garden after she died. It's sitting against a backdrop of glossy green leaves, beside the statue of a lady that also used to be hers. At the edge of its green, tepid water, a magpie is perched, dipping its beak, splashing droplets that run over its blue, teal, black and white plumage. They glitter in the sunshine.

'It's beautiful, isn't it?'

She turns to me, face stony.

'Come on,' I say, 'you don't still believe all that stuff about magpies, do you? Because if it's true, then honestly, we're doomed.

They're always in the garden here, or on the roof, or perching on the balcony. One sat on the bedroom windowsill and looked in at me the other day while I was fluffing the pillows.'

She really does not like this. She always had a thing about birds. If anyone sent a birthday card with a bird on, it went straight in the bin. I once went in December and there were Christmas cards with robins on them pinned up by the front door.

'How come these have survived?' I asked her.

'They're allowed for now,' she said, 'but anything goes wrong and they're straight out that door.'

Any bird was bad, but magpies were the worst.

'You can't really think that bad things are going to happen just because a magpie looked in at me through the bedroom window.'

She thinks about it for a bit. 'I suppose not,' she says, relaxing, 'but it doesn't mean I have to like them, does it?'

'No,' I say, 'I don't suppose it does.'

WOMAN

Have you ever walked in fog? On boggy, marshy ground? Most people find it hard – it *is* hard to walk in those conditions. You need to have your wits about you on a walk like that. You need some reserves of strength. And you also need a guide.

I was up in the Yorkshire Dales by myself last December. I needed to get away. Sometimes the air here is so thick with things that have happened that I can't stay. I needed to breathe, reassess. So I took myself off for a week of walking and writing. I sighed when I left the motorway and found the hills frosted with ice, the air alternately crisp, clear and foggy. I went straight out into the fields as soon as I could. I realise now that one of the pleasures of walking alone in December is the thick warmth of my coat and the layers beneath it. The sturdy hold of my boots around my ankles and soles. It's a kind of smugness. I have prepared for this, and now I'm out in sub-zero temperatures and I'm perfectly warm and protected.

But one day, there was a storm coming. It had been on the news the night before, and in the morning as I prepared to go down for breakfast. I did not have a compass, or a map. I don't, in truth, know how to properly use those things. But I was determined to walk. I set out, belly full of bacon and eggs, and descended the steep hill towards Aysgarth Falls. Some way ahead of me, I saw two walkers, their bright red and orange coats picked out against the muted green-brown of the graveyard. I located the small wooden gate they'd used and retraced their steps, emerging into open space where beyond a few feet nothing was visible but a hanging misty void of air, with occasional mountain peaks emerging above it. The walkers had disappeared, which was good, because I wanted to be alone. But I couldn't risk wandering off with no guide whatsoever when a blizzard might come down at any time.

I decided to follow the river and the drystone walls, tracing their lines in wet mud with my boots, stopping sometimes to admire the slim chunk of view and check how far I'd come. It was satisfying. I didn't know where I'd end up, but I had something tangible beside me, and I could turn and retrace my steps when I was ready. The hotel, with its heated tile floor and power shower, would be there waiting when I'd finished. My book and laptop, a thick pad of paper. My pen.

In the months before and since that walk, this has been my drystone wall: pain is an inevitable part of life, and some kinds of pain seem so solid that we feel like they'll never be diminished. This has been my river's edge: nothing is permanent, no course is set solid. There is always flow and the possibility of movement. This has been the solid earth beneath my feet: love flows in all of us, whatever else we've picked up along the way, whatever it looks like when it emerges.

LETTER I CAN'T SEND TO BARRIE
I'm not quite sure how I've ended up in a position of having to defend you. I'm not the last person on the list of people who should

be given that job, but I am pretty low down. I realise nobody has asked me to do it; not technically. But, as much as I try to get away from it, I feel a kind of obligation.

I think it's mostly due to my amazement at how low we seem to have sunk. And when I say *we*, I am generalising. I don't mean everyone. I don't, for example, mean me. I have not sunk so low as certain other people seem to have done, which is frankly amazing, given that I spend a lot of each day suspended only sixteen inches from the floor, on sofa cushions, waiting for enough energy to congregate below my surface, so that I can move again.

But while I'm lying there, I'm not thinking about how people in pain need to sort themselves out cos it's their own fucking fault, or how great it is when someone gets their face smashed in. I'm not thinking, *Oooh, yeah, an eye for an eye, a tooth for a tooth, a face for a face*. And I can't sit by and hear others saying those things either. Not when I've had a front-row seat on what they actually mean, in real life, and not in some cooked-up half-version of what it's like, on TV. I can't sit by and listen to reasoning that makes these things OK. It's just not in me. I know some people see that as a weakness, but it's not. It actually requires much more strength than you might think.

I don't fully blame them for their take on it. It's not easy to see the reality of it all, when you stack it up together. For the last seventeen years, I haven't been able to look at everything that happened myself. Not full in the face. I've taken little sideways glances because parts of it have had to be addressed. Some parts of it, I've examined in detail. Written about, even. Mostly the bad things. And when people expressed sadness about them or told me they were surprised I wasn't angrier, I got confused. I didn't know what to say. It's amazing the tricks you can play on yourself in your own mind, in the name of self-preservation. I told myself at the time that it was strength, but really I was not much different to all those people posting on the internet, wanting a quick, glib solution, a three-word phrase that contained something definite and final – something to cover the true extent of the damage. I didn't want to remember. I didn't want to see. But now, having seen, having really looked and felt it, I need to rest my eyes on something softer. I think we all need to be able to look at the hard stuff, but not all of the time.

I don't know why you did the terrible things you did. I can't even know for sure *which* terrible things you did. I'm not a psychologist, or a detective, and I'm sick of asking questions. I'm sick of looking for answers. I don't think it's my job any more. I think I've earned the right to some peace, and I can't get that without letting it all wash through me – all the bad things, and the good things too. I need to let it all come through, because I'm tired of holding it in. Fatigued. Chronically.

Even so, I'm almost loath to write these next things, given that they were a crucial part of your defence in your trial for a horrific attack, that I do think you were guilty of. In the witness box, you said, 'I was a firefighter at the time the attack took place, and I did not commit this cowardly act.' Those words were part of the grit in the gears that day. The salt in the system corroding the cogs. You called on everything that had been written in the newspapers about firefighters during the strikes – the presents brought to you on picket lines, the horns honking their support, the stories of bravery – everything people think they know about heroes, and let it rise up around you like a forcefield. The problem at that trial wasn't that the good things were true. It was that people don't like to see how the positive and the negative can all sit together in the same container. But that is the truth. As uncomfortable as it may be.

I've been wondering whether maybe it's enough just to make or do one beautiful thing in this world while you're here. You helped make my two beautiful boys. You also could've been instrumental in ruining their lives completely, but it didn't work out that way. I've pulled so hard against that happening that sometimes it felt like it was going to take everything I had. But it turns out that wasn't true either. Every time I think it's happened, I gradually come back to myself again. Slowly find there is something more, at the bottom of me, that I didn't know was there.

You saved lives while you were here. I don't know how many. How do you count the number of lives saved by people who run in when everyone else is running out? People whose job it is to show up where flames have flared, cars have crumpled around still-breathing bodies, water has risen into homes, offices, pub cellars, electricity supplies, gas pipes and the hundreds of tiny things in which people's reasons for being are invested? It becomes a day-to-day occurrence, and like anything, if you do it often enough, it becomes normal. You didn't talk about it much. Mostly wanted to forget about it when you walked through the front door and changed out of your uniform. But I know there was at least one little life you briefly saved – you did tell me about her.

I don't know anything much about what you did in the navy – only how you hated the smoke-filled submarines, the bed tucked up against a nuclear missile. I did meet some of the people you helped when you worked for the ex-servicemen's charity. I know about machines you helped arrange that kept people breathing, lifts to the shops, calling in for cuppas to break up lonely days.

Would things have been different if you hadn't been with me in the hospital room that day when I was bleeding out? Could lost minutes, someone who hadn't been so calm in the face of all that blood, have made a difference, shifted the balance, tipped the probable outcome more in one direction than another? It's impossible to know.

Impossible calculations are everywhere, once you start looking. Would I have preferred you did all the good things and none of the bad? Of course I would. Are any of the good things enough to balance out the bad things you did? Probably not. But they are something. They're not nothing. I can't pretend they didn't happen. I just don't feel compelled to try and build everything into some kind of definitive equation any more.

URBANPETE, *DAILY MAIL* COMMENTER
She said 'Heroes aren't always what they are cracked up to be' on reading the article I took it to mean she was actually referring to

both her late husband and Gallant. Her late husband may have been a firefighter, but as you say, violent, then again he was the father of her children, so of course she will have mixed feelings

COMMENT122345, *DAILY MAIL* COMMENTER
I don't think she was sticking up for her ex husband either, she is being considerate of her children. They were both in the wrong, two wrongs don't make a right.

RICH LEESON, *HULL LIVE* COMMENTER
Turn it in Fail, we all realise what the widow has to cope with, this guy served his time and saved people's lives, he cannot be in prison all his life, one may say he has learnt his lesson, another might say he put his life on the line to save a stranger, not the Fail dragging it all up again, its the Fail that is making it hard for his victims widow, not him. . .

WOMAN
You don't know you're the muddy Humber until someone tells you. You're just the Humber. Not able to see yourself from the outside, and never having been any other colour, you've been unaware. But if you'll allow someone to hook out a sample, let your various components rest awhile in stillness, separate, then what has been causing your brown murk becomes apparent. When the particles of soil settle, you do have some clear water in you. That's how you started, maybe in a spring, emerging from chalk into greenness.

There's an experiment they sometimes do with kids in schools. You take a bowl of clear water and stir in a cupful of mud. Then you place an empty cup inside the bowl of murky water. You cover the whole thing with clingfilm, and then you leave it out in the sun — preferably on a warm day.

When you take the kids back to look at it a few hours later, what you find, hopefully, is a bowl of damp mud containing a cup of almost-clean water. Simply put, a separation has occurred. The lesson is supposed to be about evaporation and condensation, but I think maybe it can teach someone so much more than that. It is science as magic. Science proving the possibility of transformation.

ANOTHER WOMAN

'You've been doing it again,' she says.

'Doing what?'

'Paradox two,' she says. 'These performances and assessments are all being made based on the judgements of the people who are oppressing you: men, women who support male outcomes because they benefit along the way by their collusion, people of a higher social class than you, people who have not experienced trauma / abuse. So, not only are you experiencing it at their hands, you are having to carefully consider the way in which you reflect it back to them, so that they can (possibly / maybe / maybe not) understand it, (possibly / maybe / maybe not) consider it in the future, (possibly / maybe / maybe not) change their behaviours so that these outcomes are not perpetuated, at some minuscule level of inconvenience for them. The chances are the people who matter probably aren't going to do it, and you will be left wondering why you bothered in the first place. Into the bargain, you might get called nutty, an angry feminist, too sensitive, a liar – insert your own stock phrase – as a little Brucey Bonus.'

I say nothing, so she continues: 'I think it's because of you being a goat.'

'Oh, not this again.'

'I do,' she says. 'A Libra goat. It's a terrible combination.'

'Well, thank you very much.'

'You know what I mean. Indecisive, not able to finish anything, but also, stubborn as they come.'

'Nice to know you've still got such a high opinion of me.'

'Oh, behave yourself,' she says. 'I've come all the way back here to see you, haven't I? And I know you've still got that music box I bought you on your dressing table.'

'So?'

'So, can we get past the bit where you act as though you think I don't like you?'

I can't help smiling. She sent for that music box by mail order before she died. It plays 'You Are So Beautiful To Me', and some days, when I'm not feeling so good, I wind it up and let it play out while I'm doing my make-up.

'OK,' I say. 'Point taken. But what exactly are you trying to get at?'

'Well, you're acting like a typical Libra goat. You're at the top of a mountain; it's rough. There's not much to eat, your hooves are hurting, the air's thin and you're getting dizzy. You know there's something better at the bottom but you're refusing to come down. Just because you can get up there, and survive there, doesn't mean you have to. Doesn't mean you should.'

'Do I know there's something better at the bottom?'

'You've been there before, haven't you?'

LETTER I CAN'T SEND TO BARRIE

I dreamed last night that you came to see me. Sat me down and had a little chat. You explained that it was time for me to stop being angry now. Time to let go. I don't think I said that it probably wasn't your place to tell me when I could and couldn't be angry, given, well, everything. I think it was just sort of nice. To see you. All of you. Not just a shadowy figure. You were smiling as you spoke. I told you I'd listened to that Pink Floyd song this week, all the way through, for the first time since you used to blast it out in our pink front room in our first house, while our baby slept upstairs. And you said you knew. I said it was only fair on Simon, given how much he liked it, that he be allowed to play it in the house or the car again while I was there. That it was about time I got used to listening to it, because there was a time when I used to like it myself.

The next morning, I wondered why I didn't take the opportunity to say a few things to you too. Explain that you should be grateful our children have me. That all the things you said you couldn't stand about me – my stubbornness, my inability to keep my mouth shut when I didn't agree with something, my sense of right and wrong, of justice – were the very things that had just about got us through. Maybe you should be grateful that even if I do sometimes feel as inconsequential as a ghost, as flimsy as a sheet in wind, I never quite fluttered away fully. No matter how much you might sometimes have liked me to, no matter the pressure you applied before you left. Even the ghost of me stayed.

WOMAN

My son goes away to university to study maths, and after a few weeks of wrapping his head around page-long equations, settling in to a new city, finding his way around the sprawling campus, he comes back to Hull for a few days, to see his friends, have his tea cooked, sleep in his own bed. During that one weekend, he: breaks a lamp whilst trying to bench-press the furniture; realises he's booked his train back to Manchester for the wrong month; and finds out he's accidentally been elected treasurer of a society he didn't know he'd joined after writing his name on a list to get free pizza.

Once we've arranged new train tickets for the right dates, bought a new lamp, got him safely back in his halls ready for lectures, and I'm settling into my Monday morning routine, a realisation settles on me: he is one year older than I was when I gave birth to him.

Something deep, deep down in me, softens when I realise this. It feels like the start of something. The start of beginning to think that maybe I've been much, much too hard on nineteen-year-old me.

LETTER I WILL NEVER SEND TO SG

I have to admit that some of this sadness, some of this anger, might have been lying in wait for me anyway. Two grown boys. Two grown men. Two empty spaces where my children used to live. There was bound to be a time of assessment. I would undoubtedly have had to look back over their childhoods, their still-short lives, and see how I'd fared. It was always going to be difficult to do that. I wonder if all single mothers, looking back, do it with a kind of double vision; what it could have been like a different way, what it could have been like if things were easier.

People say parenting doesn't come with a handbook, and I know that's true, but when I hear them say it now, I can feel a hard laugh bubbling up in my chest, hacking in my lungs. Oh, I think, do you want to talk about parenting and its difficulties? Do you want to talk about not having guidance, a handbook, a map of any kind? Oh, I want to shout, don't talk to me about it. But I catch myself. I am fighting a battle against bitterness now.

It's not the first time. I've done it before, when things were harder, so I know I'll win. And I want to enjoy the rest of my life. I've decided I've probably, hopefully, got at least about half of it left. Obviously, I don't take that for granted, but that's not a bad thing. I'm not deferring happiness to a later date. I'm taking it now. Or at least setting my compass in its general direction.

But still, I've had to find my way through the anger, the shame, the sadness. Unfortunately, I've realised it's the only way. Or maybe fortunately; the alternative to not doing that is the hardening. The bitter taste of it all gone fetid in your chest, the seeping of it through your pores, on your breath, settled into every word you write and speak.

Every time I think I've cleared out enough, I find another wave in waiting, but most of the time I'm now OK with that too. I'm like the super-charged version of Marie Condo – decluttering hearts for cash. Except it's only my own heart, and there is no cash for it. Just space for new stuff to come in. Hopefully good stuff. Who knows? We'll wait and see.

WOMAN

The word 'reduction' usually implies that you're taking something away, making smaller in size or amount. But when you're cooking, the meaning changes slightly. Reducing a sauce does make its mass smaller, but you also get something much bigger in return. Something most chefs would argue is much more important than quantity. You get richness. Fullness. A new sense of flavour, a new combination of tastes. Something that was once a watery undertone is suddenly amplified. Unnecessary or unwanted elements burned off. Removed from the pot to lie in particles across the kitchen ceiling. Eventually they can be washed away with a warm, soapy cloth.

LETTER I WON'T POST TO KARL TURNER, MP

Nearly three months after the final news story has gone out on Channel 4, and two years after the first ones broke across social media and the national press; after I've spent a calm, normal Christmas with my sons and my family; after I have started to accept the idea that maybe it's all over now, and things can settle, someone brings to my attention that you've been talking about Steven Gallant again. Tweeting about him. I have a look to see what you've been saying, and well, the shock is immediate this time. I'm absolutely fuming. It's not just the fact that you're saying you're 'delighted' to have had a nice catch-up with him, and how inspiring it was. It's what I see in the replies to your tweet that really shake me.

People were sharing a screenshot of something you'd deleted from earlier in the day, and I have to say that I feel now, after reading it, that my kindness towards you may have been misplaced. I see now why you might have panicked when I turned up. A kind of cognitive dissonance must have kicked in, I think. You couldn't share any of your genuine answers with me. You couldn't look me in the face and say what you really think.

It's easy to read names on paper and forget there are people attached to them. Trauma and pain and actual real blood, running out and soaking pavements, running in the veins of people left behind. You could have got in touch with me any time since I visited your office to clarify. To explain. To answer my questions. Even to check I was OK. My family were OK. But you never have, and now I see why.

There are times in my life that I've thought it was a fault of mine to be too full of the milk of human kindness. Times I've been really angry at myself. Have even almost hated myself, as the consequences for placing my trust in the wrong people have rolled out, like a slow wave, and engulfed not only me but people I love too. These feelings have been strongest during long hours spent rebuilding and gathering the strength to try again. But I don't want to waste energy on that kind of thinking any more, so I won't waste it here. It would just be anger pointed in the wrong direction, anyway. It's a funny thing, anger. Like all emotions, you need to look at it before it buggers off, and sometimes the thing that causes it is so hard to look at, that you can only see it properly by directing it away, at something else. But I'm getting quite good at looking at things straight on now. So I don't beat myself up when I see your tweets. All my anger about them is for you.

I hope that one day, in the course of your work, you'll meet someone else like me, and make the time to have a proper conversation with them. Or maybe you'll read something somewhere that sparks a thought in you, a recognition, a new kind of understanding, and you'll realise that empathy is about so much more than a well-placed word, or some shared experiences. Maybe then you'll start to think a bit more about where you stand, and the words you choose to share as you're standing there.

KARL TURNER MP (ON TWITTER), 17 FEBRUARY 2022
Retweets Channel 4 News clip from 8 January 2020, with these words:
I am delighted to have spoken with Steve Gallant last week and again today to hear how he's getting on having been released from custody. Steve is making a real contribution to society, he is a brilliant example of how rehabilitation can be hugely successful (applause emoji).

Replies:

Brandix Corporate Retreat:

> You would have had him shot

Reply contains screenshot of another of Karl Turner's tweets. It reads:

> It's a working class thing, we aren't terribly keen on terrorists or (for that matter) thugs much.

Attached to this tweet is another tweet by Karl Turner, which begins with:

> 'Shoot terrorists first, ask questions later,' says @ UKAngelaRayner.

WOMAN

The grass crunches beneath my feet, and I look down to see it is tinged white, like it's been sprayed through with liquid nitrogen. I think about moles being removed; how they are frozen, thawed and left to fall away over the coming weeks. I think about molecular gastronomy; the sight of berries made brittle, tapped with a metal implement so that they fall apart cleanly in small segments, or better still, are beaten with a pestle and mortar until they are ground to fine powder, each molecule still separate from the others – no mush, no mess. Clean powdered separation.

The river is rushing at my side. The Ure, coloured yellow by its water's journey. It is unresting, moving unstoppably, irresistibly in one direction, rushing over limestone steps, crashing, foaming. Any kind of powder dropped there now would be dispersed into banks and outlets, carried along in the rush and rumble.

GUARDIAN WEBSITE, 28 MAY 2021
Inquest into London Bridge attack deaths find police and MI5 failings

Failures by MI5, the police and the probation service all contributed to deaths in a terrorist attack at Fishmongers' Hall in London, an inquest has concluded.

Jack Merritt, 25, and Saskia Jones, 23, were unlawfully killed in the attack at a prisoner education event at the hall in November 2019, the inquest jury at the Guildhall in London found.

The jury also concluded that 'missed opportunities' in the way the attacker, Usman Khan, was investigated by the security services and the police in the run-up to the incident probably contributed to the deaths of the victims.

The Merritt family said the inquest had exposed the management of Khan as 'not fit for purpose', while Saskia's uncle Philip Jones said 'those who hide behind the cloak of secrecy' should 'search their own conscience' and review their failings.

The inquest's findings prompted the Metropolitan police to apologise for failings in the way they managed Khan, saying they were 'so deeply sorry we weren't better than this in November 2019'.

The jury agreed there was a failure in the sharing of information and guidance by those responsible for monitoring and investigating Khan. Explaining this conclusion, the jury noted 'missed opportunities for those with expertise and experience to give guidance'.

It also referred to 'unacceptable management and lack of accountability' by those monitoring Khan in the community.

The seven-week inquest heard that Khan was under priority investigation by MI5 after he was released on licence in December 2018. He had served eight years in high-security prison for trying to set up a terrorist training camp in Pakistan.

There was intelligence in late 2018 to suggest he intended to 'return to his old ways' and commit an attack after release. This intelligence was passed to special branch police but it was not shared with those responsible for managing Khan in the community, including his probation officer, Ken Skelton, and Prevent officers at Staffordshire police.

WOMAN

You have to learn your own capacity for pain. Master the art of knowing when your thresholds are about to be breached. That faraway feeling in my head is a marker, as sure as if it were hewn from stone or carved out of wood: careful here. Careful here, now. There is risk. There could be danger.

Of course, you've also got to learn to let go of the idea that you will always get the advance warning of markers. Sometimes it comes in a rush. A flood or a collapse. A rockfall. No warning until it's upon you, or at least until you have no chance of stopping it. Those days you've got to be prepared for putting yourself back together again. Doing whatever it takes. Days in bed? Takeaways instead of cooking? Ignoring your emails? Not answering your phone? Poirot on repeat? It's an emergency situation, and drastic action is required. Or maybe drastic inaction.

Those days you lie numbly by, waiting until you begin to inhabit your body again. Waiting for pain to subside, for your legs to feel like they can hold your weight again. They are both long days, and short. They hang in suspension in a place outside of normal life. People who get close to you learn that sometimes you go there.

ANOTHER WOMAN

'He just used to go in and close the curtains and sometimes he wouldn't come out for days,' she says. 'It didn't have a name then. But we all knew it was something to do with the war, and we all tried to be quiet, and we didn't disturb him, and we didn't ask about it. He was such a cheerful man the rest of the time. He just used to do what he could, with one leg and five of us kids to feed. Used to push his bike everywhere – it was holding him up, you see. There was no wheelchair or anything like that. Our Bob used to slip us bits of meat when he was a butcher's boy. And Foster was a tealeaf, there's no two ways about it. But what else can you do when you've got one leg and five kids to feed? Yeah, it was only sometimes he used to go in that room and close the door. And we never talked about it, you know? It was happy in our house. He was a good man.'

LETTER I WILL NEVER SEND TO SG

I don't want to be hard on you. I worry that if I'm too hard it could have consequences. I know what it's like to feel like you're not worthy of being here any more. Of taking up space. So, I do worry about how my anger could affect you, despite everything that's happened. I often catch myself when I feel it bubbling up – stop and think, *It's not his fault, is it, he hasn't done anything to me?* And then there's a kind of hiccup in my brain, a blank drop, a hard landing. *Oh yeah, he did do something. He murdered Jack and Harry's dad. He murdered Barrie.*

But all the same, I worry. *What if he knows deep down that whatever the prime minister or the Queen or Karl Turner or Jon Snow think, it doesn't really matter? What really matters is what I think. Or even more, what Jack and Harry think.*

HULL DAILY MAIL, TUESDAY 4 JULY 2017 (FRONT PAGE)
Rescuer received death threats from attackers of victim dumped in skip
MAN FOUND DEAD AT HOME WAS TORMENTED AFTER SAVING WOMAN
A Hull man who found a woman brutally beaten and dumped in a skip suffered years of torment and was even threatened by her attackers for saving her life.

Gary Robinson, 43, of Stanley Street, west Hull, rescued 63-year-old prostitute Carol Ives after finding her fighting for her life in a skip.

Despite his heroic actions, her attackers harassed him and as a result, he battled severe anxiety and post-traumatic stress disorder, an inquest has heard.

Mr Robinson's body was discovered at his home by his parents on January 20 this year after he suffered a head injury and went to sleep on the sofa.

At his inquest at Hull Coroners Court, his father said: 'He received threats for rescuing her and started to develop anxiety and PTSD.'

The court heard Mr Robinson had suffered PTSD and drug addiction for a number of years after he saved Ms Ives, who was left for dead in the skip in Myton Street.

[. . .]

Shortly after the attack, Ms Ives told the Mail she had been trying to shout for help for hours before Mr Robinson arrived.

'I am so grateful to him,' said Carol. 'If it wasn't for him I wouldn't be here.'

Mr Robinson told mental health professionals afterwards how he could not get the image of Ms Ives' badly beaten, bloodied face and lifeless body out of his mind and would see visions of her in the skip.

He struggled to go outside during the day when people were around as it would trigger panic attacks.

Although his actions 'undoubtedly saved her', he was even harassed by the people involved afterwards, causing him greater anxiety.

His father said: 'He would get very depressed and have episodes of anger.

'Gary would do anything to make us proud but sometimes we were blinded by his lifestyle choices.'

A post mortem examination found Mr Robinson died of a large bleed to the brain, caused by a head injury. It is not known how he came by his injury but it was not suspicious.

The toxicology report showed therapeutic levels of methadone in Mr Robinson's system, which he was prescribed, along with therapeutic levels of diazepam and temazepam.

Area Coroner Professor Paul Marks recorded a verdict of accidental death.

He said: 'He found an elderly woman who had been badly assaulted. His actions undoubtedly saved her life but he started receiving death threats.

'There were no suspicious circumstances or third party involvement. There was no evidence he had been assaulted.'

No one was ever brought to justice for the attack on Ms Ives.

LETTER FROM KIT MALTHOUSE MP, MINISTER OF STATE
FOR THE CRIMINAL JUSTICE SYSTEM

To: Dame Diana Johnson DBE, Labour Member of Parliament for
Hull North

22 March 2021

RE: MS VICKY FOSTER, x xx xxxxx, HULL, HUx xxx

Thank you for your letter of 26th February 2021, and previous
letters of 5th February 2020 and 26th October 2020, regarding your
constituent, Ms Vicky Foster and her two sons, Harry and Jack.
I am very sorry to hear of the distress being experienced by the
family as a result of unwanted contact from various organisations
and agencies.

Restorative Justice (RJ) is primarily concerned with repairing
the damage caused by crime and focused on meeting the needs of
victims. It is therefore disappointing that it appears further harm
has been caused. My officials have made detailed enquiries into the
communication that has taken place with various members of the
family at different times about RJ. It is clear that opportunities were
missed to ensure that information was passed on appropriately and
I am very sorry that the family's wishes were not respected.

In Ms Foster's correspondence, she understandably expresses
distress and concern that it seemed a serving prisoner would be able
to get a message to her. I wish to reassure you and your constituent
that HM Prison and Probation Service (HMPPS) takes its purpose
of protecting the public very seriously. There are extensive processes
in place designed to protect victims from harassment and unwanted
direct or indirect contact. These provisions include supervising the
work of partner organisations, such as RJ service providers, who
work closely with statutory agencies.

In this case it is clear that more frequent and complete
communication by the Police, Homicide Service and RJ service provider
with HMPPS would have ensured that preferences were passed on
as they should have been, key information shared appropriately with
all interested family members at the right times and any unwanted
contact prevented.

Prison and probation staff, along with Victim Liaison Officers (VLOs), who have statutory responsibility through the Victim Contact Scheme (VCS), have identified improvements that can be made to ensure specialist oversight, advice and support is more readily available to external partners, to help manage and mitigate the risk in future. External partners will be expected to liaise with the relevant Offender Management Unit (OMU) and Victim Liaison Unit (VLU). Victim Support, who deliver the Homicide Service, have welcomed the proposed improvements, as has the RJ service provider involved. Furthermore, the lessons learned will be shared and applied across HMPPS and its partners more generally.

I turn to the decision to grant Mr Gallant, exceptionally, a reduction in his minimum custodial term under the Royal Prerogative of Mercy (RPM), in recognition of the actions he took to restrain Usman Khan at Fishmongers' Hall on 29 November 2019. My officials in HMPPS headquarters made enquiries with the Humberside VLU. Unfortunately, at the time Mr Gallant was sentenced to life imprisonment for murdering Mr Barrie Jackson, the VLU did not receive a referral from the Witness Care Unit relating to Ms Foster or her children. I am truly sorry that this did not happen, and that as a direct result Ms Foster was not offered the opportunity to participate in the VCS at that stage. That did mean that only the relative who was in receipt of the VCS at the time of the decision to award Mr Gallant RPM was notified before news of the award featured in the media.

As you know, following Ms Foster's radio broadcast, the VLU was informed of Ms Foster's relationship to the victim of the offence, Barrie Jackson. Upon receiving this information, the VLU ensured Ms Foster was offered contact under the VCS. I am pleased that Ms Foster has now been able to submit a Victim Personal Statement (VPS) to the Parole Board which is considering whether to release Mr Gallant on life licence, alongside requests for no contact and exclusion zone licence conditions. It takes a huge amount of courage to write a VPS, and I respect your constituent's bravery and dignity in doing so.

Where the VLU are aware that there is likely to be media coverage relating to an offender, they endeavour to inform the victim at the earliest opportunity. Unfortunately, in this case, the information that Mr Gallant might be called as a witness at the inquests for Jack Merritt and Saskia Jones has come directly from Mr Gallant himself, and the National Probation Service (NPS) and VLU had, at that point, not received any formal notification. My officials have made enquiries and can confirm that the Inquest is due to start on 12 April, and that Mr Gallant is due to give evidence.

I am pleased to hear that Ms Foster and her sons are currently receiving support through the Homicide Service, which the Ministry of Justice funds to ensure families bereaved by homicide receive the help and support needed to cope and, as far as possible, recover from the impact of crime. Everyone involved has been genuinely concerned and deeply regrets that a series of well-intended contacts and lack of communication between organisations has ultimately caused Ms Foster and her family further distress.

Thank you for drawing my attention to these matters, enabling us to respond to your constituent and improve the coordination of services providing support to victims of crime. Given that Ms Foster is now receiving support through her VLO, who will continue to keep Ms Foster informed of developments in the offender's sentence, and current diary pressures, I will not be able to meet with you to discuss further on this occasion.

I hope that this letter reassures you that we are committed to ensuring that we learn and improve our processes accordingly.

ANOTHER WOMAN

'If these are just the things that men do, then is it always like this for women?' I say. 'This cooped-up feeling? This cooped-upness of feelings. This claustrophobic, being smothered by your own feelings, feeling. I've read a lot of stuff that tells you your feelings are within your control; that you can stop, change them, if you have enough focus. And I agree that sometimes that's true. But what is also true is that some feelings are just too big, too all-engulfing. And yet, I have never, ever tried to kill a person. So, what's the difference?'

I look at her, one arm folded across her slim tummy, clad in navy polyester trousers and a soft lilac cardigan. I've been engrossed in the carpet as I speak, but I see now that, for the first time, she looks subdued. A memory flashes up between us.

The thin kitchen of their house, the narrow distance between the opposite worktops, the open tin of evaporated milk beside the kettle, and me asking in my ten-year-old voice why she doesn't keep her knives in one of those wooden blocks. Her eyes going wide, the intake of breath: 'I don't like knives out on the sides where you can see them. That's how nasty accidents happen.'

And another time: I'm older, I've fallen off my bike, skinned my face and broken a finger. She is looking after me while I'm off school, and we've just come out of the shop where the woman behind the counter has looked at her suspiciously as she served us.

'I used to see red,' she is saying as we walk. 'Literally like a red mist, and if there had been a knife lying around at those times, I swear I would have killed someone.'

I look back at her, eyes waiting for mine to meet them.

'But you never did it,' I say. 'That's the difference. Tiny as a gnat's knackers, big as the Humber mouth. You never did do it. You were worried that you might, so you took steps. You took responsibility for yourself. You made absolutely sure that you'd never hurt anyone. And you never did do it.'

WOMAN
You're walking a very fine line. That's the thing. People say, 'Don't let your past define you,' and I agree. But you can't escape the fact that your past is etched into every cell of your body, every neural pathway that's been formed in your brain. A lot of people who say you can't let your past define you spend half their time drunk or in bad relationships or trying to buy their way out of it – if I get a car big enough, if I get those granite worktops, those

headphones, that MacBook, that house. The paradox there is that they *are* letting their past define them. It's driving their course as surely as a strong backwind. They're running away from it. Always away.

I know now that not letting your past define you is about slowing down. Really seeing it, really feeling what it's done. Acknowledging that it is going to affect you sometimes, but learning to find a way to be OK with that. Find a comfortable spot, settle down, and get to know it. Then decide what you want to do on your own terms. It's not easy. It's fucking tiring – exhausting – if the truth be told. And the days when the flashbacks come, or the crashes, or the low moods; the days when I can't go where I'm supposed to go or do what I'm supposed to do; they make it harder, of course they do. But I've done this before. I know it won't last for ever, or at least I've still got the hope it won't. And it is working. I know it's working. You've just got to not let yourself get frustrated on the days when it's not working as fast. Overall trajectory, innit? That's the thing. Eyes on the prize, and I don't mean something big and shiny, I mean a new place, where you can be the way you want to be. The way you might have been already, if all the shit didn't get in the way.

MEMORY
The raft of electric suns suspended above me floods my retinas with light. I can see nothing beyond them but vague movement in the blackness. It is quiet. A shuffle, a cough. The shaking feeling inside me. I check my hands. A tremble. I look over at the man behind the curtain on my right and he smiles, half-nods, presses a button. He has kind eyes. *Everything is going to be OK*, I think. I take a deep breath. Check my hands again. Steady.

The music begins to rise out into the auditorium, the familiar notes. I wait for my cue, plant my feet, then I begin. It is 2018, and my words travel out into the darkness, into the ears of the two hundred people who've come to hear me. There are BBC banners at the edge of the stage. I've already performed an extract of my show on *The Verb* on Radio 3, and the whole thing will be recorded and broadcast as an afternoon play for Radio 4 in a few months' time.

I'm standing in the same college I walked out of to go to court sixteen years ago. If I were to step outside now, into the cool September air, I could be by the river in about twenty steps. Check its tide, see its flow – into or out of the city. Hull Crown Court is 0.2 miles away. Hull Royal Infirmary is 1.6 miles away. Yesterday was my son's nineteenth birthday, and today I am about to tell our story. I think, as I stand there, that I've found my way to an ending.

GUARDIAN WEBSITE, 28 MAY 2021
Inquest into London Bridge attack deaths find police and MI5 failings [continued]
[. . .]
Khan's risk to the public was discussed at the regular multi-agency public protection agency arrangement (Mappa) meetings, some of which were attended by MI5. Khan's invitation to the Fishmongers' Hall event was raised at the meetings, but there was no record of any discussion about it, and none of the agencies involved raised any objections to his attendance.

Khan was allowed to attend the event unaccompanied, despite signs he was becoming increasingly isolated and frustrated at failing to find a job, the inquest heard.

The jury found 'serious deficiencies in the management of Khan by Mappa, insufficient experience and training'. It concluded deficiencies in the security arrangements at the event, which was organised by Learning Together, a prisoner education organisation run by Cambridge University, also contributed to their deaths.

The inquest heard Khan was regarded as a 'poster boy' for the Learning Together programme and recorded a promotional video at an earlier event. The jury said the authorities had a 'blind spot to Khan's unique risks due to "poster boy" image and lack of psychological assessment post release from prison'.

LETTER I WILL NEVER SEND TO SG

I thought I saw you last night, in the red-tinged, labyrinthine rooms of Napoleons Casino. I've always hated places that play with your perspective. I once cried so much in the Haunted House at Alton Towers that a member of staff took pity on me and opened a side door, briefly breaking the spell for everyone else as bright daylight flooded in for a few seconds and I walked away into it.

Napoleons isn't quite like that. It has rooms on different levels with windows and doors that give way onto them; restaurant looking onto roulette tables, bar looking onto both restaurant and games room, polished brass fixtures and mirrors reflecting light and faces, steps and dark wood doors. Red plush chairs and bench seats, polished tables. It's like going back in time. But I'm sure you know. I'm sure you've been there.

Anyway, I thought I saw you. Twice. First in a group of people sitting at the table next to ours. I didn't break my step as I took my seat. Didn't let my glance stutter. Kept moving, my feet in the cushion-soled navy-and-gold heels I bought for myself as a treat when I got my first Arts Council grant. I sat, smiled and talked, recalling in my head what that map looked like: the exclusion zone. It doesn't include the town centre, I remembered. It doesn't include this place. I don't let my mind stick on it, though. We are celebrating. I open a card. I eat prawns and salmon rillette. I drink a half-glass of wine and wait for my main course to arrive. I look up and think I see you again, walking towards me. This time I do let my gaze stick. I need to know. Time pauses as I watch the figure moving towards me. I'm convinced it's you until the angle of the head shifts, and I relax. Another slim man with a clean-shaved head in a well-cut shirt. Another man, not you. I forget about him.

But I don't forget about you all night. You and Barrie and Carol Ives. It's like I spend the night in two time zones. The smoking balcony looks out onto the bridge at the top of Holderness Road. The road where I lived when all of that stuff happened. The road that, if I followed it, would lead me down past my old houses, the kids' old school, the place where you did it, the graveyard where he's buried, the last house he and I lived in together. One straight, continuous, well-tarmacked line spooling out from here.

I know that Carol Ives loved – still loves? – this place. I know that she came here a lot. I wonder on and off all night if I might see her. I'd like to talk to her, but I know it wouldn't be fair. She almost certainly would not want to talk to me. Am I to her what you are to me? Maybe. Probably. I would never risk it. I flinch a bit about writing her name, including her, without her consent, here. But I'm trying to be honest. I think about her sometimes. I hope she's OK. I hope she's as OK as she can be.

I push a crisp twenty-pound note across the roulette table and stack a neat pile of chips at my elbow, forearms resting on the soft brown leather cushion at its edge. I win and win again, sliding plastic over felt in whatever direction my hands decide to take, hesitating over numbers, lines, corners, placing a bet or moving on. Watching with the other players when the croupier calls no more bets and the ball jumps around the spinning wheel, seems to settle, jumps again, and stays. I keep my chips neatly stacked, and as they multiply, I arrange them into five-pound piles. When I have doubled my money, I cash them in. I drink a Coke in the comfortable bar. I drive home. I am pleased with myself, and with my night and with my winnings.

I told my friend today that I'm happy, that I feel like I'm living in a dream come true. And she said, 'Good, that's good, and let's be fair, karma probably does owe you one.'

WOMAN

All that time I spent worrying that I was mad. It was my ultimate fear. The one that lurked at the bottom of all those downward arrow charts in CBT sessions. I wish I could quantify how many minutes, hours, days I've spent explaining or justifying my thoughts and behaviours, to myself and other people. Trying to reassure myself. Positive stroking. Avoiding catastrophe. Journal writing. Therapy sessions. Then this year, it felt like it finally happened anyway, after all that work. A whole year of madness. That cracking, breaking feeling in my mind. The rage that swam up and terrified me. The hours and hours and hours lying in my bed listening to audiobooks and colouring-in. The old beliefs that kept coming back, breaching the surface of my conscious mind, and me without the strength to argue any more. Larkin's 'Bridge for the Living', and its long association for me with death. Its long stretch, the pathways open to the wide air, and the rush of the river below, hanging like possibilities at the edge of my vision. I knew, living in it, that it was madness.

But now, coming out of the other side of it, I can't help but think the opposite is true. I look back at the me before all this, the one walking around with that big smile, spouting platitudes and singing and getting up on stage, and I think that maybe she is the crazy woman. Smiling madly and pretending it's all OK. All that 'everything happens for a reason' bollocks. Now I think I'd just become so efficiently obedient, that I'd taken to gaslighting myself. That year living with rage and sadness has done me a lot of good.

I didn't know it as I walked the riverbank in Aysgarth, but as that water flowed out of my sight, it travelled past Bishopdale and Walden Becks, Wensley Bridge, The Batts, The Sike, Bishop Monkton Cut, until it reached Cuddy Shaw Reach, and was joined by Ouse Gill Beck, becoming the River Ouse. It will have flowed through York, Selby, Goole, and met the River Trent, becoming the Humber. It will have flowed past the pier where I sat out the long days of the trials and the stalking, past the docks where my great-grandad used to work and will have eventually flowed out into the North Sea at Spurn, eleven miles from Withernsea.

LETTER I CAN'T SEND TO BARRIE
I didn't come to visit you in the chapel of rest. Too much churning heat and dangerous possibility. Like how I imagine it feels to stand at the edge of a volcano, looking in and not knowing what will happen next. I needed some distance. Needed to settle into shallower eruptions, fainter rumblings. Needed to be out of the hot flow for a

while. So, I didn't come. But I know there must have been softening satin at your sides, arranged by other people who could still see the good in you, who still felt close to you, and could see all of you. I didn't fall into that category.

Only now, after everything has shifted again, and settled, I find myself feeling like I need to lay you out. Tend to you. At the bottom of all the stuff I didn't want to look at, there is still a need to grieve for you. There doesn't seem much point in fighting it, or denying it. There has been too much brutality. Too much crushing and grinding and breaking. Too much deception. I need to reclaim some gentleness.

Everyone deserves some dignity in death. That is a truth almost universally acknowledged, except in the most-tainted corners of the internet and the world. And it turns out, as I begin to think about giving that to you, that I'm tending myself too; all the heat and danger has found a release, like the steam that used to rush out of the top of my granny's pressure cooker and make the kitchen a more taut place until it had finished. At the end of it all – the high-pitched, heretical howling – there is something soft, giving, warm on the tongue.

WOMAN
I worry that when I'm old I might get lost inside all these lost things. When my strength fails, when the fog descends. I worry that these things will haunt me then, the way they haunt me on the frail days now. Only there won't be the sense and knowledge that these days will lift and pass. I might be lost in them for good then. All the lost things waiting.

But so far I've never had an episode of screaming in the streets. I've never had a session of sobbing in public. There have been private places, sometimes people to hold me through it. Outposts. Stopping points. Left luggage lockers where you can place your baggage for a while before you take up your journey again. Maybe these are encouraging signs.

ANOTHER WOMAN

She hasn't spoken today, just arrived and settled a memory on me, in that way she does sometimes. I am twenty-two, and I've just told her I've begun to notice, when I look in the mirror, that I'm getting old. She laughs, of course. Of course she laughs. But it was true, I remember. I'd told her I'd begun to notice lines forming around my mouth and eyes that didn't used to be there.

'Oh, I believe you,' she'd said. 'I'm laughing because I still do the same thing. I don't feel like an old lady, you know. I pass a mirror and think, *Who's that old lady?*, and I realise it's me. But I don't feel like that on the inside.'

There is something in the oven that smells good. I think it might be chicken curry. I don't know how she does it, but whatever goes into that oven comes out smelling and tasting amazing. She once served me jacket potatoes and slices of corned beef from that oven, and they tasted like nothing I'd eaten before. Just simple things, but given so much care. Another kind of transformation. Another kind of magic.

If you asked my kids, they'd still tell you now about the amazing times they used to have there. They'd play for hours in a tent fashioned from a broom and a sheet. I don't know how she made it. How did it stand up? But she did do it, every time the kids asked for it. A washing-up bowl filled with warm water on the bright green grass of the carefully kept back garden, overlooked by the towering flats, was heaven to my boys. And the pulley system my grandad used to rig over the wide wooden slats of the open staircase in the dining room of their council house. My boys played for hours with their little men and that bit of string, once my grandad had set it up and shown them how to use it. He fixed a hook in the wall on the landing solely for that purpose. Simple things. But so much care. So much love.

LETTER I WOULD LIKE TO SEND TO PRIME MINISTER BORIS JOHNSON

We didn't pass on wealth in my family; not in the way you would probably define it. There have been no estates, no holdings, no houses, no titles, no influence in exclusive clubs and schools. When my great-grandma died, while I was still small, I inherited her cherished box of costume jewellery. I thought that was all, and it was always enough. But much later, I found out she'd passed on something else too. Her voice. A natural vibrato, which she apparently used to great advantage in pubs, standing on tables and makeshift stages, and which, it turns out, can still be traded for a fair price in the pubs and social clubs of East Yorkshire.

It might not sound like much by your standards, but it's been enough for me. It was how I managed to pay my way through university – a big loan from the government (I try to avoid checking the balance on the website, because frankly, it's terrifying) and singing. Loading my car up each weekend and some weekday afternoons, with my PA system, my vintage vanity case stuffed with sequinned skirts and dresses and glittering gold heels, and my laptop. Heading off into places where congregations of drinkers gathered, ready to sing along and chide me if I didn't do 'Sex is On Fire' or 'Humans' or one of the other songs they'd be wanting as a grand finale. Something that brought them close, in clusters, on the dancefloor before me, where their hands would touch briefly, their bodies move together in a well-known rhythm. They were demanding about it, making sure they got these moments, and I don't blame them. It's their payoff for everything else, the trade-off they make for long hours, long years, spent doing things they'd rather not be doing.

They wanted their three thirty-minute sets, or their two forty-five minutes, plus an encore, and they wanted cheesy jokes too, the bit of banter in between the singing. It's a formula, well known in the circles of pub singers. Stick to it, and you'll get booked again. You'll be back in three months or six months and if you're lucky, they'll want you for Christmas Eve or New Year's Eve, when it's two or three times the usual rate. But I never took those gigs. I'd done the calculations, my own trade-off: I would leave my teenage kids to take care of themselves on weekend evenings, and in return we'd be able to afford to do things at other times in the week – Wednesday-night teas at Mexican restaurants and burger places, a few nights in Whitby, cinema trips, bowling, shopping trips to the places slightly better than Primark, the odd designer item. We couldn't have it all. We were down one parent, and I had to do the best I could.

When I was trying to find a way into a new kind of future, I decided that finally getting myself inside a university was something I needed to do. One of the keys. But it was going to take years to rack up the degrees I wanted, and in the meantime, I had to make tough decisions. Sacrifices had to be made. But Christmas Eve and New Year's Eve were always sacred times to me. Times when, I'd decided, my kids needed at least one parent to be there, marking the passing time, trying to draw in some good luck, store up some good memories for the coming twelve months.

But we weren't together on 31 December 2019. My boys were old enough to be doing their own thing by then, and I was at a party without them. As midnight approached, I started to get a sense of foreboding. I went outside to calm myself, to talk myself out of a sneaking superstitious dread. To smoke. A man approached me – a homeless man. There are lots of homeless people on Princes Avenue in Hull. When I first moved here, I used to sit down with them on the pavement, and talk. They all had a story about why they were there, on the cold tarmac in the rain, and not tucked up in a family home, or a flat or even a hostel. They all had some shadowy tangle of trauma that had chased them out.

The systems don't work. That's the crux of it. Personal responsibility is bollocks in the face of the things they'd tell you if you lowered your buttocks to the pavement on a winter's night in Hull, to sit beside them. I'd usually slip them a tenner as I left, and when this man approached me, I slid one out of my pocket to pass to him. But a friend stopped me, told me it wasn't the right thing, and unusually for me, I listened. Didn't do it. As I climbed the stairs back to the party though, I felt bad, thinking about him walking away, empty-handed, into the darkness. And selfishly, I thought, *That's bad karma, especially on New Year's Eve.*

I don't suppose you're superstitious. It seems to me it's mostly people who don't have much control over things who start believing in green cars being unlucky, or not stepping on the cracks in pavements. Nevertheless, my feeling that night was justified. A tough year was coming. It was just over a week later when I watched you say those things in the House of Commons, and only a couple of months after that it became apparent that we were heading into a pandemic, and you were the one I was supposed to trust to steer the ship.

MEMORY

The landlady of my house is a nice woman. She comes every month to collect the top-up rent payment I need to make in cash. We always have a cuppa. I've told her how one day I'd like to buy my own house, and she has said that when I'm ready to go back to work, maybe I can buy this one from her. Sometimes I've daydreamed about building an extension in the small back yard – a dining room and an extra bedroom for when the boys are bigger.

In the days following Barrie's murder, she arrives as usual, and she's sort of hyper. Het-up. She says, 'I've just been to pick up some rent on Bilton Grange and it was the house of the cousin of one of the men who did that murder that's in the news—'

I hold up one hand, and she doesn't finish her sentence. I say, 'Let me just stop you there. That was my kids' dad they murdered. We weren't on good terms, but it's probably best you know.'

Her face goes slack. All the life has drained out of it. Her mouth opens and closes slowly as she looks at me.

'It was you,' she says.

'What was me?'

My heart is beating fast. I have already had to prove my whereabouts to the police. Rule myself out of their investigations.

'It was you,' she repeats.

I laugh to disperse the anxiety that's building up in my head.

'My panic attacks are bad enough already,' I say. 'Spit it out. What was me?'

'He was trying to get his ex-girlfriend killed,' she says. 'That's one of the reasons they did it. It must have been you.'

'He's had other ex-girlfriends,' I say. 'It might not have been me.'

'Has he got kids with them?' she asks.

'No,' I say.

'It was you,' she says.

LETTER I WILL NEVER SEND TO SG

This will be the last letter I write to you. You and I are done now, as well as we can be. I decided this after the walk – the one by the river. I imagined myself shaking something off as I moved. It was like something loosening. Really. I could almost feel it. Something letting go of me. Something that had been clinging. Something heavy. Something hindering me.

I'm not saying I believe in things like exorcisms, but I'm not saying I don't either. All I can tell you is I felt this loosening; this shaking off. And the thing that I was shaking off was you. I came back to my room afterwards, showered, wrote in my journal, and sat down at the desk by the window while I waited for the kettle to boil. The window looked out towards mountains, white-topped, and in the foreground were fields, rolling away to where the river ran beyond them. I thought about the energy in that river, remembered its crashing motion over the rocks. I thought that anything thrown in that river would not climb back out.

I didn't know then about the course the river took. Didn't know it would wind its way back within a few miles of my house. But even now, knowing, it feels OK. It's months now since it passed by and flowed out of the muddy estuary into the sea. It had travelled a long way by then, changed from yellow to dark cocoa brown as it picked up fragments of the heavy dark mud it flowed over around here.

As I was sitting in my room, thinking about this new sense of lightness and freedom, my phone rang. A mobile number I didn't recognise. It was probation. They were calling about you. Letting me know about your upcoming media engagements and interviews. I didn't quite manage to gather my thoughts before she told me the first of them, but it didn't take me long.

'Sorry,' I said. 'Can I just stop you there? I'm wondering if you can update my details, please? I don't want to know any more about what he's doing. I'll take my chances. I might never see them.'

'Yes,' she said. 'I understand. None of us thought it would go on this long.'

'No,' I said, 'none of us did. I've just had enough now. But thank you. Thanks for all your help.'

'I'm sorry,' she said.

'It's not your fault,' I said.

People talk a lot about forgiveness, but honestly, I don't think I even know what it is any more. I used to think I knew, but I thought about it too much these last couple of years. You know how if you say a word over and over, even a word as familiar as your own name, it becomes nonsensical? It's like that. Forgiveness. Forgiveness. Forgiveness. A hollowing of the cheeks, a hard catch in the throat, a hissing on the tongue. There's a lot of it in the Bible. I know that. We used to say it at school every day in assembly, and again before we ate our lunch: 'Forgive us our trespasses, as we forgive those who trespass against us.'

It's interesting what a change in perspective can do to words. Because although I can no longer catch hold of what I thought was important in that sentence when I was small, I find that the almost-unnoticed part of it has taken on new meaning. Trespassing. That's what it feels like you've been doing. One year and ten months where you've stretched out across the whole of my life. But it stops here. I don't know what forgiveness is, but I do know what boundaries are. Might sound silly, but that's been hard-won knowledge for me. And this is where my boundaries lie, as far as you're concerned: a thick black line around some of my favourite places, a do-not-inform note on the probation records, a no-contact order that says you can't seek to approach me or my kids. Other than that, I'll take my chances. You go your way. I'll go mine.

I actually do hope you do some good. If you really do want to make some difference to some people who've lost their way somewhere, then I wish you luck with that. Of course I do. We both know there are people, right now, lost in places so dark and uncharted that only someone who's been there before can find a way in to help them. If you can be that person, then good. It's just that I don't need to know about it. I don't need to know about you. In fact, I need to *not* know about you any more.

But I hope that somewhere, out beyond the muddy Humber, and the flat blue-brown North Sea off the coast, there is a place where all things settle. A quiet little cove, where the water is disturbed only by the faint swelling tide and shifting breeze. Where, as it settles, it clears, all it's been carrying falling away, to lie undisturbed on a sandy bottom, where it can't trouble anyone. Where you can look in and remember only these new, flat, quiet versions of them, like they were things that happened to someone else.

WOMAN

Turns out relapses aren't as bad now. They're less intense. They don't last as long. Maybe it's because my kids are grown up, and I'm able to look after myself a bit better when I need to. Maybe it's because I've learnt what to do when it happens, and because I've built myself a job where I don't have to be in the same place at the same time every day, moving my body and making my brain work in a certain way for a certain number of hours. Whatever it is – one of these things or all of them together – it's easier to manage, easier to recover. I'm beginning to feel relief, like maybe it's beginning to pass again now. Maybe I'm coming through it. Maybe I am going to get another chance at feeling normal again. At functioning out in the world.

I've developed a new appreciation of dandelions. I've stopped pulling them out from between the block paving in the front garden. Instead, now I look at them and think, *You know what, little yellow flower, who says you shouldn't be there? Turn those tiny golden fingers up towards the sun and make the most of it. We don't all get a specially laid-out flower bed, a particular breeding, labelling and appreciation society. But don't let that stop you. You're all right where you are.*

LETTER I WOULD LIKE TO SEND TO PRIME MINISTER BORIS JOHNSON

It's two and a half years since I started writing to you, and time has changed things, as it always will. It looks like you won't be prime minister for much longer. It looks like your days are numbered, as we move through a summer of heatwaves and energy crises, and news of more deaths, more violence, more failures in more systems. It looks like you're winding down from high office, but we'll know for certain in a month or so. Whether you let go or keep pushing remains to be seen. I've learnt you can never predict accurately what men like you might do under pressure, but I expect you'll probably go. You'll have other things to attend to. TV shows to appear on. Books to write.

I expect we'll finally see the one you're intending to write on Shakespeare. Long-awaited, eagerly anticipated, and maybe it is in Shakespeare that we can finally find that common ground I've been searching for. Some people think we shouldn't be reading him any more – that it's time to move on, that things from the past should stay in the past. But I don't agree with that. The past is never really dead, and Shakespeare's words have never been dead to me. They have always lived, from the first time I picked up *Romeo and Juliet* when I was eleven years old, clapping out iambic pentameter, and letting metaphors unfold like rose petals in my head. I won't claim to be an expert, though. I haven't seen all his plays performed at the Globe or studied endless essays exploring his themes and ideas. I haven't read the histories or many of the comedies. I'm limited mostly to a handful of tragedies. I had to be excused from the module on Shakespeare and Early Modern Drama during my degree, because the first lecture on the revenge plays gave me flashbacks.

But this week I've been reacquainting myself with Cordelia, who for the last twenty-five years has remained as my favourite of his characters. The first time I read *I cannot heave my heart into my mouth*, I had to tilt my head to hide my tears behind the book, while the room of sixteen-year-olds and my teacher carried on without me. I knew that feeling well – already, at sixteen – the powerlessness, the sense of frustration, of being manipulated. Reading *Lear* again now though, I also feel a new affinity with Kent: *Think'st thou that Duty shall have dread to speak / When Power to flattery bows?*

There's always something new to see, or a different way of seeing what's already there – as it filters through new experience, new understandings of the world. There will always be new, interesting interpretations, but I'm not sure I want to read any of yours. For a man who claims to love Shakespeare so much, it's amazing to me that you understand so little about responsibility, about the way actions can unfurl into consequence, the endless ripples we all make, especially when we move selfishly or with malice. Maybe you'll have learnt something about that in the last few months, but I doubt it. You might have to give up 'the best job in the world' but as for other inconveniences and real repercussions – I expect you'll be protected from those.

Shakespeare can sometimes seem prophetic, but even he probably couldn't have predicted what the world would look like four hundred years after he was writing. I do hope though, that even in a world he might not have fully understood, some of his observations hold true. There's one in particular I think about a lot:

'Time shall unfold what plighted Cunning hides,
Who Covers faults, at last with Shame derides.'

LETTER I WILL NEVER SEND TO SG
Actually, there is one final thing I need to say to you. One final thing I want to explain. Because the time at which you arrived in my living room is relevant to how I felt about you coming, I think. The places I'd been on the day you appeared might not be important,

but the reason why I was feeling good is worth explaining. Because there was a particular reason for the lightness. The happiness. Something unusual was happening. The kind of thing you think will never happen to you. The kind of thing you don't even dream about happening to you when you've grown up in the places where we grew up. The kind of thing you don't even know *does* happen.

A year or so before the day when you arrived, I'd told our story – mine and my boys' – and I had thought, in doing it, that I'd cleared out the closet. Closed the lid on it, the best you ever can on a story like that. It turned out people quite liked the way I'd chosen to tell it, and millions of them had listened to it on Radio 4. It was published in a book. I'd performed it live. I was thinking of touring it. Then just before Christmas I got a call to say it had been shortlisted for an award. I was invited to the BBC Radio Theatre for the ceremony, but I couldn't really tell anyone until the official announcement was made.

The announcement was going to be made the next morning. That's why I was so happy – a secret I'd been hugging to myself for the past couple of months was about to be revealed. I'd been walking around feeling like it was Christmas Eve. I knew people would be pleased for me. People have been so kind to me since I started writing and getting up on stage. I don't think it would be an exaggeration to say they've probably saved my life, and the next day I was going to be able to tell them all about this new, lovely thing that was happening.

But when I got home, Simon had to tell me about your announcement instead. Your big reveal. He's a journalist, and one of his friends at the local paper knew who I was. Knew what this would mean to me, had somehow realised that nobody else had told us – not the government, not your solicitor, not anyone I knew – despite the press releases and statements that had gone out to just about every media outlet in the country. He decided that we should probably get a bit of a heads-up, and I was grateful to him for that. But it meant that the night I should have spent excitedly, eagerly awaiting the tweets and Facebook posts with my good news, was spent instead checking news websites, waiting for your story to break.

I won the award at the BBC, on 2 February 2020. I was given a glass trophy with my name engraved. I met famous people, writers I respect, who said lovely things to me. Who encouraged me to go on writing. But I spent the night in two places. When they read out my name, when I walked up onstage and gave a short speech, when I shook hands with people, and sipped wine, and smiled, I was in two places. I was half in the radio theatre, and half on London Bridge, 3.1 miles away, 174 miles from Hull.

WOMAN

I am flowing back into my own life. I touch things and know they're really there — the thick black curls of my dog's fur in my fingers, the warmth of my son's shoulders under my palms as I hug him, the texture of paper in my hands as I read, the ripe resistance of red tomatoes just before I slice them. It's a relief to have substance again. To speak and know my words find their landing place. To call up air from my lungs, have it pass through my larynx, vibrate in vocal folds, be shaped by my lips and tongue, and travel in waves, like an ocean of my own making, to find a home in the soft swirling cave of someone's ear. Trembling through tiny bones — the hammer, anvil, stirrup — before meeting fluid, setting off nerve responses, being translated into electrical impulses, that find meaning in the brains of other people. In real physical beings.

In the mornings I piece together my life as I wake; lining up securities and escapes, checking what I've got to face before I decide whether or not I will open my eyes yet. The tally is favourable at the moment. My sons are safe. The man lying beside me is a good man, who has never threatened or abused me, who is gentle and kind. The bills are paid, and I know how I will pay them in the coming few months. My edges are all tucked in. I am neat again. I can predict with relative accuracy what my energy will allow me to do today, and I have a choice about what that will be. I spend my time doing things that I love – even my chores are palatable to me. I like making things shine, hoovering debris from carpets, the order of a properly loaded dishwasher and clean crockery in cupboards.

I share my life with people I love, who make me laugh, who share my interests and passions, who make beautiful things, who have overcome obstacles in their lives that I can't imagine, but whose eyes I can look into and see understanding, warmth, common ground. Who have known me when I was an unravelled thing, and have stood by me, holding frayed threads and helping me pick out an order as I reconvened.

I am lucky. We all make the best life we can for ourselves, and if my wishes seem to run out ahead of my capabilities at the moment, I take that as a good thing. It will move me forward now that I am recovering, instead of weighing me down. It has begun to feel like good things are possible again.

ANOTHER WOMAN

She says: 'So that's how it works, really. That's it in a nutshell. You do a million little things, and sometimes you do nothing at all. It's not big or grand. You don't get any applause. It's not about that. It's about what it adds up to, in the end. All those times when you're tired and there's no one there to help, when you need a hand on your shoulder or a hand with the tea or someone to tell you that you aren't the bad things your brain tries to say you are, but you just keep going. Just keep plodding. And the times when you want to walk away, or worse, some other darker way of getting away from everything, and you do nothing. Nothing or a million little things. Both of those are enough to save a life, and who knows how many have been saved that way? How do you unpick the fibres that hold people together? That hold them up when they could be sinking.

'But people think that if no one is looking, it doesn't count. Well, I'm here to say that it does count. And you can't compare five minutes of bravery to a whole lifetime. It doesn't add up. The books don't balance, and don't let anyone tell you they do. Not ever.'

Then she shifts in the semi-darkness, and I see a movement of light, somewhere up under her ribs, puncturing the delicate weave of her lilac jumper. She leans forward and lifts her arms. And then she grows, expanding towards the ceiling, and as she does, a space is revealed. A glittering black space where a constellation hovers. Pinpricks of gold and silver, the contours of clifftops, the black tarmac path of Holderness Road, the sycamore tree in the park, waving autumn leaves in the breeze. Pulsing red planets of pain, and the flashing of all our faces. Mine, peering at her over my dad's shoulder, newly born, and her saying, 'She's been here before.' And then it all starts to fade, until it's just me again, sitting in my dark office, like a loon. The air all around holding a sort of shimmer.

Oh, I think, understanding at last. *It was all in there. All the time. There was space for everything.*

I know she won't come back again, but that's OK. I had her for a long time. My whole life. And this time she's allowed to not come back. She's got the right to let go. The same as I have. The same as we all have.

MEMORY

I am sitting in the front bedroom of my friend's house. Women gather below us, in the living room, and from the window I can see, across the road, another window behind which my first child, my baby son, is sleeping. Barrie is watching him. The car is on the drive, behind the green picket fence and bursting blood-red poppy heads, the lupins. Washing is drying on the line in the back garden, the dishwasher is loaded, the carpets hoovered.

The woman sitting opposite me closes her eyes, takes a breath, spreads out an arc of glossy black, gilt-edged cards, and asks me to pick five.

'I see difficult times ahead for you,' she says. 'A lot of difficulty. A long time.'

'Oh,' I say.

'Yes,' she says. She looks up, into my eyes, a slight pucker in her brow. Her whole face full of sympathy. 'You've got a lot of difficulty to get through. It lasts a long time.'

She lifts one of the cards, shows me The Tower, the lightning strike, the tumbling brick and the grey clouds gathering.

But beyond that, she says, 'I see blue skies. I see you in a happy place. I see certificates of achievement going up on the walls around you. You are happy. You are loved. You will need to remember what I'm telling you. It's important. There is a place beyond all the difficulty. A happy place. Blue skies. Where your children will love you so much. Where they'll understand. There is so much love between you all. There are certificates on the walls, and blue skies.'

WOMAN
I open my eyes and wonder if maybe I am finally there.

SUPPORT SECTION

If you have been affected by any of the issues raised in this book, I'm sending you love and hope, because there is hope whatever is happening, and the following organisations may be able to help you find your way through it all:

People affected by homicide, including family members and eyewitnesses, can contact the National Homicide Service by phone on 0300 303 1984.

Anyone suffering from Chronic Fatigue Syndrome / ME can visit the ME Association website for information – meassociation.org.uk

Anyone who thinks they, or someone they know, may be experiencing domestic abuse can visit the Women's Aid website for information – http://www.womensaid.org.uk

For advice on stalking, visit the Suzy Lamplugh Trust website – https://www.suzylamplugh.org

For advice about online abuse, visit https://glitchcharity.co.uk

If you think you may have an issue with addiction to drugs or alcohol, there is guidance and further information available on the Narcotics Anonymous website – ukna.org, and the Alcoholics Anonymous website – http://www.alcoholics-anonymous.org.uk

If you think someone you care about may have an issue with addiction to drink or drugs, there is advice available at https://adfam.org.uk/help-for-families/you-and-your-loved-one/

PERMISSION CREDITS

The following kindly gave permission to reproduce copyright material.

- The Sun / News Licensing
- The Guardian / Guardian News & Media Ltd
- Daily Mail Online / dmg media licencing
- Hull Live
- Hull Daily Mail
- Metro / dmg media licensing
- ITV / ITVx

The extracts from the *Living with Loss* report (2019) are taken from the Victim Support National Homicide Service and are in the public domain.

Other extracts were reproduced under the following licences.

- Lord Justice Latham speaking during SG's appeal against his murder conviction: R v Gallant, England and Wales Court of Appeal (Criminal Division), 21 May 2008, contains information licensed under the Open Justice – Licence v1.0.
- Home Office Domestic Abuse Statutory Guidance contains public sector information licensed under the Open Government Licence v3.0.
- Extracts from The ME Association website were taken by The ME Association directly from the National Institute for Health and Care Excellence, and Guideline on ME/CFS (NG206)

ACKNOWLEDGEMENTS

This book began life as my MA dissertation at the University of Hull. It was inspired by all the reading, writing and conversations I had during seminars and workshops delivered on Teams, while we were still in and out of lockdowns during 2021. Thanks are due to everyone in both the English and the Creative Writing departments there during that time, many of whom I am now very proud to call my colleagues. In particular though, to Sarah-Jane Dickenson, who was my personal supervisor while I was writing for my MA, and to Martin Goodman, who was my personal supervisor during the turbulent years when I was studying for my first degree, and who introduced me to the concept of creative non-fiction writing and all the possibilities it could hold.

I would never have written this story at all were it not for the support of my superstar agent, Cathryn Summerhayes, who waited patiently while I figured out a way to start writing it all down, and then read and advised on my false starts before I finally found a way that worked. She's often been the recipient of my panicked texts and emails and has always steered me in the right direction.

Long before I had an agent I was supported by a whole network of wonderful Northerners, who hopefully know what they mean to me, because I try to make sure I tell them every chance I get. They are: Sue Roberts, Kate Fox, Louise Wallwein, Pat Dooner and Carl Conway-Davis of Broken Orchestra, Adelle Stripe, Toria Garbutt, Shane Rhodes, Russ Litten, Dave Windass, Dean Wilson, Mikey Martins, Louise Yates, Louise Beech, Julie Corbett, Cassandra Parkin, Michelle Dee, Lynda Harrison, Helen Mort, Ralph Dartford (honorary Northener) and everyone who hosted an open mic where I read, invited me to read as a guest, or put on work and shows that made me understand the reason why writing and sharing our words is such a powerful and important thing.

Everyone at Bloomsbury has been amazing, especially Alexis Kirschbaum, who believed in my strange book before I even finished writing it, and encouraged and supported me through its various forms. Fabrice Wilmann has shown unending patience through the long process of permissions and copyedits and many other processes I didn't understand, and he had to explain to me. Victoria Goldman made sure it all made sense with her suggestions and exceptional attention to detail.

Dame Diana Johnson, my local MP, was unwaveringly kind, supportive and helpful throughout the most difficult of these times. She helped me keep faith that there are still good people in the world and in politics, at a time when I really was beginning to question those things.

Most of all though, thanks are due to my family and friends, who not only lived through all of this with me, but don't mind that I write about it and share it with the world. My sons, Jack and Harry, are the best things I'll ever make in this world, and two of the best men I know. My mum, Sandra Archer, who could write her own book, and has shown me how to enjoy life even when the difficult stuff is pouring down on us, as well as how to wear the unfair criticism that sort of behaviour brings. Jo Newby, who cooked my tea and picked me up more times than I can count. Louise Craft, who posted money and fags through my letterbox and brought me groceries when I couldn't buy them myself. Every woman I've laughed with and cried with, even those I only met when we shared stories in the toilets on drunken nights out. Chrissy Lewis, Jess Fear, Jo Charlton, Sian Humphries, Kath Wilson, Laura Flowers, Sam Leighton – you are all awesome and I really don't know what I'd do without you.

Simon Bristow literally saved my life when I thought I couldn't take any more and remains one of the kindest men I've ever met, even though we've separated. He's sat by me in hospital waiting rooms, police stations, recovery rooms and doctors' surgeries, as well as posh restaurants and holiday flights. Those kinds of things create a bond that will never break.

Edna and Doreen, my dad's mum and my mum's mum, are the two real women who make up my 'Another Woman'. They taught me about love, hardship, how to get by in this life and how important the so-called small kindnesses we share can be. They are the people I have dedicated this book to.

A NOTE ON THE AUTHOR

Vicky Foster is an award-winning writer, performer and poet from Hull who has broadcast extensively across the BBC. She has published two collections of writing and is currently working on her first novel whilst studying for a PhD in English and Creative Writing. She won The Society of Authors' Imison Award at the 2020 BBC Audio Drama Awards for her Radio 4 play *Bathwater*, and in 2020 her Radio 4 documentary, *Can I Talk About Heroes?*, was reviewed in the national media. She has written poetry for radio, podcasts and TV, delivered writing projects and creative writing workshops for a wide range of organisations, and performed at festivals and events across the North. She is a writer-in-residence for First Story, working with schools to help young people write their own stories.

A NOTE ON THE TYPE

The text of this book is set in Perpetua. This typeface is an adaptation of a style of letter that had been popularised for monumental work in stone by Eric Gill. Large scale drawings by Gill were given to Charles Malin, a Parisian punch-cutter, and his hand-cut punches were the basis for the font issued by Monotype. First used in a private translation called 'The Passion of Perpetua and Felicity', the italic was originally called Felicity.